THE NEVER-ENDING FEAST

THE NEVER-ENDING FEAST

THE ANTHROPOLOGY AND ARCHAEOLOGY OF FEASTING

KAORI O'CONNOR

Bloomsbury Academic
An imprint of Bloomsbury Publishing Plc

B L O O M S B U R Y
LONDON • NEW DELHI • NEW YORK • SYDNEY

Bloomsbury Academic
An imprint of Bloomsbury Publishing Plc

50 Bedford Square	1385 Broadway
London	New York
WC1B 3DP	NY 10018
UK	USA

www.bloomsbury.com

BLOOMSBURY and the Diana logo are trademarks of Bloomsbury Publishing Plc

First published 2015

British Library Cataloguing-in-Publication Data
A catalogue record for this book is available from the British Library.

ISBN: HB: 978-1-8478-8926-3
PB: 978-1-8478-8925-6
ePDF: 978-1-4725-2093-7
ePub: 978-1-8478-8927-0

Library of Congress Cataloging-in-Publication Data
A catalog record for this book is available from the Library of Congress.

Typeset by Fakenham Prepress Solutions, Fakenham, Norfolk NR21 8NN
Printed and bound in India

CONTENTS

CONTENTS

For my daughter

Kira Eva Tokiko Kalihilihiokekaiokanaloa Ffion Lusela
Hopkins

With never-ending love

Acknowledgments

A feast involves many people. Thanks are due to The Trustees of the British Museum, and to my publisher Bloomsbury, especially Louise Butler, Molly Beck and Ken Bruce, my three anonymous reviewers, Kim Storry and all copyeditors, proof-readers, designers and others who have been involved in the production, along with the Department of Anthropology at the University College London (UCL). Seats of honour at *The Never-Ending Feast* go to my daughter Kira, Noel Rees, Paul Sidey, Timothy O'Sullivan, my merry culinary companions Gillian Riley and Helen Saberi, Max Carocci who was the inadvertent catalyst for this book, my aunt Martha Yamashiro and my grandmother Kato Yamashiro, who first took me over the bridge of dreams to Heian Japan. Panserban and Mah-Jongg were frequent uninvited guests who particularly relished the imperial cat banquet. A special toast is hereby made to the many scholars and writers past and present whose work is woven into this account, and to those peoples of antiquity whose feasts we have shared.

List of Illustrations

CHAPTER ONE

Introduction: Invitation to the Feast

How is it that there is no wreath before the doors, no savour of cooking strikes the tip end of the projecting nose, though the feast of the Amphidromia is on? For then it is the custom to toast slices of cheese from the Chersonese, to boil a cabbage glistening in oil, to broil some fat lamb chops, to pluck the feathers from ringdoves, thrushes and finches withal, at the same time to devour cuttle-fish and squids, to pound with care many wriggling polyps and drink many a cup not too diluted.

(Epippus in *Geryones*, in Athenaeus IV: 370c–d, in Garnsey 1999: 128)

The tall doors of the British Museum in London, the world's first and most famous public Temple of the Arts, are flanked by a colonnade of forty-four great stone columns copied from the sanctuaries of the goddess Athena at Priene and the god Dionysius at Teos, topped by a pediment of Grecian figures that symbolize the progress of civilization (Mordaunt Crook 1972). The Museum was built to house treasures that document human cultures from early times to the present and inside, under ceilings so high they are perpetually in soft shadow, rooms open into rooms and grand staircases wind inexorably upwards, leading to things that bespeak the long ago and the faraway. Time gives way to things as some 7,000,000 pieces compete for attention, mounted on plinths or displayed in cases—kraters and kylixes from ancient Greece, silver vessels from Achaemenid Persia, golden bowls from Ur in Mesopotamia, bronze cauldrons from Shang China, lacquer ware from Japan and much more, all with museum labels that call attention to the elegance of their shapes, the sophistication of their colors and the artistry of the designs worked upon their surfaces. The exhibits suggest that here, in all its variety, is Art—the universal essence and epitome of human culture and civilization. But is it?

If you stop thinking of these things as "Art," what do you see? Although they are now empty, stripped of their function and context, these are dishes that once bore rich foods and splendid roasts, pitchers from which choice wines were poured, tall jars that held beer sipped through long straws set with gold and lapis, platters that were piled high with fruits and sweet cakes, cylinder seals engraved with scenes of banquets, carved friezes showing servants hastening to serve guests, moving so quickly that their clothes flutter behind them. The Museum is full, not of "Art," but of the remains of countless ghostly feasts.

Feast! Few words are as full of anticipation and excitement, infused with implicit meanings and associations that arise from the common understanding of "feast" defined in the Oxford English Dictionary (2010) as an event of rejoicing and commemoration, held to honor a person or mark a religious or secular anniversary; a festival connected to a place; a sumptuous meal or entertainment given to a number of guests; a banquet especially of a more or less public nature; an unusually abundant and delicious meal. But is this all there is, and was, to feasting?

The collections in the British Museum and establishments like it great and small the world over signify that feasts and feasting are "an extremely significant aspect of social life on a worldwide scale" (Dietler and Hayden 2001b: 2), something that all humans have in common, in all periods of history. Yet despite their ubiquity, the details of feasts past—certainly non-European feasts of the pre-modern period—remain little known outside highly specialized academic fields. Museum curators like to say that "every object tells a story," but as far as feasts and feasting go, it is more the case that "every object poses questions." In what social and historical contexts were the feast objects in museums used? What were these feasts of antiquity like, and why were they so important?

Not long ago, these would not have been regarded as serious academic questions. Up until the 1960s, and with the exception of scholars of the Graeco-Roman world (Wilkins 2012; Wilkins, Harvey and Dobson 1995; Halstead and Barrett 2004; Gold and Donahue 2005), along with economic historians and folklorists (Scholliers 2012: 59; Scholliers and Clafin 2012), the lack of interest by historians of antiquity in food, drink and feasts was "attested by their eloquent silence" (Bottéro 2004: 2). There were exceptions, notably Bottéro himself, a French historian and Assyriologist who devoted years to studying the food and drink of ancient Mesopotamia and translated the world's oldest known recipes, a selection of rich dishes emblematic of palatial cuisine (2004, 2001, 1999, 1995, 1987, 1985). There is also the molecular archaeologist Patrick E. McGovern (2009, 2003; McGovern et al. 1995) who traces the origins and practice of viniculture and brewing and advises breweries and heritage events on recreating the drinks consumed in antiquity, notably reconstructing those served at "King Midas's Funeral Feast." Both Bottéro and McGovern placed food and drink in a larger social and historical context, and the fact that their recipes could be reproduced and consumed added another dimension to the field. But on the whole, if mentioned at all, food and feasts were footnotes to history.

Literature was another matter. The Graeco-Roman corpus of works from classical antiquity is full of descriptions like that with which this chapter begins, and this passage from Europe's oldest cookery book, the *Life of Luxury* by Archestratus of Gela, fourth century BC, rendered into prose here (Wilkins and Hill 2011) but originally in verse:

> Always festoon the head with all kinds of garland at the feast, with whatever the fruitful floor of the earth brings into flower; dress your hair with fine distilled perfumes and all day long throw on the soft ashes myrrh and incense, the fragrant fruits of Syria. And while you are drinking, let these tasty dishes be brought to you: the belly and boiled womb of a sow in cumin and sharp vinegar and silphium; the tender race of roasted birds, and whatever may be in season.
>
> (Archestratus, fragment 62 in Wilkins 2014: 181)

However, this work and countless others were seen as literature, or in some cases as medical texts, not as historical documentation. In literary analyses, food was not sustenance but metaphor, a vehicle for morality and values, and a discourse on its own, distanced from history and from everyday life. Persistent themes were the dangers of pleasure and the disapproval of luxury and excess.

This view entered the Western literary tradition and became an embedded cultural attitude which persists down to the present, its legacy seen in the deep-seated academic fear, still with us, that dwelling upon food and feasting will result in work seen as an "ill-digested fad" (Dietler and Hayden 2001b: 2), superficial and frivolous. Holzman (2006: 164) warned that a popular food-centered analysis would lower the study of taste to merely the study of "tasty things" feeding on Western "Epicurean" sensibilities, while Sutton (2010) cautioned that although the celebration of food is to be lauded, it is vital that the research does not fall prey to "Epicureanism" which he understands to mean the unbridled pursuit of pleasure through all things luxurious, sensual or gluttonous. The Greek philosopher Epicurus (341–270 BC) was actually an advocate of restraint and the simple life, who valued sociability over mere consumption saying: "We should look for someone to eat and drink with before looking for something to eat and drink, for dining alone is leading the life of a lion or wolf."

However, the misunderstanding and misuse of "Epicureanism" persists. Here can be detected an academic longing for what Sherratt (1999: 13) called "a utopian world without ostentation and cupidity," along with elements of what Elias (1983) identified as the European bourgeois disapproval of elite splendor and "indulgence" that emerged in the early modern period and for long impeded the study of courtly societies. Under this cloud of disdain and disapproval, it is not surprising that the displays of feasting wares in museums were stripped of context, rendered mute and displayed as "Art." In sum, "regarded as a trivial or inconsequential activity unrelated to the more serious issues," feasting was "a critical element almost entirely overlooked in the past" (Hayden and Villeneuve 2011: 435) as a way of understanding human society, until the changes described below.

The Cultural/Material Turn

In the 1970s and 1980s, long-established academic paradigms were subjected to fundamental re-evaluation, transforming the humanities and social sciences (for the initial effects of these movements within anthropology see Ortner 1984 and more broadly Hicks 2010), especially conventional history and literature. The grand narratives and developmental sequences that had characterized the former were discredited, and the prevailing model of official history as "unique and unrepeated sequences of events … an accumulation of discrete actions by individual people" (Elias 1983: 3)—the "great men" approach—was discarded in favor of a search for social patterns and dynamics. The authority of official texts was challenged; they were now seen to be partial, only dealing with elites, and biased, giving only one viewpoint. For historians, "anthropology helped to provide insights into features of the past that were so strange that modern historians had found them difficult to comprehend or examine" (MacFarlane 1988), such as complex rituals, blood-feuds, the Divine Right of Kings, magic and witchcraft; it introduced them to the importance of symbols, the agency of material things, the dynamics of different forms of social organization and the importance of holism. Instead of timeless and objective truths, "tradition" now came to be seen as cultural constructs and interpretations in response to particular times and places, as demonstrated in *The Invention of Tradition* (Hobsbawm and Ranger 1984), a highly influential work in what came to be called the New History. The former focus on politics, diplomacy and economics was replaced by a wider perspective that took in the whole of cultural and material life, a notable example being the social history, developed by French scholars of the *Annales* school, which focused on the late medieval and early modern periods. Works that had previously been considered purely "literary" were now seen as social documents, a shift that allowed historians to draw liberally on what James Davidson (1998: xvi) calls "scraps that have fallen from the tables of ancient literature" to illuminate their analysis, using food and drink as lenses through which to see the peoples, events, cultures and environments that produced them. The concept of mentalities emerged—distinctive and persistent worldviews and ways of thought, analogous to what anthropologists call "culture." Instead of macro-studies on the grand scale, local micro-studies or micro-histories became fashionable, great events were replaced by the ordinary, and the focus turned to the common people, previously invisible in official accounts, often illiterate, cut off from literary high culture and unable to contribute to it.

A pioneering work was Ladurie's *Montaillou* (1978), a study of peasants in a medieval village in the Languedoc, France, which drew on Inquisition records that contained the direct testimonies of illiterate peasants, supplemented by the inventories of their material goods as described in the records. The coarse bread, bacon and cabbage soup and provisions like snails gathered from the wild along with the lack of imported goods like sugar and wine, bespoke their lowly position and isolation from networks of trade. As Ladurie demonstrated, to conjure these faceless and voiceless folk from their dark past, new kinds of non-literary "documents" needed to be consulted—administrative records previously considered of little interest, demography and, notably, the non-written record provided by material objects, everything from baskets and furniture to architecture and food. In addition, the symbolic aspects of culture and the cosmologies revealed through ordinary objects and everyday life became important, a key work of the period being *The Interpretation of Cultures* (Geertz 1973).

Taken together, this was the beginning of what came to be called the Cultural/ Material Turn. Non-literate cultures and the everyday material world were new territory for most historians, and many turned to the discipline that had long specialized in them—anthropology.

The Early Anthropology of Food and Feasting

Although some anthropologists would contend that anthropology is older than history (Sahlins 2004), systematic and "scientific" anthropology arose during the era of Western colonization. Detailed descriptions of places and peoples in the new territorial possessions were called for, and in Britain from 1874 onwards many of the necessary observations were carried out with the aid of a remarkable volume called *Notes and Queries on Anthropology,* the self-stated aim of which was "to promote accurate anthropological observations on the part of travellers" among the indigenous populations that made up the British Empire in its heyday. Small enough to fit into a commodious pocket, it had a ruler in inches and centimetres embossed on the cover, to allow observers to take on-the-spot measurements. The contents consisted of key topics and lists of questions that could be used to construct a detailed description of any society encountered, with the findings to be sent back to the Royal Anthropological Institute in London.

Ultimately becoming a manual for professional anthropologists, *Notes and Queries* purposely avoided theoretical matters, stating:

These are undoubtedly of great importance, but the immediate duty of an observer is to observe and record, and the mingling of theories with ascertained facts should be rigorously avoided ... If the recorder wishes to indulge in hypotheses, these should be relegated to an appendix, so that no ambiguity should arise.

(*Notes and Queries* 1929: 17)

Instead of theory, *Notes and Queries* focused on two broad categories—social organization and material culture—not as separate entities, but as parts of an interrelated whole, embracing everything from economics, agriculture and rules of hospitality, to dancing, stimulants and cooking in meticulous detail. Were baskets twined or twilled? How were boats constructed? What kinds of fishhooks were used? In addition, *Notes and Queries* instructed its readers:

It is important that the study of the artefacts and material culture of a people should not be viewed solely from their material aspects ... [there is] an organic connection of ritual practices with the arts and crafts of daily life. Indeed, the practices are considered to be as essential to the industries as are the technical processes themselves, and therefore it is as necessary to record the one as the other. Most, if not all, of the more important ceremonies ... socio-religious in character ... have also a distinctly practical aim; they serve not only to maintain and increase social well-being, but frequently they have a definite purpose in causing the increase of crops, or success in hunting, fishing and warfare. Therefore, every description of the occupations of a people must take note, not only of their material aspects, but also of the minor ritual acts and the major ceremonies ... Further the myths and folk tales connected with any occupation should be recorded ... it sometimes happens that particular plants are cultivated with much more ritual than others, some without any at all, and an endeavour should be made to discover which are so treated and why.

(*Notes and Queries* 1929: 187)

Here, *Notes and Queries* (1929: 188) pointed out, material culture had an additional use: "There are times when the investigator of socio-religious matters may find that he cannot get information and he will then find that a study of material culture provides him with a convenient avenue of approach." As material culture threw light on belief, so it revealed social organization. It quickly became apparent that simple questions about material life—such as "Is the food ready cut up or does each help himself?" and "Is there any order observed in serving the persons present or giving drink?" could reveal complex social hierarchies and dynamics of inclusion and exclusion not otherwise easily observable.

The questions in *Notes and Queries* were not intended to be asked of the people under observation. As the manual explained—"They are framed to draw the observer's attention to facts which he might otherwise ignore, and are founded on the practical experience of fieldworkers throughout the world. An attempt has been made to open all possible fields of investigation" (*Notes and Queries* 1929: 19).

Through reading the manual, the observer was irresistibly drawn into unknown material worlds, learning to see them in new ways, especially from the point of view of the people being observed.

The material culture relating to food proved an especially rich resource for, as *Notes and Queries* (1929: 218) put it, the provision of an adequate food supply "was the first charge upon the time and energies of all peoples." In early editions, there were five sections devoted to food—mode of cooking, articles of food, fires, manufacture of drinks and meals. Questions included "What are the staple and the accessory articles of diet ... anything from worms or grubs to man?" (Special queries were provided should the observer encounter cannibalism: "Is it frequent or exceptional? Is human flesh looked upon in the same light as other animal food, or partaken of as a matter of ritual? What parts of the body are eaten and why? Are any parts considered delicacies?") Among hundreds upon hundreds of other questions were: "Is beer known and how is it made? How were the spoils of hunting and fishing divided? Are men and women allowed to have their meals together? Is there any particular sequence in the order of dishes? Are there special ceremonies connected with food? Is there any mode of preserving fruit or vegetables by cooking with sugar, fermenting, pickling, etc.? Are great feasts held, and if so, on what occasions?"

No society large or small, materially simple or complex, was without feasts and descriptions came flooding in: the great feast that preceded the yam harvest in Old Calabar, Southern Nigeria; the Midwinter Festival of the North American Iroquois which centered around a feast and the sacrifice of a white dog; celebratory feasts among New Guinea head hunters where triumphant warriors in full regalia ate special food from a wooden trough carved like a crocodile; elsewhere in New Guinea the nine-day feasts in which kindred tribes and allies gathered to pledge loyalty sealed by gifts of pigs followed by a procession of masked figures and dancing; the feasts held in Zululand after the death of elders and chiefs, to remove the "darkness" produced by death; the great meat feasts held to celebrate weddings among the Bakene of East Africa; the headhunting feasts of the Sagai of Borneo, at which the successful hunter made a speech about his victim whose head was on display, and then claimed the bride of his choice; the feasts held by the Fulani of West Africa, who only killed their own cattle when the first son of a newly married couple was born, and then only the infant's father, his best man at the wedding and one chosen male friend were allowed to partake; the three days of feasting and gifting held to celebrate Muslim betrothals in the Punjab; the feasts of beef and sugar beer served at rainmaking ceremonies among the Akamba of East Africa; the famous potlatch feasts of the Pacific Northwest Coast of North America at which piles of valuables were destroyed in competitive displays in front of the assembled guests, and further examples beyond count. Across time, space and cultures, the feast was never-ending.

It quickly became apparent that feasts and food were what the social theorist Marcel Mauss (1966: 76–7) called a "total social phenomenon," usually rendered today as "total social fact":

> These phenomena are at once legal, economic, religious, aesthetic, morphological and so on. They are legal in that they concern individual and collective right, organized and diffuse morality; they may be entirely obligatory, or subject simply to praise or disapproval. They are at once political and domestic, being of interest both to classes and to clans and families. They are religious; they concern true religion, animism, magic and diffuse religious mentality. They are economic, for the notions of value, utility, interest, luxury, wealth, acquisition, accumulation, consumption and liberal and sumptuous expenditure are all present, although perhaps not in their modern senses. Moreover, these institutions have an important aesthetic side which we have left unstudied; but the dances performed, the songs and shows, the dramatic representations given between camps or partners, the objects made, used, decorated, polished, amassed and transmitted with affection, received with joy, given away in triumph, the feasts in which everyone participates – all these, the food, objects and services, are the source of aesthetic emotions as well as those aroused by interest.

This totality lay at the heart of what became a distinctive feature of anthropological analysis and description—holism—meaning the study of all aspects of a society and their interrelations. In the words of Marcel Mauss (1966: 78): "the study of the concrete, which is the study of the whole ... furnishes more explanations ... than the study of the abstract."

The aim of anthropology was not simply the amassing of descriptions of exotic folk and their practices. The foundational objective of the discipline according to the anthropologist Bronislaw Malinowski (1922: 517–8) was "the study of other cultures with the ultimate aim of understanding our own." Or as the anthropologist Franz Boas (1928: 522) put it, anthropology must study human culture in all the variety of its forms past and present, including ours.

Out of the mass of description, patterns began to emerge. In all cultures, food was at the intersection of the biophysical and the sociocultural. Different forms of food production were associated with certain kinds of social organization, and vice versa. Food was symbol as well as sustenance, linking body and spirit, past and present, place and person, self and society. These meanings and values were embodied in the cuisine as a whole, in particular meals or foods, or even in a single dish, giving them symbolic power. In addition to the material aspects of food, there was an associated cosmology that connected food to religion, myth, magic and belief. Food linked the social, the material and the sacred, and at its heart was the feast.

In all parts of the world, feasts were the primary arena for:

- The display of hierarchy, status and power including gender distinctions
- The expression of competition and conflict
- The negotiation of loyalty and alliance
- The creation and consolidation of community and identity through inclusion and exclusion
- The cultural recognition and regulation of the natural world, time and the life cycle
- The enactment of public rituals
- The linking of sacred and secular
- The celebration of life and death
- The honoring of the gods
- The commemoration of specific events and personages
- The mobilization and exploitation of resources.

It became axiomatic in anthropology that one of the best ways of engaging with and understanding a society was to attend a feast, and then to follow up the networks, hierarchies, rituals and objects there displayed. On a smaller scale, focusing on a particular meal or key symbolic food was also instructive.

The significance of symbolic food was well known in antiquity, the best-known example being the "black broth" of the Spartans made of pork, blood and vinegar. Sustaining for a society of warriors, it caused a citizen of Sybaris, a city-state known for its luxurious ways, to say after tasting it that he understood why the Spartans were so willing to die in battle. In another account, the ruler of Pontus, on first tasting the broth, spat it out, only to be told "Your Majesty, in order to appreciate this broth, it is necessary to have exercised in the Spartan manner, and to have bathed in the Eurotas" (the river on whose bank the city of Sparta was built). Here is an expression of what we call *terroir* today—the belief in the mystical and consti-tutive properties of the ancestral soil, embodied in the food it produced, consumed by its people.

A book published in the 1970s was a pioneering work in the anthropology of food as it then was, in which leading anthropologists of the day used local food and cooking as a lens through which to describe the societies they had studied during fieldwork. It also provided recipes at a time when "ethnic" recipes of any kind were rarely obtainable outside the communities of origin, there was little general interest in exotic food and cookbooks and recipes had not yet been recognized as key social documents. Entitled *The Anthropologists' Cookbook* (Kuper 1977), it included chapters such as Le Stockfish [of the Quercy Region, France] by Julian Pitt-Rivers; Green Chile Stew of the American South West by Robin Fox; Ghanaian Ground-Nut Stew by Esther Goody; Maroon Jerk Pork and other Jamaican Cooking by Barbara Kopytoff; and Roast Dog or a Substitute by Naomichi Ishige. Beyond these specific cases, it was an invitation to think more generally about food, feasts, what we eat, why and the consequences. In her Introduction to the book, the anthropologist Mary Douglas (1977: 7) wrote, "Let this be a beginning to a systematic anthropology of food." But then anthropology began to change.

Originally, anthropologists focused on small-scale societies, usually those at what was called the "tribal" level of social organization, illiterate, in remote locations where the people appeared free of outside influences, and in a kind of "anthropological present" where nothing changed over time. Societies and fieldwork sites like these disappeared rapidly in the twentieth century, and increasingly after World War II anthropology was seen to be tainted by colonialism and imperialism and out of date as regards mechanization, urbanization and other aspects of modernity. "Traditional" food came to seem of little importance in the face of the sweeping social and political changes of the time, the effects of globalization on local diets and the rise of newly independent nations. By the 1970s, the ethnographic authority and objectivity once taken for granted had been called into question, as had the authority of anthropologists to represent other cultures. While much of anthropology succumbed to a period of disciplinary self-doubt, the nascent interest in food and feasting took root elsewhere.

The Emergence of Food and Feasting Studies in History and Archaeology

The temporary eclipse of anthropology coincided with the Cultural/Material Turn referred to above, which saw the emergence of the New History in all its forms, including women's history and cultural history. There was a period of "borrowings" (Scholliers and Clafin 2012: 4) in which historians drew upon the social sciences and especially anthropology, as has been described, to give dynamism, depth and breadth to their customary primary resource, written text. When the authority of official texts was challenged, interest shifted toward other kinds of records and material culture. Initially, the quantitative methods of sociology—things tangible and enumerable—were easier for historians to work with than anthropological intangibles such as "symbols" and "culture," but eventually these too were appropriated. The complexity of food and its centrality to all aspects of human life as established by anthropologists then became the basis of a field that is now global in scope and rapidly evolving (Mintz and Dubois 2002; Hayden and Villeneuve 2011). The first Food Studies departments appeared in universities in America in the mid-1990s, although reservations about the subject persisted. As scholarly works on the historical, social and cultural meanings of food began to appear, critics charged that it was not a "real" subject, but "scholarship Lite" (Ruark 1999).

Today, food history flourishes in America (Bentley 2012) and further afield, while in modern Europe the field has been well compared to a house with many rooms (Scholliers 2012) each of which accommodates different groups of residents who focus on food in some way, usually as a lens through which to address larger issues and questions. In addition to those who consider themselves "historians" albeit informed by the cultural turn to some degree, there are socio-economic historians, agricultural historians, gender historians, environmental historians, commodity historians, historians of medicine and of science, cultural historians, art historians and historians interested in advancing critical theory. Other rooms hold anthropologists, ethnologists, sociologists, geographers, philosophers, psychologists and natural scientists. Most of the foregoing are academics, but other rooms are populated by the large non-academic group that distinguishes the food field—specialists that include journalists, cookery writers, bloggers, artists of various kinds (see Machida 2013), heritage curators and re-enactors, chefs and other people with professional culinary training, artisanal food producers, food activists and environmentalists, foragers, writers and novelists, enthusiasts, collectors, technologists and those historians who combine research with practice, like Ivan Day (2014), who recreates cooking and dining in medieval England, the technology, food and presentation of the Victorian Christmas, and the courtly cuisine of the Italian Renaissance. Everyone in the house is further differentiated by national, regional and period interests. In some cases, the doors between the rooms are firmly closed, while in others the walls seem to be porous, facilitating communication and collaboration. Is it all food history, or is there a core "food history" within the broader interdisciplinary field of "food studies," and if the latter, just what makes up the core? These questions are highly contested and the answers ever-changing with the field definitely a work in progress, but what about the distant past and the archaeology of food?

Initially, the relationship between history and the archaeology of the remote past, which grew out of antiquarianism and collecting, was close but distinctly unequal in character. Among classicists and specialists in the Ancient Near East and medieval Europe, archaeology was seen as subservient to history, with objects constituting a kind of mute record that could never challenge the authenticity, authority and direct access to the past provided by text. The primary use of archaeological artifacts was to validate text (Moreland 2001). For this, a favored method was the collection of artifacts and their arrangement into typologies or developmental sequences—still seen in museum display cases—in apparent confirmation of the written record. To supplement this restricted use of objects, aesthetics and style—usually in developmental terms—took on importance. Historians set the agenda for the study of the past, with archaeology acting as the handmaid of history (Moreland 2006: 136).

All this changed with the Cultural/Material Turn, which had a profound effect on the discipline. The discrediting of text liberated archaeology from history's shadow, and led to the emergence of what outsiders gloss as the New Archaeology but which archaeologists themselves see as contesting submovements or as successive stages— processual and post-processual—in the on-going development of their discipline. With objects, artifacts and whole sites now seen by many archaeologists as the only—or at least the primary—direct contact with the past, everything hinged on interpretation. As had happened in the New History, because of its centrality to all aspects of human life, food became a key focus.

In America, early processualists asserted "American archaeology is anthropology, or it is nothing" (Willey and Phillips in Binford 1962: 217) and, informed by the anthropology of the period, sought to reconstitute past societies from the archaeo- logical record in an objective and "scientific" manner, concentrating on provisioning, environmental exploitation and the types of social structure and functional identities associated with them (Joyce 2012). "Postprocessualism" is a very diverse and divisive movement, the best-known arm of which approached the past and its material record in a subjective and politicized fashion, from a range of theoretical perspectives that included Marxist and neo-Marxist archaeology, practice theory, engendered archaeology and phenomenology (Twiss 2012: 360). Their interest lay in the ways in which politics, ideologies, belief, economy, ethnicity, gender, hierarchies, and other forms of diversity (Twiss 2012: 357–8) could be inferred from such things as the production, preparation, consumption and material accoutrements of food, feasting and drinking (Dietler 2006). In addition, there developed "processual-plus" archaeology, which combined the two in different ways (Hegmon 2003).

By "moving beyond the traditional concerns with typology, chronology and distribution" (Wright 2004b: 123) and applying the anthropological patterns and principles set out above to artifacts and sites, archaeologists were able to animate the material remains, recover social aspects of ancient societies, and create a dynamic new understanding of past societies that was not dependent on text. For example, the forms, patterns of distribution and contexts of elite Inca pottery vessels become "a window into the ways in which food, feasting and gender figured in the negotiation of state power and imperial expansion" (Bray 2003a: 93), while the visual images of feast and drinking scenes on cylinder seals throw light on "the politics of the distri- bution and consumption of food and drink as they contribute to state power and policies in the urbanized landscape of southern Mesopotamia in the Early Dynastic period, c. 2900–2350" (Pollock 2003: 17). As was general in other disciplines at the time, after an early emphasis on elite food and feasting, the archaeological focus widened from the wealthy and powerful to include those previously excluded. In Egyptology, long focused on Pharaonic burials and elite culture in which the New Kingdom rich had over forty kinds of bread and cake and twenty-three kinds of beer to choose from (Tyson Smith 2003), interest shifted to "settlement archaeology" and the everyday lives, humble homes and monotonous diet of the faceless, nameless workers who built the fine tombs, palaces and monuments. Despite these changes, the archaeological penchant for typologies remains, as seen in the tendency to categorize feasts by function—for example Hayden's (2001: 38) alliance and cooperation feasts (for solidarity), economic feasts (for gain) and diacritical feasts (for display)—which are then imposed as templates. These may be a useful heuristic device, but tend to flatten the cultural landscape and de-contextualize, rendering all feasts the same.

As with food history, food archaeology today can be compared to a house with many rooms, generating studies as varied as the gendered production of pounded acorns in pre-contact California, burnt animal sacrifice at Mycenae, slave diet in colonial America, the economics and politics of Maya meat eating, crop choice and social change in early China, and bread-making and social interaction in the workmen's village at Amarna, Egypt. A particular interest among prehistorians is the role feasting may have played in early plant and animal domestication and the emergence of complex societies and inequality (Flannery and Marcus 2012; Wright 2014).

Increasingly, archaeological studies incorporate scientific techniques like isotope analysis that give information about long-term diet in the past. Research is beginning to reveal regional preference patterns—such as those for sticky rather than non-sticky rice—that go much further back in time than previously suspected, and are embedded in sociocultural practices and values (Fuller and Rowlands 2011). The remarkable stability and persistence of these preferences over time indicate that, although it is only beginning to be known, cuisine has a *cultural* prehistory that underlies the way we eat and feast today. Molecular archaeology is used to investigate the composition of residue in cooking pots and drinking vessels which previously could only be guessed at, while the field of archaeobotany explores the consequences of human–plant interactions over time. Much has been learned about the movement of plants and animals, and about the early role of food in human origins and physical development, but since the Cultural/Material turn due attention is paid to the social. As the archaeologist Andrew Sherratt (1999: 29–30) put it:

> The spread of new crops and of newly domesticated forms of livestock, is a *social* process: that is to say, part of the sphere of competition, emulation, negotiation, performance and communication like the rest of material culture. Simply because its products are consumable in the literal sense should not exclude them from the field of the anthropology of consumption!

Which brings us back to anthropology.

Consumption and the Later Anthropology of Food and Feasting

During anthropology's period of postcolonial self-doubt in the 1980s and 1990s while the old paradigms were being deconstructed, "consumption" emerged across the humanities and social sciences. Hailed as "a major transformation in anthropology" and as "the vanguard of history" (Miller 1995a: 141, 1995b), it involved applying anthropological knowledge to the problems and processes of life in the developed world. A pioneering work in the field was Mary Douglas's *The World of Goods* (1979) in which she argued that mass produced contemporary goods—like the handcrafted objects and food produced by natives on the old fieldwork sites— were social values in material form, making visible and stable the categories of culture, communicating social meaning and drawing the lines of social relationships. Objects were not inert, but had agency, reflecting social values and formations and also influencing and creating them. Or as Sahlins (1976) put it, social categories corresponded to categories of things, and when one changed, so did the other. Consumption was not the mere act of acquisition—it was "the very arena in which culture is fought over and licked into shape" (Douglas 1979: 37). Text came into it too; Appadurai (1981, 1988) showed how the creation of a standard "Indian" cuisine, supported by a new genre of popular cookery books and key recipes, was a major factor in achieving national unity: recipes and cookery books both created and perpetuated the new social order, for the commensality produced by eating the same food welded community and identity in a way that political rhetoric alone could not. This was the traditional material culture of *Notes and Queries* re-envisioned for the contemporary world. Although it seems obvious and taken for granted today, it was revolutionary at the time, making anthropological techniques accessible to inter-disciplinary scholars, introducing a new kind of dynamism to contemporary history and opening up the study of food within anthropology.

In his seminal *Cooking, Cuisine and Class* (1982), Jack Goody set out the three main anthropological approaches to food, drink and feasting developed on the basis of ethnographic observations over time, now applicable to all societies and periods in history: the functional, the cultural and the structural. These remain major modes of analysis, supplemented by new fields like sensory anthropology and the anthropology of memory (Holzman 2006, Sutton 2010) and ecologically oriented post-development anthropology (Klein, Pottier and West 2010). The differences between the functional, cultural and structural approaches often lead to academic disagreement and the boundaries frequently blur, but all have been drawn on in this work. Implicit in the three is a key anthropological distinction between *etic* and *emic*. *Etic* is the exterior, "objective," universalistic perspective of an outside observer, epitomized by culturally non-specific studies of technology and politics. *Emic* is the culturally specific, inside view—the way the people themselves see things, drawn from their own written words, representations and oral accounts. Although they use the term *"emic,"* archaeologists have found it somewhat problematic because their access to people is not direct in the same way that text and observation are—although they can now argue that the new scientific techniques they use add another dimension to the meaning of *emic*. Introduced in 1954 by Kenneth Pike, the terms have sometimes been called "dated" but the distinction is vital, and has been given new currency by studies of globalization to which they are central. Both *emic and etic* are essential to holistic analyses.

Anthropology: The Functional Approach

This *etic* approach sees feasting as an activity with adaptive, *practical* benefits for human reproduction and survival on the physical and social levels (Hayden 2014 and see Wiessner and Schiefenhovel 1996). Its starting point is subsistence, and it can be summed up in these words attributed to the food writer M. F. K. Fisher—*"First we eat, then we do everything else."* This is the domain of *homo economicus*, of the "natural economy" and of utilitarianism. In this view, feasts are a means by which people transform food surpluses into other kinds of useful or desirable goods and services (Hayden 2001: 27), and studies focus on the way surpluses are produced, used, transformed, controlled and distributed. Commensality, the very act of eating together, is seen as promoting solidarity and community unproblematically. This segues into social technology—feasts mobilize labor, extract surplus produce from the general population for elite use and create political power. Everything is seen as proceeding from functional principles and the emphasis is on production. For example, from this perspective, studies of the ancient history of wine tend to focus on the domestication of early grape varieties and how vines were tended and the fruit processed, rather than on when and how wine was consumed and used in rituals. Food functionalists are dismissive of studies that look at feasts through what they see as "a fog of ideology and symbolism" (Hayden 2001: 28). Human action is assumed to be rational and pragmatic. Anything seemingly irrational or illogical, like ceremonies and rituals, are thought to be "functional" in some way, and generally disregarded. Food and drink are of little importance in themselves, serving primarily to facilitate social relations. Societies are seen from an *etic* perspective, "from the outside," largely shorn of cultural specificities. This is the most universalistic of the approaches, "objective" and interested in societies on a general level.

Anthropology: The Cultural Approach

In contrast to the universalism and utilitarianism of Functionalism, this approach was summed up by Mary Douglas (1977: 7) in just four words: *"Food is not feed."* Food is *culturally* defined. Beyond basic subsistence, each society decides for itself what is edible and what is not, and how things should be prepared and eaten. These decisions develop into foodways or cuisines—"highly formalized and typically normative culinary systems [that] sustain cohesive and coherent cuisines" (Ferguson

2004: 22)—which are cosmological and symbolic systems as well as culinary ones. Cuisines make categories of culture visible and embody social meanings and values that become one with the eater through the act of consumption. The emphasis is on what Marshall Sahlins (1976: 170) called "the cultural reason in our food habits"— the distinctive practices, preferences and categories that define a particular society or group, and show how they think about the world, themselves and others. Food is a fundamental part of identity, a way of distinguishing between "we" and "they," "self" and "Other." Because food is essential to life, it is the most direct way of demonstrating power and status, making this the domain of what Louis Dumont called *homo hierarchicus*. Different types or categories of food, drink, dishes and feast gifts correspond to different types or categories of people. Socio-spatial placement is significant—what do furniture, posture, seating and placement say about the diners and the society as a whole? The cultural approach lends itself to studies of taste and of memory and, instead of treating food simply as sustenance, it deals with the fine points of cuisine, of changing ways of eating, and the significance of specific meals and feasts, along with ceremonies and etiquette. In the case of ancient wine, cultural interest lies not in production, but in the sacred and social significance of drinking and related practices. Ritual, myth and belief play an important role in the cultural approach, providing insight into past events and present social formations. It is concerned too with how feasts materialize and perpetuate the structures of power, while also challenging them. This approach is predominantly *emic*, seeing feasting, food and drink from an "inside" perspective, focusing on the meaning and significance they have within particular societies, although when these are compared cross-culturally at a higher level of analysis, an *etic* dimension is involved.

Anthropology: The Structural/Symbolic Approach

This is the domain of *homo symbolicus*, and the source of one of the classic anthropological quotations—food is *"good to think with"*—by the noted French structuralist Claude Levi-Strauss. Its fundamental premise is that humans perceive their world and distinguish culture from nature using categories or symbolic codes which are reflected in language. The assumption is that, by analyzing linguistic terms, the way people think and how they experience and order their lives should become apparent. Arising in the 1960s during the academic heyday of semiotics, it is driven by a search for the universal "deep structures" of human thought as revealed through language relating to such key cultural phenomena as kinship, ideology, mythology, ritual, art, etiquette and cooking (Levi-Strauss 1967: 84). Mediating between nature and culture, food and cooking are particularly appropriate for this kind of study. Applying the structural approach to cuisine, Levi-Strauss began by isolating what he called "gustemes," constituent elements of culinary meaning, which he organized into three oppositions: national/exotic ingredients; staple food/ accompaniments; and savory/bland, providing an initial basis for comparing and "understanding" different cuisines. Levi-Strauss then elaborated this treatment to include the meanings associated with the "culinary triangle" of raw, cooked and rotted food, along with additional food and drink oppositions such as roasted/boiled and hot/cold. Using these oppositions and others, Levi-Strauss analyzed language and myth to arrive at insights such as "Boiling provides a means of complete conservation of the meat and its juices, whereas rotting is accompanied by destruction and loss. Thus one denotes economy, the other prodigality; the latter is aristocratic, the former plebeian" (Leach 1989: 23). Although some scholars take issue with the style of structural discourse which tends to be highly abstruse, this approach demonstrated that the processes of food preparation and categories of food are everywhere elaborately structured. Of the three, the structural approach is the least used as a method of analysis today, but it continues to be influential by encouraging scholars to go beyond the functional and the descriptive and to *think* with and through food, drink and feasting. Proponents would say this was the most *emic* of the approaches, although critics say it is *etic*, a mode of interpretation imposed from outside.

These models have been criticized for being essentialist, static, synchronic and normative (Hicks 2010: 27), but this is to misunderstand how the models work. Dynamism is their very essence with things always in the process of change, and the synchronic element is removed when the models or aspects are compared across time or space, anthropology's "comparative method." Anti-essentialism became fashionable after the Turn, but it is now clear that, in the past and in the present, we continue to be constrained by norms. As for not being "new"—a charge leveled by neophiles—these approaches have stood the test of time, and continue to inform current historical and archaeological studies, their presence often disguised by secondary source citations and sometimes by reinvention under different terms (see Ingold in Hicks 2010: 79–80). For example, today's combined "new" cultural ecology/archaeology (Hayden 2014) corresponds to anthropology's traditional functional approach.

Alone or in combination, these approaches reveal recurrent anthropological themes relating to food—the importance of myth, and the feast as sacrifice or gift—features anthropologists look for in the field, in texts and at feasts.

Food: Ritual, Myth, Symbol and the Sacred

The ethnographic record discloses the deep connections between food, the sacred and the origins of life—what the anthropologist A. M. Hocart called "The Life-Giving Myth." As he wrote, what really mattered to the ancients, as to us, was life—not merely keeping alive but living well:

Life depends on many things—on food, and food on rain and sun; on victory, and victory on skill and strength; on unity, and unity on wise rules and obedience. An elaborate ritual grew up designed to secure all these good things, all that contributed to the full life.

(Hocart 1970: 11)

The beginnings of these good things—their original creation—are recorded in myths which set the precedent on which the rituals are based. Existence is uncertain, ritual aims to remove that uncertainty by ensuring abundance through the proper observations. The myth describes the ritual, and the ritual enacts the myth (Hocart 1970: 22). Instead of being mere fables or fictions, myths are about what Hocart calls the serious business of life—secret and sacred knowledge that confers abundance, health, wealth and victory over enemies for the community as a whole.

It is not only secular pragmatism that drives ceremonies, rituals and feasts, but sacred power and fear of or love for the gods. The anthropologist studying feasts is interested in how religious sanctions expressed through ritual as a series of obligations to the gods dictate the expenditure of foods and labor, and also in how the belief that the feast and the proper performance of its rites are essential to maintaining fertility, security and general welfare through divine favor (Firth 1967: 27) expresses and perpetuates the secular structures of power. It is often in myth that the origins of the meanings, associations and symbolism attached to particular foods, drinks and feasts are to be found.

"Symbol" is an elusive concept. All cultures construct their own subjective and distinctive systems of meanings and values that define and organize their worlds. These meanings and values come to be embodied in objects and actions called "symbols" that stand for or represent them. Symbols are able to evoke strong emotions, mobilize social action, communicate values and mores and serve as vehicles of culture, giving insights into what is going on beneath the functional level of everyday life. The difference between ritual and symbol is one of degree rather than of kind. Turner (1967) described symbols as the smallest units of ritual behavior, while Kertzer (1988: 9, 11) defined ritual as "action wrapped in a web of symbolism," with symbols providing the content of ritual. Usually a symbol is thought of as an object, and a ritual as an action or cultural performance involving symbols—for example, a national flag (symbol) and a parade in which the flag is carried (ritual/cultural performance)—but the boundaries between them blur in practice. What interests anthropologists is the role of symbols and rituals in the social process, and what they can tell us about the societies and groups of which they are part. Symbols and rituals are dynamic; old symbols can disappear and new ones emerge, established rituals can be appropriated and given new meanings, and symbols and rituals can be used to foment rebellion and revolution as well as promote stability and continuity. As Mary Douglas put it, "social rituals create a reality which would be nothing without them" (in Kertzer 1988: 12). That the meaning of symbols is complex and ambiguous seems only to enhance their power and their potential for manipulation and mystification.

The Feast as Gift and Sacrifice

The correct verb relating to "feast" is "to give." A feast is something that is not just "held," but given, in the manner of a gift. "Gift" is one of the foundational concepts in anthropology, associated with Marcel Mauss. Not the spontaneous and ostensibly disinterested present the word calls to mind today, the Maussian "gift" is part of a social contract based on reciprocal exchange involving three obligations: to give, to receive and to repay. The principle is summed up in the Latin phrase *do ut des*—I give that you may give. No gift comes without strings that tie the recipient to the giver in some way. Whether the relationship is between equals or non-equals, whether it is direct or indirect, some kind of return is expected and it is the cycle of giving, return and giving again that keeps the relationship active, and helps to hold the society together, with connections between societies maintained through reciprocal exchanges in the same manner. What is given away is deemed to include something of the giver, thus strengthening, deepening and prolonging the gift bond. Commercial transactions in which commodities are bought and sold are considered not to have these qualities and the relationship does not extend beyond the transaction, although in practice the distinction can blur (Wengrow 2008). Feasts are a gift in themselves and a primary arena in which the economy of gift exchange was transacted in public.

Sacrifice is a special form of the gift and, according to Mauss, the oldest—a contract between man and the gods and ancestors. As with other gifts, sacrifices and offerings are made in hope and expectation of a return gift in the form of victory, fertility, wealth, health, protection and other signs of divine favor. As an old Mesopotamian text *A Father's Advice to his Son* put it:

> Every day worship your god.
> Sacrifice and benediction are the proper accompaniment of incense
> Present your free-will offering to your god,
> For this is proper toward the god.
> Prayer, supplication and prostration
> Offer him daily and you *will* get your reward.
>
> (Bottéro, 2001: 113, original emphasis)

There are many kinds of sacrifice, including the well-known blood sacrifice in which living things are despatched upon the altar; libations in which liquids such as wine and beer are poured out for the gods; offerings of first fruits or of specially prepared foods, often followed by a feast. It was common for food and drink to be offered to the god, and then to be treated as divine leftovers, to be shared out in some way, frequently at a public feast in which the relationship between men and gods was further consolidated, and social hierarchy made manifest through who was allowed to perform and be present at the rites, and how the consecrated food and drink were apportioned and consumed.

Toward Synthesis

Despite the developments in history, archaeology and anthropology described above, and the immense and ever-growing corpus of specialized academic work on food, the answers to the questions: In what social and historical context were the feast objects in museums used and enjoyed? What were these feasts of antiquity like, why were they ubiquitous and important?—remain elusive. This is because they cannot be answered coherently by a single discipline.

Before the Cultural/Material Turn, the simplified differences between the disciplines can be represented in this way:

History/past/texts

Archaeology/past/things

Anthropology/present/people

After the Turn, the boundaries blurred and continue to do so, while at the same time there are intermittent attempts in some quarters to put up barriers, in order to protect disciplinary identity. This is particularly true of anthropology and archaeology. In 1929, *Notes and Queries* (363) declared:

> Archaeology and Ethnology (here used as synonymous with Anthropology) are the same subject considered from different aspects. The latter deals with existing conditions, the former with those that are past; but the past may be remote, or even quite recent.

Some archaeologists have been happy to embrace this duality, while others strive to establish archaeology as an entirely separate discipline, closely connected to which is the rise of theory in all fields.

Since the advent of postmodernism, there has been an evolutionary hegemonic view among academics that if a discipline is to advance it must move beyond the descriptive to the theoretical, and that developing or substantiating theory is the sole worthy object of scholarly production. Theory is indeed important and valuable, but taken to extremes it can become, as the anthropologist Tim Ingold has pointed out, a kind of an elaborate academic game, a charade in which practitioners "talk past each other in largely incommensurate theoretical languages" (Ingold 2012: 427; see also Ingold in Hicks 2010: 79–80), spinning abstractions that are ever-more divorced from the material, a danger against which *Notes and Queries* warned long ago. In the field, there is the associated problem of over-determination—arriving on site with the specific aim of substantiating a particular theory. As one critic put it,

> by investing heavily in a model, the archaeologist may find himself merely telling the same story over and over again. The tales told, for example, by archaeologists devoted

to critical theory may be "true" in that they reflect a portion of the historical reality of a time and place, but they lose their power through constant repetition. Every site becomes merely another opportunity to identify one particular historical process at work.

(Praetzellis 1998: 2)

There is also the risk of becoming tied to a micro-site, instead of dealing with larger regions. The result is an incomplete picture of sites and societies and fragmentation of the field as a whole, a predicament that is now common in archaeology, anthropology and many branches of history. Above all, it has meant the loss of anthropological holism—the broad, integrated picture needed to answer the questions above. The pre- and post-Cultural/Material Turn present a classic pattern of thesis and antithesis, from one extreme to the other. What is needed now is synthesis—a coming together of different disciplines, not as a denial of theory, but to consolidate and revitalize the foundation upon which theory should be grounded.

In order to achieve this, the present study looks at feasts and feasting from the perspective of the "anthropology of history" developed by the anthropologist Marshall Sahlins, both in his own work and through collaboration with the archaeologist Patrick Kirch (see Kirch and Sahlins 1992). The anthropology of history is, as Sahlins (1992: 1) explains, "a synthetic discipline in the broad sense ... combining archaeology and social anthropology to construct an integrated history," in which culture is history and vice versa.

The linchpin of Sahlins' approach is the redefinition of "history" or rather its restoration to what Sahlins contends is an earlier meaning that embraces both *logos* and *mythos*, the former usually defined as logical, universalistic, objective thinking characteristic of pre-Turn history, and the latter as mythical, particularistic and subjective thinking distinctive of anthropology. In Sahlins' view, history began as anthropology. The text that established narrative written history in the West was *The Histories* by the Greek writer Herodotus (c. 485–425 BC). Epic in scope, it was intended in his words to "prevent the traces of human events being erased by time" and "to preserve the remarkable achievements of Greeks and non-Greeks." *The Histories* can be seen as the first example of what Geertz (1973) later called thick description—a culturally informed materially conscious account in which gods, omens, religious beliefs, dynastic relations, animate landscapes, different voices, strange customs and costumes, foreign ways of thought, sacred and significant objects and much more were interwoven with an examination of the causes of the hostilities between the Greeks and the Persians and other non-Greeks, in which politics was only one factor. On the basis of this great work, Cicero acclaimed Herodotus as the Father of History and, because of his ethnographic sensibilities, anthropologists consider Herodotus the first anthropologist as well.

Because Herodotus presented non-Greek values, objects and achievements in their own terms and offered a culturally nuanced interpretation of events instead of insisting on Greek superiority, he was vilified by Plutarch and other later historians who called him *philobarbaros*—"lover of barbarians"—a label that has stuck to anthropologists ever since. The Greeks preferred the writer Thucydides (c. 460–395 BC), whose *History of the Peloponnesian War* was the antithesis of Herodotus' *Histories*. Seen entirely from the Greek perspective, it aimed to present what Thucydides called "an exact knowledge of the past," focusing on pragmatic political decisions and the detailed movements of soldiers on the battlefield, portraying the victory over the Persians as the inevitable result of the superiority of Greek civilization and military strategy. There were no nuances, no multiplicity of voices, no sense of dynamic encounters. Historical thought now became *logos*, while everything else was dismissed as *mythos*—fable or the stuff of literature and poetry. Material things retreated before text. As Sahlins (2004) put it—history became cultureless.

Did Thucydides give an exact account of the past, as he claimed? On the one hand, his descriptions of battles are so clear that military strategists can use them today. On the other hand, reading Thucydides you would never know that in ancient Greece all military and political undertakings, campaigns, enemy engagements, the conclusion of treaties and the opening of assemblies had to begin with a sacrifice followed by a meal (Detienne 1989: 3), and that all military campaigns had a sacred as well as a secular dimension. *Logos* accounts give only a partial view, *etic* rather than *emic*, divorced from the full context. To restore anthropological holism and dynamism to an understanding of the past, Sahlins advocates a return to the cultural landscape of Herodotus. These are worlds in which divinity and politics are entangled, ritual is an instrument of power, and the ruler—often seen as a god or a semi-divine being—mediates the relations between society and the cosmos. A purely *mythos* perspective is no more satisfactory than a completely *logos* one; both are necessary. As Sahlins (2004: 2) puts it: "If the past is a foreign country, then it is another culture. *Autre temps, autre moeurs*. And if it is another culture, then discovering it takes some anthropology."

This means going into the past, equipped with what anthropologists know about culture and society, but drawing on archaeology and texts as well—"going among the texts" in Sahlins' phrase, or "doing anthropology in the archives" as the Comaroffs (1992: 11) put it. Initially, many anthropologists had reservations about using texts after they had been discredited, but archives have now become a legitimate fieldwork site and subject in their own right (Zeitlyn 2012). The use of text requires a literate society, or at least written descriptions of non-literate ones. Archaeologists and many historians have found it difficult to apply anthropological models taken from tribal culture to the complex hierarchical societies of antiquity, enshrined in text and whose elaborate material remains fill museums. To avoid this problem, Sahlins focused on complex societies of the past, particularly that of ancient Greece during the Peloponnesian Wars, in developing his anthropology of history, along with the hierarchical society of Hawaii. The societies in this study are also complex and hierarchical, with text and with substantial material remains. As described above, history and archaeology have borrowed liberally from anthropology in their post-Turn approach to the past. Anthropology has been slow to return the compliment; *The Never-Ending Feast* is a step in that direction.

To the Feast

At present, human history is reckoned to extend some 2,000,000 years backwards from today, beginning with the earliest human remains and first artifacts. The sequence proceeds through hunter-gathering to the independent emergence of agriculture in several places around the globe. From about 4000 BC, cities begin to emerge, although new discoveries in present-day Syria and Turkey suggest the date may be much earlier. Pastoral nomad societies developed in Eurasia on lands unsuitable for agriculture, supported by the domestication of the horse on the steppes. On-going research focusing on the Arabian Gulf, the Red Sea and all the earth's oceans substantiates the need to think of the past in terms of marine connectivity as well as in terms of terrestrial relations. On the Eurasian Steppe, along the Silk Road and in the Pacific, it is becoming clear that societies long thought of as separate were in fact linked from early times, and regions previously dismissed as unimportant and peripheral from a Eurocentric perspective were centers of complexity and technological innovation. Where in all of this should an historical anthropology of feasts begin?

In establishments like the British Museum, with all the world and 2,000,000 years of time to choose from, curators have devised a menu that carves out what they see as the choice cut—the prime sirloin—of human cultural history. This slice takes in the broad middle of the globe where the core areas of agriculture, animal husbandry and increasingly complex social organization are situated. These are the same places where the earliest writing systems developed, making possible the development of administrative accounts and legal codes, written literature, religious texts, and mathematical and scientific knowledge. Generally, the focus in the great traditional museums is on the period 4000 BC to AD 1600 and the menu consists of the artifactual remains of elite formations, courtly societies and great empires separated in time and space, but comparable as centers of power, influence, affluence—and feasting—from an elite perspective. After the Turn, during the elevation of the everyday, the museums' focus on elites was criticized, but that view is shifting. Within anthropology, Laura Nader has long argued (1972, 1997) that, instead of concentrating on the poor, the disadvantaged, the marginal and the colonized, it is necessary for academics to "study up," and to focus on the colonizers, and the mainstream cultures of affluence and power, if they are to understand the dynamics of societies past or present. George E. Marcus is currently working on what he calls the "belated speciality" of elites, reinvigorating the field through ethnographic and historical study and critical analysis.

So we will follow the menu of the great museums, with one difference. Until relatively recently "ancient history" has been Eurocentric. This is still reflected in museum collections, but this study adopts the emerging perspective in which Europe is seen as Western Asia, and the field of enquiry shifts eastwards. The following chapters deal with Mesopotamia, Assyria and Achaemenid Persia, the early Greeks, the Eurasian nomads at the time of Genghis Khan, Shang China, and Heian Japan. Chapters Two and Three deal with the same wide region, but very different cultures and periods, to introduce a longitudinal dimension. Occasionally context touches on the early modern or present periods, when a broader scope is warranted. Limitations on length prevented the inclusion of chapters on Africa, Oceania and the New World, although these may be dealt with in a future volume. There have been archaeological and historical studies of feasts and feasting (Hayden 2014; Hayden and Villeneuve 2011; Jones 2008; Bray 2003; Strong 2002; Dietler and Hayden 2001a) and many anthropological accounts of feasting in the ethnographic present, but this is the first historical anthropology of its kind on feasting in antiquity.

What follows is the "anthropology of history" as envisaged by Sahlins—a synthetic combination of archaeology and history led by anthropology, and drawing on literature and art—that approaches the textual and material sources mindful of the sort of questions asked in *Notes and Queries*, and of the models and dynamics that are part of the anthropological canon. In particular anthropology is able to provide insights into belief, religion and myth that archaeologists find difficult because many are "not comfortable with exploring social practices which are difficult to document through the material record" (Wright 2004b: 122) and have not yet embraced what the anthropologists John and Jean Comaroff (1992: 27) call the "historical imagi-nation" in which culture is seen to be "a historically situated, historically unfolding ensemble of signifiers in action, signifiers at once material and symbolic, social and aesthetic," which anthropologists and many historians use to move beyond the material evidence. It may also involve using ethnographic knowledge imaginatively (Willerslev 2011) to show, in the present absence of archaeological evidence or text, how things might have been, in order to stimulate future work.

In presentation, this study is a return to the narrative style, *emic* perspective and holistic approach of *mythos* history and the classic anthropological monographs in a world in which "The elementary forms of kinship, politics and religion are all one" (Sahlins 2008: 199). Overall, it aims to bridge the divides that have separated disciplines, and provide a foundation for those interested in cuisine and feasting in complex societies, now working in isolation without common ground. Explication of theory is kept to a minimum. It should be implicit in the text, and has in any case been set out above. This is not a refusal, but an invitation to develop further theory, once a degree of synthesis has been achieved. Where not mentioned, the archaeology is also implicit—it is responsible for the objects in museums, for the chronologies woven into the narrative, and for ways of "reading" monuments and visual representations, as well as for on-going discoveries that will add further detail to the accounts presented here. However, the charts, drawings and tables of objects, and distribution maps common to archaeological studies, have not been included. No standardizing template has been imposed—as with classic anthropological ethnography, each society takes its own shape and speaks with its own voice whenever possible. Instead of mortuary feasts and grave goods, the terrain of archaeologists, the emphasis is on the feasts and objects of the living. Many chapters are linked to objects in the British Museum, which stands as representative of grand museums everywhere, the sites where most people encounter the past through things. In what follows, the terms "feast" and "banquet" are both used, reflecting the sources. Their precise meaning in each case will be clear from the context.

As Aristotle (384–322 BC) observed in his *Politics*, writing of King Midas of Gordium who could not eat or drink because everything he touched turned to gold—"surely it is absurd that a thing should be counted as wealth, which a man may possess in abundance, and yet nonetheless die of starvation." Because of its centrality to human life, food and drink connect everything and are the ultimate form of value, with the feast at its heart. In what social and historical contexts were they held, and why were they so ubiquitous and important? To find out, let us hasten to the never-ending feast.

CHAPTER TWO

Mesopotamia: The Pursuit of Abundance

While I feel wonderful, I feel wonderful
Drinking beer in a blissful mood,
Drinking liquor, feeling exhilarated
With joy in the heart and a happy liver.

> (Hymn to Ninkasi, the goddess of brewing. Dating from c. 1800 BC,
> in Jennings et al., 2005)

From the beginning, the Mesopotamians had a very clear idea of themselves, as their origin myths and literature show (Cohen 2007: 417; Black 2002). While savages went naked or wrapped themselves in animal skins, lived in the wilderness, ate raw meat or grass and drank water, they—the civilized Mesopotamians—wore clothes of linen or wool. They lived in cities: "Good like the city"; they would say, "there is nothing so good" (Kramer 1963: 504). They delighted in consuming bread and beer, the defining food and drink of civilization, the triumph of culture over nature, celebrated in the joyous hymn to Ninkasi above. The Sumerian word for banquet translates literally as "the place of beer and bread" (Michalowski 1994: 29). And they loved feasting. As a Mesopotamian servant exhorted his master: "Feast my lord, feast! A round of banquets is the heart's relief" (Spieser 1954: 98).

To archaeologists, epigraphers and historians of the ancient world, "Mesopotamia" is not only the geographical region that takes in all of present-day Iraq along with parts of Syria and Iran stretching back some six millennia. It is also a gloss for a complex mosaic of cultures and peoples. Among the best known are those we call the Sumerians, including the people of Ur, and the Babylonians, but there were many others. The legacy of Mesopotamia includes the oldest writing system presently known which also served as the first information processing system; astronomy; mathematics; complex accountancy; some of the world's earliest cities and urban planning; the first ancient empires; centralized administration; large-scale flow irrigation; the first written law code; several genres of literature; the first example of work by a named female author, the royal high priestess Enheduanna (c. 2350 BC); foundational religious and philosophical beliefs; innovative monumental architecture; distinctive art; what has been called the world's first cuisine (Bottéro 2004); a complex brewing industry and the first known recipe for beer; possibly the reclining eating position that later became associated with Greece and Rome (Dentzer 1971); the mass production and consumption of food that we take for granted today and certainly feasting on an unprecedented scale. The study of Mesopotamia is in its infancy compared to that of ancient Greece, but it is increasingly claimed that Mesopotamia can "be placed firmly as the ancestor of the Western world" (Black and Green 1992: 7), and that it is the distant source of Western civilization, "at the extreme horizon of history" (Bottéro 1995: 1), influencing Greece and Rome to an extent that is only beginning to be acknowledged.

Context: The Mesopotamian Pasts

The broad sweep of Mesopotamian history has been well characterized as "the alternation of centralized political control with periods of turmoil" (Postgate 1992: 22) throughout its long duration. While the oldest prehistoric remains now known from Mesopotamia date from the sixth millennium BC, the main scholarly focus has fallen on the period between c. 3100 BC when writing emerged, and the incorporation of the region into the Persian Empire in 539 BC (see Chapter Three). Historians and archaeologists have conventionally divided the Mesopotamian past into complex classificatory schemes based on specific dynasties, sites or remains such as pottery which are only meaningful to specialists, and have further fragmented an already discontinuous field (van de Mieroop 1997: 7). In order to achieve a more unified view of Mesopotamia in antiquity, there has been a movement toward the use of simplified schemes in which the main peoples, personages, events and places presently known are placed within a framework of the latter three millennia. Briefly and broadly, for the purposes of this study, the anthropological narrative of the Mesopotamian past is as follows.

The Sumerian peoples, whose origins have yet to be determined, arrived on the lower southern plain of Mesopotamia in the prehistoric period. During their ascendency writing emerged, systematic irrigation was implemented and urbanism developed, ultimately taking the form of more or less independent and competing city-states of which the pre-eminent were Uruk and then Ur. Subsequently, Semitic peoples began to move into the plain and, after a period of co-existence with the Sumerians, became dominant following the conquest of Sumer by King Sargon I of Akkad (reigned c. 2270–2215 BC), who consolidated the previously independent city-states and administered them from his capital. Sargon I is considered to be a central figure in the formation of Mesopotamia as a social and cultural entity. Among his innovations were the installation of his daughter Enheduanna as high priestess of the moon-god Nanna at Ur (see Suter 2007), an appointment that from then on would be a royal prerogative, and the appointment of royal officials to "assist" rulers of conquered city-states. These new administrators were charged with breaking down the boundaries between city-states and furnishing material support, mainly foodstuffs, to the army including a single delivery of 60,000 dried fish. Centralized production of goods like pottery was established, and workers were conscripted and paid rations (Yoffee 1995: 292).

Under Sargon's aegis and that of his immediate successors, the cities of the plain were welded into something resembling a nation state for the first time. After the fall of the Akkadian dynasty within a few generations, centralized administration broke down, independent city-states reasserted themselves and there was a period of efflorescence known as "Ur III" centered on Ur. King Sulgi of Ur, whose reign lasted 48 years, further transformed social, political and economic life, creating a standing army, introducing systematic weights and measures, and establishing a system of provincial administration and a bureaucracy of unparalleled size that managed taxation and the flow of goods (Yoffee 1995: 295). Then came another collapse, the arrival of a new wave of incomers and a transitional period before southern Mesopotamia was reunited under Hammurabi (reigned 1792–1750 BC), whose capital was at Babylon in the central plain, and centralized government was eventually re-established. In the nearly five centuries of consolidation and expansion that followed, despite regime changes, Babylon enjoyed a period of cultural growth, social development, economic expansion and political hegemony until about 1300 BC. Then the city-state of Assur in the north, a vassal of Babylon, rebelled, setting off two centuries of conflict and conquest as described in Chapter Three.

In this climate of pervasive political instability, exacerbated, as will be seen, by the requirements of a highly sensitive ecosystem which needed constant maintenance and vigilance, and with an increasingly heterogeneous population, the question arises—how can "Mesopotamia" be considered a meaningful whole in any sense? And yet it was seen as such—both by the Mesopotamians and by their contemporaries—for over three thousand years. What held it together? The sharing of writing and a scholarly tradition (Dalley 1998: 7), the institution of the city (van de Mieroop 1997) and the economic administration system (Nissen et al. 1993) have all been seen as contributory and explanatory factors, but from an anthropological perspective—and reflecting the Mesopotamians' own view—it is possible to see Mesopotamian identity and society as held together by food, feasting and the gods.

Bread and Beer

The great cities of southern Mesopotamia were literally and metaphorically built on bread and beer. The prehistoric period saw the emergence of "a model of culturally situated dietary practice" involving "accounting systems, beer and leavened bread" (Sherratt 2006, in Goulder 2010: 359) that laid the foundation for the future development of Mesopotamia. In parts of the ancient Near East, the search for food security led to the cultivation of barley, which had been exploited in the wild state for several millennia previously (Wilcox 1999). Cereal cultivation required settled communities and collective labor, ultimately bringing cities into being. Robert Braidwood, a pioneer of scientific archaeology, asserted that the invention of barley bread in particular acted as an agent of history by supporting large populations, while the botanist Jonathan D. Sauer argued that the invention of barley-beer came before that of bread (see McGovern 2009). The question remains unresolved, but barley bread and beer were the culinary keystones of Mesopotamian life for three millennia, giving rise to a culture in which sacred and social technology were fused to a remarkable degree in the relentless pursuit of abundance.

The cereals that were the Mesopotamian staple were first roasted, and then boiled and eaten as porridges and gruels, brewed as beer or ground into flour, and made into bread (Ellison 1983: 146). In ritual as well as material terms, bread and beer had the same divine origins, celebrated in this hymn to Ninkasi, goddess of brewing, which describes the process by which water and baked *bappir* (barley bread) were mixed with honey and dates, fermented and filtered to make beer. Although it does not give quantities, the text is generally considered the earliest recipe for beer:

> Ninkasi, you are the one who handles dough (and) … with a big shovel,
> Mixing in a pit, the *bappir* with sweet aromatics …
> You are the one who bakes the *bappir* in the big oven
> Puts in order the piles of hulled grain …
> Ninkasi, you are the one who waters the earth-covered malt …
> You are the one who soaks the malt in a jar,
> The waves rise, the waves fall …
> You are the one who spreads the cooked mash on large reed mats,
> Coolness overcomes …
> You are the one who holds with both hands the great sweetwort
> Brewing it with honey (and) wine …
> You … the sweetwort to the vessel …
> The fermenting vat which makes a pleasant sound,

> You place appropriately on [top of] a large collector vat ...
> You are the one who pours out the filtered beer of the collector vat,
> It is like the onrush of the Tigris and the Euphrates.
>
> (adapted from Civil 1964: 72–3)

As in all cereal-based agricultural societies, bread was the consummate food, "*the* early Mesopotamian symbol" (Cohen, 2007: 418) of being human and civilized, a food with implicitly mystical and sacral qualities, always offered to the gods as part of their daily meals. The techniques of bread-making are often given mythic origins as a divine gift from the gods along with grain itself, and the onerous process of cultivation, harvesting, processing and backbreaking grinding represented the triumph of man and culture over nature. Flour was so highly esteemed that it was used in libations, the pouring of drink or the sprinkling of flour being the most basic offering and honor acceptable to the gods. The Mesopotamians used *tannûr*-type ovens for baking unleavened bread and dome ovens for leavened breads and cakes. As Waines (1987: 256) observed, bread possessed "a 'dynamic' character changing shape, as it were, from one cultural and social context to another." Some three hundred kinds of bread are mentioned, including seed bread, soft bread and cupcakes (Donbaz 1988), sourdough and "blistered" bread (Sasson 2004: 190), and the baking repertoire involved the use of different grades of flour, spices and fruits, and the addition of oil, milk, beer or sweeteners, with baked goods ranging in size from "very large" to "tiny," and including novelty items shaped like a heart, a hand, or a woman's breast (Bottéro 1985: 38).

For those at the bottom of society, coarse unleavened bread would have been the staple, along with gruel or porridge, commonly eaten out of large communal bowls, but "prestige breads" may have developed as early as the fourth millennium, to supply the new administrative cadre that made up the emerging bureaucracy needed for centralized production and distribution, with this superior bread serving as "salary" and as part of their cultural identity (Goulder 2010: 359). In later periods, the different kinds of bread consumed continued to mark social distinctions, and the following recipe gives the ingredients added to high quality flour to make cakes that were "sent to the royal palace": 1 *sila* of butter; 1/3 *sila* of white cheese; 3 *sila* of first quality dates; 1/3 *sila* of Smyrna raisins (a *sila* is generally reckoned to be a litre, but for different definitions see Gelb 1982). Another elite cake recipe from the city of Nippur dating from the time of Hammurabi calls for flour, dates, butter, white cheese, grape juice, apples and figs, while a special honey cake made with dates and figs was frequently offered to the gods (Limet 1987: 134).

As "liquid bread" (see Schiefenhovel and Macbeth 2011), the nutritional benefits of beer are commendable, with barley-beer containing more B vitamins and the essential amino acid lysine than barley bread. However, with a 4 to 5 percent alcohol content (McGovern 2009: 72), the consciousness-altering, recreational and medicinal qualities of beer would have been equally appreciated. As regards the latter, beer was mixed with herbs and other substances and taken internally or used externally; one prescription directs that powdered minerals and juniper oil should be mixed with beer, exposed to the stars overnight, and then rubbed onto the patient's body (Reiner 1995: 63). It has been suggested that not all "beer" was pure barley; drinks may have been made from fermented mixtures of cereal and fruit, notably dates (Stol 1994), and some of what was brewed might have been *kvass*, a fermented drink with a lower (0.5–1 percent) alcohol content (Powell 1994). In any case, what is translated simply as "beer" covers a range of malted liquors now known as beer, ale, stout, porter and lager, and there were fruit flavored beers, *alappanu* being flavored with pomegranates (Ellison 1984: 92). Whatever its composition, cuneiform texts of various kinds (Neumann 1994: 321) dating mainly from the Ur III period (c. 2111–2003 BC) and proverbs like the following show that the Mesopotamians were well aware of the perils and joys of drink:

> He who drinks much beer must drink much water! (Gordon, 1959: 96)
> When you drink beer, don't pass judgement! (Alster 2005: 78)
> No children without sex—no drunkenness without beer (Hornsey 2003: 107)
> Pleasure—it is beer. (Gordon 1959: 264)

Many different types of beer were brewed: "dark," "sweet dark," "reddish-brown" and "golden" are among those referred to—and there were grades of each, starting with "best" and "first class." Brewing took place on a grand scale, judging by the amounts of malt mentioned in the ration lists and other records and the ubiquity of references to beer and drinking in the literature, which also reflects a significant gendered social shift. The brewing divinity, Ninkasi, was one of a number of early Mesopotamian "Mother Goddesses," and initially brewing was carried out by women, who also sold beer in taverns. Wine made from dates, raisins and dried figs was also sold in the streets by wandering vendors (Bottéro 1985: 40). Later, the beer operations (Jennings et al. 2005) were taken over by men, and although home brewing may have continued, the main, large-scale production was carried out by the "great organizations." When this happened, Ninkasi, like many early goddesses, was demoted to a lesser place in the pantheon, reflecting a decline in the status of women when they lost control of brewing and other productive activities. Myths depicted the gods as drinking and being drunk, and even in the later periods when wine was commonly drunk by the elite, beer remained the drink of the gods, always offered to them in their temples along with other beverages. Wine, as Bottéro notes, was "a foreigner, a latecomer ... eventually naturalized but with roots elsewhere" (Bottéro 2004: 95). There was never a god or goddess of wine in Mesopotamia, as there was elsewhere in the ancient world.

The range and qualities of beers brewed bespeaks a hierarchically differentiated society, but even the best were not refined by modern standards. In the earliest representations, beer is shown served in large jars set on the floor. During the brewing process, bits of barley husks and stalks would float to the surface, so people would take their places around the beer jar and, sitting on low stools, sip from the bottom through long drinking straws that strained out the flotsam. Drinking through straws may also enable the drinker to feel the effects of the drink more rapidly (Homan 2004). In addition, "strained" beer that could be drunk from cups was also available (Powell 1994), along with the sweet date drink often translated as "syrup," and bibulous sociability tied people and gods together. On the everyday level, there are enough references to production, consumption excess and enjoyment to know that this was a drinking culture in which drink and its consumption acted in several ways. First, it gave expression to the structure and distinctions of social life; second, it served as an economic activity of consequence; third, through its ceremonials it constructed an ideal world (Douglas 1987: 8); and fourth, it was food for the gods. But beer, bread and all other foods had to be wrested from a challenging environment.

"Fear In a Handful of Dust"

Thorkild Jacobsen (1970), the historian and scholar of Sumerian literature, used T. S. Eliot's phrase "fear in a handful of dust" from *The Waste Land* to convey the abiding dread that lay at the heart of the Mesopotamians' relation to the cosmos, the world and the gods: the specter of starvation. These people who relished abundance were, he believed, driven by its opposite, haunted perhaps by the prehistoric famines that may have brought cities into being, and certainly by the challenges of the ecosystem in which they lived and the perpetual threat of warfare. It was this funda-mental fear, and the Mesopotamians' devotion to their gods of food, he believed, that drove them for three millennia.

The physical environment over which the gods of Mesopotamia ruled was charac-terized by long summers of searing heat and equally harsh winters when "the north wind and the south wind howled at each other, and lightning, together with the Seven Winds, devoured everything in heaven", in the words of a poem praising King Shulgi of Ur (reigned c. 2029–1982 BC, in Black 2002: 42). Mesopotamia falls into three geographical zones, the differences between them influencing social, political, economic, religious and culinary development, with the south coming to be associated with the Sumerians and Akkadians, the southern central part with the Babylonians, and the northern part with the Assyrians. It was in the southern-most part—sometimes called the "Land of Sumer"—that intensive, irrigation-fed agriculture and the first city-states of Mesopotamia emerged. Comprising the land lying between the Tigris and Euphrates rivers, much of it was an alluvial plain where initially "the only natural resource of importance was dirt" (McBride 1977). Here, away from the immediate environs of the rivers, dry farming was impossible without irrigation, which became more complex and intensive over time. Mesopotamian flow irrigation was one of the technological marvels of the ancient world, a network of canals and channels that utilized the gentle gradient of the plain to carry water, mainly from the Euphrates and its now vanished tributaries (Jacobsen 1960), and also helped to control seasonal river flooding by setting up run-off channels and reservoirs that became established as wetlands, supplementing the natural riverine swamps, marshlands and grazing areas. Through three millennia, the rulers of Mesopotamia would boast of three things; their service to the gods, their military conquests and their construction of foodscapes, as stated below by the Sumerian king Ur-Nammu (reigned c. 2047–2030 BC), founder of the Ur III dynasty:

> In my city I dug a canal of abundance ... The watercourse of my city is full of fish, and the air above it is full of birds. In my city honey-plants are planted, and the carp grow fat. The *gizi* reed of my city is so sweet that the cows eat them. May the watercourse bring them [the fish] into my canal, may they be carried in baskets to him [the god En-lil].
> (http: //www.humanistictexts.org/sumer.htm)

Farming in the delicately balanced man-made Mesopotamian ecosystem became a fine art, recorded in agricultural texts that covered every aspect in meticulous detail. One such farmer's manual, dating from c. 1750 BC but believed to draw on older versions, gave exhaustive instructions for the cereal production chain: flood irrigation and drainage; preparation of tools and implements; plowing and harrowing; fieldwork; sowing, furrows and their maintenance; irrigation and care of the crops; harvesting; threshing, winnowing, measuring and release of the grain for transportation and storage (Civil 1994: 1–3). When sowing, the farmer was exhorted to "Make eight furrows per *ninda* ... keep your eye on the man who drops the seed. The grain should fall two fingers deep of width ... " (Civil 1994: 31). The burden of maintaining the canals and keeping them clear of silt was relentless and heavy, with the threats of water theft and malicious damage ever-present. "Wisdom literature," consisting of maxims and precepts, was a popular Mesopotamian genre, and *A Father's Advice to His Son*, written in about 2600 BC, urged: "Do not beat a farmer's son, or he will beat your irrigation canal" (Bottéro 2001: 113). In the early period, all Mesopotamian city-dwellers were required to provide labor and other resources to maintain the irrigation system and carry out other public works. Under the Neo-Assyrian and Neo-Babylonian empires, large numbers of captive peoples whose leaders had rebelled, refused to submit, withheld tribute or broken treaties were transported to distant parts of Mesopotamia to perform *corvée* or forced labor in agriculture, on canal-building and irrigation work, and on public projects. Most buildings and the city walls were made of mud brick, requiring constant maintenance in order to avoid crumbling into the dreaded "ruin heaps." The evocative Mesopotamian term for *corvée* translates literally as "spade, bucket and hoe" (Grayson et al. 1987: 136), and the Babylonian captivity (c. 597–520 BC) of the people of the Kingdom of Judah, then a rebellious client state, is today the best-known example of many such exiles.

The man-made landscape that resulted from irrigation, along with the resources of the river system, produced for the Mesopotamians the richest and most varied harvest of domesticated and wild foods in the early ancient world. Depending on location, there were fish and shellfish; wild fowl and game; barley, emmer wheat, wheat and millet; fruits and vegetables; and meat from domesticated goats, sheep, pigs and cattle, along with luxuries imported from abroad. The Mesopotamian pleasure in food and drink is apparent in early accounts, with the literature relating to palace or temple food abounding with words like "finest," "best" and "first class," and displaying a well-developed concept of *terroir* and of connoisseurship—the choicest foods from particular places. The dates of Dilmun, present-day Bahrain, were renowned, as were the sweet wines of Simum. Sweet things were enjoyed by all and plants like lettuce that had to be grown by the water were especially esteemed, entering Sumerian poetry as terms of endearment—"honey of my eye ... lettuce of my heart" (Kramer 1963: 508). People wrote asking to be sent special fish, fruit and produce, promising other foods in return. One letter begs, "If you really care for me, send me lean and nice shanks, from one to two pounds, that I may in this way appreciate your friendship" (Sasson 2004: 195 n. 49), while another wheedles, "send me some nuts, some *crevettes* and a present" (Lion et al. 2000: 56).

Something of what the Mesopotamians thought about food and feasts can also be gained from the literary corpus known as "the debate poems" (Vanstiphout 1992), in which a banquet is often the setting for debates in which pairs of food-related protagonists—for example the Ox and the Horse, the Tamarisk and the Palm, the Bird and the Fish or the Ewe and the Wheat—argue the relative merits of their contributions to human wellbeing. In the debate between the Hoe and the Plough, the latter scorns Hoe for "digging miserably, weeding miserably with your teeth ... burrowing in the mud ... wood of the poor man's hands, not fit for the hands of high-ranking persons, the hand of a man's slave is the only adornment of your head," to which Hoe retorts, "I build ditches, I fill the meadows with water ... The fowler gathers eggs. The fisherman catches fish. People empty bird-traps. Thus the abundance I create spreads over all the lands" (http://etcsl.orinst.ox.ac.uk/cgi-bin/etcsl.cgi?text=t.5.3.1#).

Because of its agricultural achievements, the animal wealth of Mesopotamia has tended to be overlooked, but pastoralism and its products expanded in tandem with irrigation, as did pisciculture in rivers, canals, marshes and ponds, enriching the diet, expanding the range of goods available for trade or exchange, providing a medium for the display of wealth and status, and supporting the development of a differentiated cuisine based on quality, complexity and varied ingredients (Goody 1982: 99) suitable for the tables of the elite and the gods.

However, in an early example of the paradox of plenty, the proverbial industry and fertility of ancient Mesopotamia carried the seeds of its own destruction.

Over time, as a result of urbanization and population growth, which demanded intensive production and pushed irrigated cultivation to its limits, the soil became increasingly saline (Jacobsen and Adams 1958), a disaster for food security. As one Mesopotamian curse put it: "may the salt rise in your furrows!" (Cooper 1983: 48). "Salty fields" was a simile for ruin, as in the conqueror's boast: "I subdued the land and sowed salty plants over it" (Grayson 1987: 136). Even when it did not result in outright abandonment of the fields, salinity dictated the choice of what was planted, exposing the Mesopotamians to the dangers of relying on a single crop. Because it was more salt-resistant and higher-yielding than wheat, barley became the most widely planted cereal (Gibson 1974) in the southern alluvium, followed by emmer, although there is evidence that before the era of intensive irrigation and rising salinity, wheat and barley had been planted there in equal quantities. It has been suggested that salinity was responsible for the northward movement of the major centers of political power from southern Mesopotamia into the central zone during the early second millennium BC (Jacobsen and Adam 1958: 1252), and certainly the long-term consequences of Mesopotamian irrigation continue to bedevil the region today. In the short term, however, it was the success of irrigation that proved more problematic. Rich harvests, full storehouses, extensive fields and access to water provoked envy and aggression among other cities and led to the conflicts referred to above. The foundation of abundance in times of peace, the irrigation system was the weak point in a city's defenses in times of war, as seen in the ruthless simplicity of royal inscriptions that use this formula to describe the havoc wrought: "I uprooted his harvest, cut down his gardens, and stopped up his canals" (Grayson 1996: 30). This passage from *The Curse of Agade*, which dates from the late third millennium, reflects a recurrent theme in Mesopotamian life and literature down through the centuries:

> May this make the city die of hunger! May your citizens, who used to eat fine food, lie hungry in the grass and herbs ... May the grass grow long on your canal-bank tow-paths, may the grass of mourning grow on your highways laid for wagons! Moreover, may ... wild rams and alert snakes of the mountains allow no one to pass on your tow-paths built up with canal sediment! In your plains where fine grass grows, may the reed of lamentation grow!

The city-states were constantly contending with each other, and the consequence for the losers was starvation:

> The king who used to eat marvellous food grabbed at a mere ration. As the day grew dark, the eye of the sun was eclipsing, the people experienced hunger. There was no beer in the beer-hall, there was no more malt for it. There was no food for him in his palace, it was unsuitable to live in. Grain did not fill his lofty storehouse, he could not save his life. The grain-piles and granaries of [the goddess] Nanna held no grain. The evening meal in the great dining hall of the gods was defiled. Wine and syrup ceased

to flow in the great dining hall. The butcher's knife that used to slay oxen and sheep lay hungry in the grass. Its mighty oven no longer cooked oxen and sheep, it no longer emitted the aroma of roasting meat.

(http: //www.etcsl.orient.ox.ac.uk/section2/tr223.htm)

It was in order to avoid this "fear in a handful of dust" that the people, in their different ways, devoted themselves to the gods.

The gods of Mesopotamia were omnipresent: all-seeing, all-knowing and, as will be seen, all-consuming. Among the best known are En-lil, Nanna, Asser, Marduk and Ishtar, but there were countless others. With some 3,000 to 4,000 deities the Mesopotamian pantheon seems to stretch the meaning of pluralism to its limits (Jacobsen 1970: 16), embracing gods and goddess, demons, spirits and ghosts as well as the whole of the natural world, which was considered to be animate. New deities were introduced and the pantheon became ever more hierarchical, reflecting increasing social complexity and the rise of kingship. No gods were ever discarded, just gently shifted to the heavenly periphery. Divinities were capricious, fighting among themselves and sometimes withdrawing their favor and patronage if a city or ruler gave offence. Lesser deities were legion, there was a fear that the shades of the dead could return as evil spirits if not propitiated, and the threat of harm from supernatural forces seemed to overshadow everyday life, a danger that people fought through the use of oracles, omens, amulets, magic, curses and charms such as this Sumerian spell against the *utukkus* or demons:

Seven are they, seven are they!
In the channel of the deep seven are they!
In the radiance of heaven seven are they!
In the channel of the deep in a palace grew they up.
Male they are not, female they are not.
In the midst of the deep are their paths.
Wife they have not, son they have not.
Order and kindness know they not.
Prayer and supplication hear they not.
The cavern in the mountain they enter.
The throne-bearers of the gods are they.
Disturbing the lily in the torrents are they.
Baleful are they, baleful are they.
Seven are they, seven are they, seven twice again are they.

(Thompson 1903)

Some of these demons were shadowy specters, others were beings of terrifying aspect which had not lost their eerie power millennia later. In the early twentieth century, archaeological discoveries in Mespotamia captured the public imagination and a translation of this spell, then newly discovered, inspired the Russian composer Sergei

Prokofiev to write his 1917 cantata *Seven, They Are Seven,* which is still hauntingly evocative of demonic menace. To placate the gods, the Mesopotamians had to feed them.

The Work of the Gods in Mesopotamia

Whether agriculture gave rise to urbanism or vice versa has been much debated by academics and remains undetermined, but from the viewpoint of the Mesopotamians, what mattered is that the gods came before both. By the time the Sumerians entered written history, their relationship with the gods had already been established. In Sumerian cosmology, the world and everything in it had been created by the gods and belonged wholly to them. As the Sumerian origin myth of *Enki and Ninmah* described it:

> The gods were dredging the rivers,
> were piling up their silt
> on projecting bends
> and the gods lugging the clay
> began complaining
> About the *corvée.*

(Jacobsen 1987: 154)

Finding the labor of irrigation, agriculture and clearing the rivers and canals onerous, the gods fashioned the first people from clay as servants to do their work for them, marking the act of creation by feasting on bread and roasted kid and by drinking beer which made the gods begin "to feel good inside" (Jacobsen 1987: 158). Service, feasting and drinking were thus central to the relationship between the gods and people of Mesopotamia from the beginning. The service obligation is reiterated in the later Babylonian creation epic *Enuma Elis,* in which the old gods tell the young god Marduk that if he becomes head of the Babylonian pantheon, he must hence-forth supply their food and drink, stating "Provisioning is the need of the shrines of the gods ... Henceforth you will be the provisioner of our shrines" (Lambert 1993: 197–8), a duty that Marduk passed on to his devotees. There are numerous variations of the same theme in Mesopotamian myths, literature and ritual from all periods and regions. The foundation of Mesopotamian life was the belief that the human race had been created for the sole purpose of serving the gods by providing them with food and drink. It was only by feeding the gods that the people themselves could eat, as caring for the gods was essential to gaining the divine favor that perpetuated the fertility of the land, the flow of the waters and abundance for all. This ideology was so deeply embedded that the whole of life was seen by the Mesopotamians as what Oppenheim (1977) called "the care and feeding of the gods."

The work of the gods in Mesopotamia involved a fusion of social and sacred technology, the balance and expression of which varied slightly over time but which remained overall as the dominant organizational form and dynamic for social action, as well as the foundation of a belief system in a society in which the gods were seen as omniscient and all-powerful, influencing the outcome of war and national and personal fortunes, as well as controlling the forces of nature. On the one hand, there was the sacred or ritual cycle in which the gods in their temples were treated as living beings. On the other hand there was the secular cycle in which social, political and economic life was seen or presented in terms of the need to feed and care for the gods and their principal servant the king, and to carry out the gods' "wishes" which embraced everything from the cultivation of "their" land to military campaigns, represented as the protection of the gods' domain or revenge upon the gods' enemies. In this sense, the sacred and secular were as one; "the work of the gods was performed as much for the sake of society as for that of religion" (Firth 1967: 19), and at the center of the work of the gods was the city. Mesopotamian cities were regarded as the property and dwelling of the gods, with each city having its own patron god or goddess, in addition to hosting other deities of the wider divine pantheon. It was never simply a city, but the city *of* a god—Ur of Nanna, Babylon of Marduk and the eponymous Assur of Assur—supported by secondary city gods often considered the principal god's "family." In time, kingship itself came to be seen as divine: "when the kingship was lowered from heaven" as the Sumerian King List put it, adding "and the kingship was in a city" (Buccellati 1964: 54). Gods, kings, cities and people were inseparable, and the link between them was food. For above all else, cities were machines for producing, distributing and consuming food—and in order for the people to eat, the gods had to be fed.

Mesopotamian Temple and Palace Economies

Mesopotamia saw the earliest and most extensive and intensive development of what are called "the temple economy" and "the palace economy," which mobilized large populations in demanding productive enterprises. In principle, the land, the waters and the produce thereof belonged to the gods, with humans—led by priests and increasingly by the city rulers and ultimately the king—acting as the gods' servants and stewards. Wealth was in the control of a centralized administration based in temple or palace, which took in and redistributed food rations and other goods to a population who were reliant on these distributions to a greater or lesser degree, which varied over time. "Rations" is a very wide category, which was used in Mesopotamia to cover everything from cereal for serfs to wine for palace administrators, and served both as subsistence and as "wages" in a complex economic system that functioned for millennia entirely without coinage (Powell 1996: 225), and which in the archaeological record are represented by the remains of vast numbers of standardized bowls and other containers used to dispense barley or

prepared food and drink to workers (Pollock 2003). Here rations are to be understood in a general way as the disbursements from temple and palace that kept the
Mesopotamian physical and social body going. The basic barley ration provided the
foundation of the diet, supported the personnel of public institutions and private
estates, and provided an instrument of taxation, of rent and of credit, thereby
defining central relations of social and political power (Edens 1992: 122), and
enmeshing the population in a web of food and drink (Neumann 1994). Rations, as
Joffee (1998: 298) has noted, are materializations of the fine line between coercion
and provision of benefits treaded by emergent elites and early state institutions in
their relationships with agricultural producers.

Loyalty-building was also central to rationing, as seen in this letter from the father
of King Yasma Addu of Mari (reigned c. 1782–1774 BC) in response to a request for
money to spend on slaves and beer installations:

> Rather than opening beer-vats and spending money, satisfy the troops themselves,
> natives *of the region*, who might come to Mari and *defend the city*. Ration handsomely
> those who cannot farm for lack of oxen, those who have no flour, who have no wool,
> who have no oil, who have no beer. Set them by your side, for them to defend you and
> thus strengthen Mari's foundation. They should regularly be at a meal with you. Don't
> have them eat anything outrageous, yet always do feed them liberally.
>
> (Sasson 2004: 181, original italics)

There was a private sector which increased in size in the later periods but which
remains shadowy, as excavations have so far focused on temple and palace complexes,
and private operations do not feature in official accounts, except peripherally. Of the
large labor force required for centralized activities on behalf of temple and palace,
it is unclear how many were slaves, how many were persons with restricted freedom
who received rations as slaves did, and how many were free laborers who worked
for wages and whose number increased from the Old Babylonian period onwards
(Gelb 1965). For now, it is only possible to say that a high percentage of the
Mesopotamian population was dependent on the "great organizations" (Oppenheim
1977) in some way. It is assumed that, in prehistory, the temple and religious leaders
came first, supported and later to a degree supplanted by military or secular leaders
who assumed responsibility for defending the temples, city and people and ensuring
food security through maintaining the canals and administering the land. But
although the palace and the ruler came to be the primary source of abundance and
security, the temple and gods continued to be honored, and the dual temple/palace
economies remained overall as the dominant organizational form and dynamic for
social action. Temple and palace comprised the seat of multiple activities; administrative, bureaucratic, industrial, ceremonial and residential (Winter 1993: 27). The
first written accounts were part of an elaborate system of surveillance and administration intended to achieve efficient control of temple and palace goods (Nissen et al.

1993: x. Also Schmandt-Besserat 1992, Michalowski 1990), which came in and were then disbursed as rations and supplies to support temple and palace personnel, laborers, craftspeople and suppliers of all kinds, and above all the priests, kings and gods themselves.

Rations are particularly interesting on two counts. First, the different kinds and quantities of disbursements give at least an outline of social organization, an example of the way in which, as the anthropologist Mary Douglas (1979: 37) put it, food and consumption make "visible and stable the categories of culture," particularly important in Mesopotamia where there are no narrative chronicles or annals in the early periods (Cooper 1983: 39). In the ration texts, quantities of barley disbursed to workers are broken down into units for "men," "women" and "old women," along with sons, daughters, children and infants. Also provided for differentially were: soldiers; weavers; farmers; foremen—and forewomen—of workshops; household personnel and servants; scribes; craftspeople including goldsmiths and silversmiths; carpenters; leather-workers; reed-mat makers; stone-cutters; potters; fullers; smiths; boat-makers; shepherds; gardeners; fishermen; fowlers, bakers and cooks, grain-grinders, brewers and maltsters, among others (Gelb 1965). Rations could be issued on a daily or monthly basis, or for the duration of a specific activity such as the harvesting of a particular field (Ellison 1981). Tantalizingly, but all too rarely, more detailed descriptions are given, such as the sweetmeat boy, the salt boy, the fruit gardener, the vegetable man, the honey-cake-makers and the servants who specialized in cleaning the long drinking straws used for beer, or in grilling kebab-style meats. Later, a new group appeared in the ration lists—eunuchs, differentiated as adult and boy eunuchs—who became influential in the palace in Neo-Assyrian times (Mallowan 1972).

The second point of interest about rations is the calculations of which they were a part. For example, estimates for fieldwork jobs were drawn up for the number of laborers needed for various kinds of projects such as irrigation work or sowing, the length of time the work should take, how many workers were required for the specific projects, and what their rations in barley would be—calculations like size of field x man days required x barley per man per day. Even more complex calculations were made for things like woollen textiles, where raw wool and the various processes to which it was subjected before emerging as finished cloth were stated in terms of the rations needed for all those involved in the commodity chain. These calculations treat food as the driver of production on the one hand, and as the product on the other, people being mere intermediaries, an interesting and thought-provoking perspective which the modern wage system tends to obscure. Particularly in the later periods, they set out finely judged distinctions in the reckoning of a person's worth in food, in terms of both quality and quantity, making the social hierarchy explicit and material. Feasts were where these hierarchies were on display, but only after the gods had been fed.

Feeding the Gods

Situated at the center of Mesopotamian cities, the temples were imposing buildings that had incense and honey mixed into their very mortar, and silver, gold and precious stones buried under their foundations so the entire structure was an offering (see Grayson et al. 1987: 49 n. 39). The public was not normally admitted to the temple, and their main opportunity to see the gods was when their images were taken out of the temple and carried in processions connected to cultic events and festivals. The gods were considered present in their images, which were "born"—the word "made" was not used in this context—in temple workshops under conditions of great secrecy, using the most valuable materials. When ready, in ceremonies that took place by night, the images underwent ritual procedures that brought them to life, "opening" their eyes and—most important—"opening their mouth," so they could eat. The god was then placed in the inner sanctuary of his or her temple, and dressed in splendid garments onto which golden discs and rosettes and beads made of precious stones (Oppenheim 1949) were sewn, and further adorned with tiaras and pectorals. As one early poem described the cosmological significance of this sanctum—"inside the innermost part of the house [temple] is the heart of the country, inside its back rooms is the life breath of Sumer" (Jacobsen 1987: 383). The images of the gods were treated as living beings: they received visits from other gods, had offerings presented to them, had the god images of defeated peoples make submission to them, were put to bed nightly and awakened at dawn and, above all, they were fed.

"Feeding the gods" was the metaphor applied to daily deliveries of food to the temple, only part of which was used in temple ceremonial, the rest being used as wages or rations for temple administrators and workers, or stored and used for export or exchange. The earliest archaic Mesopotamian clay tablets carry records of deliveries to temples using signs that translate as "total amount of product," "receiving official," "institution" and "purpose"—for example, a delivery of grain to the temple of Inanna, patron goddess of the city of Uruk, for the purpose of celebrating the goddess's festival of the evening star, or regular deliveries of barley to the temple granaries (Nissen et al. 1993). Records of animal husbandry show that cattle, sheep and goats were delivered to temple and palace live and on the hoof, or as carcasses along with component parts—horns, hooves, hide and tail in the case of cattle—all meticulously listed separately. Herdsmen and other suppliers were held strictly to account. If there were any discrepancies such as missing horns and hooves or short measures of cereals, the herdsmen or farmers would be held responsible for making them up, and if they died before they could, their families would be pursued for the debt and made to serve as laborers or even slaves if the payment could not be made. As writing evolved, records of deliveries and disbursements became more detailed, tracking different kinds of cereal products—barley, groats and malt, jugs of beer and loaves of bread—along with other goods, and occasionally there are records of the goods served to the gods. The most detailed accounts are from later periods, but due to their ritualistic character it is assumed that they correspond to earlier practice.

The gods were served two meals daily, one in the morning and one at night, each consisting of two courses, called "main" and "second" (Oppenheim 1977: 188), the difference between them being unclear as no temple menu has as yet come to light. On festivals and during cultic celebrations, additional meals or special foods would be served. First, a bowl of water for washing was offered; afterwards this water was considered sacred, and was sometimes sprinkled over the ruler. Food and drink were then arranged on trays and brought to the sanctuary, presented to the god or goddess behind a linen curtain, and removed after the deity had "eaten." Although it was unseen and solitary, in ritual terms these daily feedings of the god can be considered a perpetual feast. These are part of the instructions for the rites carried out daily in the temple at Uruk for the benefit of the city's gods (Sachs 1969: 343–4):

> Every day in the year, for the main meal of the morning you shall prepare eighteen gold *sappu*-vessels on the tray of the god Anu seven *sappu*-vessels on the right—three for barley-beer and four for mixed beer—and seven *sappu*-vessels on the left—three for barley-beer, and one for mixed beer, one for *masu* beer, one for *zarbabu* beer, and one alabaster sappu-vessel for milk—and four gold *sappu*-vessels for "pressed" wine. Similar preparations shall be made for the second meal of the morning and second meals of the evening. No milk shall be served at the main and second meals of the evening … These vessels do not include the food … Below are enumerated the bulls and rams for the regular offerings to be made every day of the year to the deities Anu, Antu, Istar, Nanna and the other gods dwelling in the temple … For the main meal of the morning, throughout the year: seven first-class clean rams which have been fed barley for two years; one fat, milk-fed *kalu*-ram … Furthermore one large bull, one milk-fed bullock, and ten fat rams which, unlike the others, have not been fed barley … While slaughtering the bulls and the rams, the slaughterer shall recite the words – "the son of the god Samas, the lord of cattle, has created the pasturage on the plain" … similarly while slaughtering the bull and rams, the chief slaughterer will speak a prayer for the deities … For the second meal of the morning, daily throughout the year: six fat, clean rams which have been fed barley for two years; one fat, milk-fed ram … and five fat rams which, unlike the others, have not been fed barley, one large bull; eight lambs; five ducks which have been fed grain, two ducks, of a lower quality than those just mentioned; three cranes which have been fed flour, four wild boars, thirty *marratu*-birds, twenty … birds, three ostrich eggs and three duck eggs …

Similar quantities of meat are specified for the first and second meals of the evening. Then followed the specifications for bread and cakes. These baked goods would have been made in temple premises, where blessings were pronounced throughout the process. At Uruk, the miller had to recite the formula "the heavenly plowman has harnessed the seed plow" as the grain for the gods' bread was ground, and the baker had to chant "O Nisaba (god)—exuberant abundance and pure food" while kneading the dough and when the loaves were taken from the oven (Thureau-Dangin 1921: 82–3 my translation).

> Every day of the whole year, for the principal regular offerings ... there will be needed 648 litres of barley and spelt which the millers ... will provide daily to the temple cooks, in order to prepare the four meals for (the gods) Anu, Antu, Istar and Nanaya, as well as for the other minor gods around them. From the above they will take 486 litres of barley flour and 162 litres of spelt flour, from the mixture of which the cooks will prepare and bake 243 "round loaves." Out of that total, the same cooks will prepare and deliver 30 round loaves for the table of Anu: that is, each time 8 loaves for the large and the small morning meals, and 7 for the large and small afternoon meals. 30 loaves will also be needed for the meals of Antu; 30 for those of Istar; 30 for Nanaya; and 15 for the four meals of the divinities in their company. Also to prepare: 1200 "biscuits" (fried?) in oil, to accompany the cakes of fine dates ... .
>
> (Thureau-Dangin 1921: 81–2, in Bottéro 2001: 129)

The temples were abundantly supplied with oil, dates, fruit, vegetables and all the requirements of a great household. In addition to the produce of the temple's own estates, offerings came in from the palace, from subordinate temples and—both voluntary and obligatory—from the people. Temple accounts show how these goods were redistributed to workers differentially according to status, but are less clear on the matter of what happened to the food presented to the gods and the animals slaughtered for the gods. However, it is known that after the gods had finished their meals, divine "leftovers" were sent to the king (Parpola 2004) or shared out among the leading personnel of the temple, while the distribution of temple meat followed a strict order of precedence.

Apportionment was a matter of importance, carefully specified. In the time of the Babylonian king Nabu-apla-iddin (reigned 888–855 BC), the distribution of meat from the regular offering slaughtered daily at the Uruk temple was as follows (McEwan 1983):

> *For the king*: a shoulder, the rump, the back, a leg and a rib roast.
> *For the chief priest*: the heart, a kidney, the *nasrapu* and a choice shoulder cut.
> *For the priests*: a shoulder, a rib roast, the breast and the *harmil*, a choice shoulder cut, one half of a leg, a kidney and the spleen, most of the internal organs and one half of the hide.
> *For the chief administrator*: one half of a leg
> *For the singer*: the head.
> *For the cooks*: the penis.

At Uruk, other portions went to the chariot priest, to other specialized priests, and to the singer, the brewer and the baker among others (McEwan 1983: 191). Larger and richer temples enjoyed more substantial offerings, and in smaller or provincial cities the king's portion would go to the king's local representative or someone designated by the king. The consistency of records and references from different periods, even fragmentary ones, indicates that the scale and frequency of these offerings was not exaggerated. The full details of how these goods were redistributed are at present unclear, although some may have been resold in the private sphere, possibly using a form of "temple" commodity branding as suggested by Wengrow (2008, 2010).

On festival days and occasions of public celebrations, the ration texts tell us, special provisions were given out by temple and palace in honor of the gods. Over and above the standard measures, there would be distributions of bread and beer, such as described for the festival of the god Dagan in the city of Satappu, when "all the men and women of the city, each and every one of them, takes in their presence the breads made from thirty of those dough strips and the buckets of bitters, sweets and barley-beer" (Cohen 1993: 390). There might also be issues of sheep meat and cattle meat; fish, milk, cheese, butter and other daily products; onions, legumes, cucumbers and other vegetables; dates, figs, apples and other fruit; condiments; and beer and wine (Gelb 1965: 237, 240; Ellison 1981, 1983). But even as these things were going out (Schmandt-Besserat 2001), they were also flowing in, because people were required to make regular offerings of goods to the gods, although it is not yet clear what these were or how and how often they were tendered. The following, a late account of a procession by the god Nabu at Calah-Nimrud during the *Akitu* festival, provides a rare glimpse of public feasting:

> From Calah the deity goes out to the threshing floor of the palace, and from the threshing floor of the palace he proceeds to the gardens where the sacrifices are carried out ... Temple agents and vendors selling animals for personal sacrifices will be present and a person may then offer such sacrifice, while anyone who places on the altar his 1 *qû* of bread flour is permitted to eat in the compound of Nabu.

The account goes on to mention other people present, including the "firewood man," there to supply wood for roasting the sacrificial meat. It is calculated that it takes three hours or more to roast a sheep, the number of fires required for this and the bread ovens would have been considerable, requiring storing up in advance of the festival. When the cooking was completed, the public are seen feasting in the open air with the costs of the feast defrayed to some degree by the bread-flour offering that served as entrance fee (Kinnier Wilson 1972: 31).

Because of the lack of narrative sources, we can only see early Mesopotamian sacred feasts in broad outline, as given above. Because all food and drink were gifts from the gods, everyday consumption had something of the feast-as-gift about it and certainly in the early Sumerian period references to eating and drinking celebrate divine abundance in a rejoicing manner, although this would change in time. Even if all the details are presently unknown, it is clear that in early Mesopotamia there were frequent opportunities great and small to feast in honor of the gods, facilitated by the temple. But while feasting would continue, the context would change, as seen dramatically at Ur.

From Temple to Palace—The Feasts of Ur

On an upper floor of the British Museum are artifacts from feasts that shocked the world when they were excavated between 1926 and 1932, and continue to mystify. One of the Museum's great treasures is the so-called "Standard of Ur." Dating from c. 2600 BC, the Ur III period, it is a box-like framework of uncertain purpose covered with inlays of shell, highly prized lapis lazuli and red stone which is thought to have come from India. Discovered in a fragmentary condition in the "Royal Cemetery of Ur" by Sir Leonard Woolley, the reassembled fragments capture significant changes in Mesopotamian feasting and society. Originating in a period of military conflicts and shifting alliances among and between the southern Mesopotamian city-states, the two major panels are conventionally called "War" and "Peace" following Woolley's (1938) names for them, although it would be more accurate to call them "War" and "Feast." On the "War" side, the Standard shows heavy four-wheeled chariot wagons drawn by equids being driven over fallen enemies. Uniformed soldiers confront the enemy, who are vanquished, stripped naked and led away as captives in the top register.

On the "Peace" side the top register shows a large figure and smaller companions, seated and holding drinking cups, attended by cupbearers, a musician with a lyre and, next to him, possibly one of the cross-dressing male singers known as *gala*. At the

2.1 The "Standard of Ur," showing the king banqueting with friends, c. 2600 BC. © *The Trustees of the British Museum. Museum number 121201, Image number AN 631923*

bottom, a procession of even smaller people brings goods for presentation, including sheep, goats, cattle and fish. In the artistic convention of the time, important people are depicted as larger than subordinates, and the position of the figures relative to each other is also significant. Subordinates do not turn their backs on the dominant figure, but face him, and subordinates sit with others of their ranks, with the most important being closest to the major personage. The grave goods discovered with the Standard evidenced great wealth, a well-developed social hierarchy and human sacrifice—sixteen elite tombs were found with attendants who had accompanied the tombs' main occupants into the afterlife. The specter of sacrificial death and the richness of the grave goods and jewelery have drawn attention away from what the burials, objects and standard reveal about early Mesopotamian feasting and society. These Mesopotamian "human sacrifice" burials in large tombs with rich grave goods took place during a period of significant social and economic change when local rulers were in constant conflict, competing with each other for good agricultural land and trade routes, especially along the rivers (Yoffee 1995: 290), inevitably causing the balance of power between the sacred and the secular to shift. Although there are vessels among the grave goods, there is no evidence mortuary feasting has taken place, although every occupant of the tomb, including the sacrificial victims, has drinking cups in their hands or next to them. This can be interpreted (Cohen 2005) as an indication of the growing ascendency of "palace ideology" over "temple ideology." Instead of earlier images which show the gods and emphasize the sacred and the role of the gods in human affairs and provisioning, the Standard of Ur presents a secular panorama of a strong leader, triumphant on the battlefield, whose victory and the spoils and tribute it brings are celebrated and consumed at a feast which is hierarchical in nature, contradicting the older "temple ideology" that "all people are the same before the divine" (Cohen 2005: 142).

More suggestive evidence is presented by the four hundred cylinder seals found by Woolley in the Royal Tombs at Ur, an unprecedented quantity that suggests they had a special significance in this time and place. Almost without exception they showed conflict and banquet scenes (Pittman 1998). During the early period, seals often depicted deities, and what were called "banqueting seals" usually showed seated participants of equal size and status, drinking companionably together through long tubes from a vessel set on the floor between them (Collon 1992: 23), without food. On the Ur seals, the drinking scenes change in character. More participants are shown, indicating larger drinking or feasting groups. Hierarchy is emphasized through different-sized figures and the increased presence of servants, while drinking beer through straws is eclipsed by drinking from small individual cups, and social distance becomes the rule since people no longer share a common vessel. Food now begins to be shown regularly, taking the iconographic form of bread and haunches of meat displayed on high side tables. The remains of food and drinking vessels in the royal tombs of Ur were not analyzed for some 30 years after excavation, and when examined those in Queen Pu-Abi's tomb were found to include the earliest examples of chickpeas then found in lowland Mesopotamia, along with barley and wheat grains; charred bread; peas and dates; dried crab apples threaded on a string; the remains of oxen, sheep and caprovids as marrow bones and in pots suggesting they were ingredients in stews; perch and shark; and the vertebrae of a large tuna fish, which would have been especially prized and imported from the Mediterranean (Ellison et al. 1978, and see Van Buren 1948). This trend carried on into the Akkadian and Post-Akkadian periods (c. 2330–2110 BC), with banquet scenes continuing to show hierarchical drinking from cups as opposed to the more egalitarian drinking from a shared vessel through straws, and Winter (1986) has asserted that the cup itself was an emblem of the power of the king.

Taken together, all of this suggests that, in the period of the Royal Tombs of Ur, the new ideal world actualized and celebrated through what appears to be intensive drinking and feasting and the introduction of new modes of doing so was

2.2 Gold cup with integrated drinking straw, possibly transitional, excavated at the "Royal Cemetery of Ur" by Sir Leonard Woolley. 2600 BC. © The Trustees of the British Museum. Museum number 1928 10106. Image number AN 860768

increasingly hierarchical, in which the palace sought to appropriate the leading role of the temple. The king or ruler, supported by an emergent elite, strove to emphasize his secular power and roles as deliverer of abundance and as chief servant of the gods, acting in their name, and increased feasting and drinking appears to have been one of the primary means by which this was accomplished. Feasting and the new social order it consolidated were so important to the burying group—the royal family—that in mounting these post-mortem feasts, they were seemingly seeking to establish their hegemony in the next world as well as in this. Although a fuller picture awaits further discoveries, changes in feasting and drinking were clearly central to the transition, a striking example of the way in which, in early complex societies, drink and communal consumption can be used to forge "formal links between emerging socio-political orders, ontological cosmogonies and cosmologies, and agricultural producers" (Joffe 1998: 298). Later, banqueting-theme seals lost their popularity and were replaced by representations of the king with deities that further emphasized royal power.

Palace Cuisine

After Ur, more detailed records of cuisine become available, usually associated with palaces. The two most detailed accounts of elite cuisine and dining practices that have come to light so far are roughly contemporary. The first dates from the palace archive of Zimri-Lim (reigned c. 1775–1761 BC), king of the Old Babylonian city-state of Mari. One part of the archive consists of food allocation records, documenting the flow of raw and pre-processed foods rather than the preparation of elite meals. However, some insight is provided in references to "pantry-women" in charge of preserving figs, medlars, plums, pears and crab apples, steeping them in honey to make a thick conserve. There were also specialists charged with making pickles and possibly of pickling or curing fresh meat and fish. Fish were salted, dried, and steeped in brine or oil and crayfish were also preserved, as were locusts, the latter considered a delicacy and roasted over the fire like shish-kebab when fresh. There are records of ice, "floated downstream from the mountains, for the delectation of the royal palate" (Postgate 1992: 146). The second part of the archive concerns the "king's meal" more specifically. Ceremonies connected to royal dining are alluded to and, although they are not described in detail, it is clear that at Mari, meal-taking "was central to an alimentary communion meant to bind hosts and guests and to instil solidarity among them" (Sasson 2004: 199). These communal feasts could take place wherever the king found himself in the course of his travels, on which the full battery of vessels, bowls, jars, cups, saucers and cutlery required for royal feasting accompanied him. In the Mari palace itself, numerous decorative moulds were found, used to shape food and possibly bread for royal feasts, and a document refers to "moving palm trees in the orchard into the Palm Courtyard ... for the banquet" (Sasson 2004: 200 n. 58). The size of banquets held at Mari varied from twenty-six guests up to a thousand when entertaining a large visiting delegation. Those who regularly shared the king's meal included his retinue of bodyguards and the inner circle of secretary scribes, diviners and chief administrators. Occasionally, the king was joined by his wife but, as in all polygamous societies, multiple consorts caused problems. The primary wife was supposed to sit with the king, but sometimes it was the current favorite who was so honored. One surviving letter in the archive is a complaint from a Mari princess about her royal husband's failure to treat her as the primary queen of his city of Aslakka. Instead, her husband treated another woman as queen—"his meals and drinks are constantly taken in the presence of this woman," she wrote to her father (Sasson 2004: 200 n. 60).

But this was as nothing in comparison to the jealousies and problems of precedence on a large scale that arose during feasts for visiting envoys and delegations. From the time of the first city-states, diplomacy had been an important part of statecraft, the process through which political alliances and land and water agreements were negotiated and maintained and trade facilitated, through frequent meetings marked by rituals and feasting. The remains at Mari reveal a palace with a constellation of richly decorated suites suitable for grand receptions and banquets (Winter 1993: 30), an arrangement that served as a model for future palace architecture, and these rooms acted as arenas in which social status and power were contested and displayed. Court and diplomatic etiquette was strict, dictating who must squat or stand, and who was entitled to sit and where. Envoys were treated according to the prestige of the king or lord they represented and their ranking within the delegation—"the potential for public humiliation was infinite and the Mari letters reveal how thin were the skins of diplomats" (Sasson 2004: 201). A number of ceremonies preceded and followed the eating and drinking. There was a parade of standards before the guests were seated, oaths were sworn and treaties announced, and honored guests were presented by the king with gifts and new garments, each different, bespeaking the way they were valued and esteemed, and offering many opportunities for comparison. Where people were seated relative to the king was another mark of distinction, as was what they were given to eat. Subordinates would "eat less, and less well" (Finet 1992: 38) than the chief dignitaries, which was facilitated by the method of serving on individual tables which were presented to the feasters with elaborate courtesies. This mode of presentation meant that each meal could be slightly different in its composition and in the quality and number of dishes and the type of cup: grades of status that were visible for all to see. Guests were alert to the type of wine they were offered, and whether their meat was grass- or grain-fed. All slights, real or imagined—the opportunities for both were legion—were reported back to the ruler of the envoys' home country, where they were treated with great seriousness, it being appreciated that these feasts were statements of power in which the dynamics of inclusion and exclusion were made explicit. Rulers also toured their domains, holding feasts for local administrators and provincial officials. As

Sasson (2004: 210) notes, "in a society in which political instability was the norm and loyalty was achieved through formal oaths, sitting together during meals must have created obligation and nourished allegiances at all levels of the culture." As to what was eaten and how it was prepared, the Mari records are silent, apart from tantalizing references to seasonal harvests of truffles and eels, and plentiful supplies of game.

The second main source on elite cuisine presently available are the so-called "Yale Culinary Tablets," which originated in Southern Babylonia c. 1700 BC (Bottéro 1987, 1995a, 1995b). Instead of mere lists of provisions, they are the earliest cookery recipes presently known, antedating the Roman Apicius's cookbook *On Cookery (De Re Coquinaria)* by two millennia. It is thought they come from a larger corpus that covered all aspects of cuisine, but the surviving tablets—likened by Bottéro (1999: 254) to the remains "of a vast shipwreck," the bare bones of a lost culinary literature—mainly deal with stews, broths and pot roasts, of which two sample recipes from the tablets follow (and see Slotsky 2007):

> *Tarru* Stew (a *tarru* is an unidentified small bird, possibly wild pigeon, quail or partridge). Besides the bird, there has to be a fresh leg of lamb. Prepare the water. Add fat. Truss the *tarrus*, salt, hulled malt, onions, *samidu* (unidentified), leeks, and garlic, which are crushed together with milk. Having cooked the *tarrus* once in the water of the pot, next crack them and place them to braise in a vessel with the broth before returning the whole lot to the pot. To be presented for carving.
>
> (Bottéro 1985: 42)

> *Tuhu* beet broth. Lamb meat is used. Prepare water; add fat. Peel the vegetables. Add salt; beer; onion; arugula; coriander, *samidu*, cumin and the beets. Assemble all the ingredients in the cooking vessel and add mashed leeks and garlic. Sprinkle the cooked mixture with coriander and *suhutinnu* (unidentified).
>
> (Bottéro 2004: 28)

There are also recipes for stews of stag, gazelle, kid, lamb and mutton, for boiled leg of lamb and many kinds of broth and, partial though they are, the tablets reveal a rich cuisine requiring highly skilled cooks, specialized cooking vessels and stoves and expensive provisions. These are meals, as Bottéro (1985: 254) observed, for the gods, the kings and the rich. Roasting would have been an impractical way of cooking all the meat brought in to temple and palace, and the importance of stews and broths in elite dining is attested by the many large cooking and serving containers for them that were the pride of royal and temple households. Large cauldrons of hot liquid were not without their dangers—King Erra-Ismitti of Isin (reigned c. 1860 BC) died as a result of being scalded with hot broth—but in Bottéro's view it was the simmering, stewing and braising techniques that were the foundation of advanced cuisine in Mesopotamia, providing opportunities for refinements in seasoning, texture and saucing that lifted dishes above the basic level of what could be achieved through roasting and grilling. The distinctions between food for the elite and for the poor are clear and the symbolic aspects of bread and beer are apparent, as is the enjoyment of consumption, but the cultural meanings associated with Mesopotamian cuisine have not yet come to light.

Among the techniques used by Mesopotamian chefs—the palace cooks appear to have been mainly male—were the pre-cooking and browning of meats, the reduction of liquid to produce a more fully flavored cooking broth, the meticulous matching of particular cuts of meat to specific dishes, cooking in several stages requiring changes of pot, and the inclusion of vegetables that could be served as a side dish or used to make a sauce. Herbs and spices were used, although many remain unidentified, and a favored liquid condiment was *suqqu*, made of fermented fish, shellfish or grasshoppers in brine, presumably similar to the later Graeco-Roman *garum* which was used to enhance the taste of cooked and raw food (Bottéro 2004: 70–1). But here the Yale tablets come to an end, and until more material emerges, Bottéro suggests that something of the "demanding and subtle taste and genuine interest in gastronomy" (Bottéro 1995: 194, my translation) found in Mesopotamia in antiquity survives in some measure in the Arabo-Turkish, Lebanese and "Middle Eastern" cuisine of today.

Only the city could produce and amass this amount of food, and only the city could disperse it through sacred and secular consumption on a grand scale. The city and the production and trade systems that supported it and were supported by it in return was the acme of food security in the ancient world. From this perspective, no records would have been so pleasing as inventories, no sight more satisfying to the gods and comforting to the people than a flow of goods coming in and being disbursed, which explains the care with which the records were drawn up, the flourishing of accountancy and the recurrence through all periods, and on all forms of art from cylinder seals to large *stelae*, of seemingly endless images of processions of edible goods, reiterating the paramount importance of food and feasting. After the fall of the last of the Mesopotamian city-states, the never-ending feast continued, but on a larger scale. In the next chapter, we remain in the same geographical area, but follow the feast centuries into the future among new peoples who came to occupy the lands of the Mesopotamians. We tend to think of the civilizations of antiquity as entirely separate, but here we are able to see continuities and differences—both cultural and those imposed by the environment—a rare opportunity to take a longitudinal view of feasting.

CHAPTER THREE

The Assyrians and Achaemenid Persians: Empires of Feasting

I dug out a canal from the Upper Zab, cutting through a mountain at its peak ... I irrigated the meadows of the Tigris and planted orchards with all kinds of fruit trees in its environs. I pressed wine and offered first fruit offerings to Assur, my lord, and the temples of my land. I dedicated this city of Assur, my lord. In the lands through which I marched and the highlands which I traversed, the trees and plants which I saw were cedar, cypress ... juniper, almond, date, ebony, olive ... oak, tamarisk, terebinth, pomegranate, pear, quince, fig, grapevines ... and swamp-apple. The canal cascades from above into the gardens. Fragrance pervades the walkways. Streams of water as numerous as the stars of heaven flow in the pleasure gardens ... I Ashurnasirpal, in the delightful garden, pick fruit ...

(Grayson 1991: 290)

Not far inside the entrance to the British Museum stand great gates of cedar wood twenty feet high, embellished with bronze taken from the Balawat Palace of King Shalmaneser III (reigned 858–824 BC), flanked on either side by two colossal stone statues of winged lions with human heads. Nearby stand another vigilant pair—strong of sinew and stern of eye, embellished with elegantly curled beards and the horned crowns worn by gods and kings—that once guarded the entrance to the throne room in the palace of King Ashurnasirpal II (reigned c. 883–859 BC). It was in the grandeur of settings like these that Mesopotamian feasting reached its late acme. In the ancient world, as in many places today, doors had a special significance as portals where good or evil influences could enter, so magical protection was provided by figures like these. Here, they stand at the entrance to the Museum's renowned Assyrian sculpture galleries comprised of room upon room of stone obelisks, casts, statues and finely carved wall panels from the cities of Nineveh, Nimrud and Khorsabad which once served as backdrops for royal feasts, for under the Assyrians there was a renewed interest in banqueting scenes in art, and in feasting as social practice, political propaganda and visual ideology.

The first Assyrians were the people of the city state of Assur, named for their god, who rebelled against Babylon as noted in Chapter Two. Over the following two centuries, the new power became, through conquest, the nation of Assyria, then a proto-empire (Grayson 1987: 4) and finally the Neo-Assyrian Empire, stretching into southwest Asia. Assyria's hegemony was not uncontested. There were two peaks of Assyrian military might under Tiglath-Pileser I (reigned 1114–1076 BC) and Ashurnasirpal II (reigned 883–859 BC), the latter the giver of the grandest feast yet known in antiquity. In between, the Babylonians and their allies along with self-interested neighbors and new incomers continually challenged the Assyrians. In 609 BC, Babylon seized control of Mesopotamia and the Neo-Assyrian Empire became the Neo-Babylonian Empire, lasting until AD 539 when Cyrus captured Babylon and Mesopotamia became part of the Persian Empire.

The Neo-Assyrian Empire was the most powerful in the ancient world in its time, and the expansive Assyrian vision and the methods used to achieve it resound in royal inscriptions of the Neo-Assyrian period, this of Tiglath-Pileser I being representative:

> ... at the command of the god Assur, [my] lord, I marched to the lands Nairi whose distant kings, on the shore of the Upper Sea in the west, had not known submission. I pushed through rugged paths and perilous passes, the interior of which no king had previously known ... I rode my chariot over smooth terrain and I hacked out the rough terrain with copper picks ... With the onslaught of my fierce weapons I approached [the enemy] and destroyed their extensive army like a storm of the god Adad. I laid out like grain heaps the corpses of their warriors in the open country, the plains of the mountains, and the environs of their cities ... . I conquered their great towns [and] brought out their booty, possessions [and] property. I burnt, razed [and] destroyed their cities and turned them into ruin hills ... I captured all of the kings of the lands Nairi alive. I had mercy on those kings and spared their lives ... and made them swear by my great gods an oath of eternal vassaldom. I took their natural, royal sons as hostages. I imposed upon them a tribute ...
>
> (Grayson 1991: 21–2)

The violence of these campaigns has come down through history, their scale and savagery increasing with time, especially after the introduction of the horse by the first half of the second millennium and the development of horse-drawn chariot warfare for which the Assyrians became renowned and feared. Campaigns were not waged only against foreign and faraway peoples. Near neighbors and relatives could be targeted if they became troublesome, and even in the third millennium when urbanization was on a smaller scale and politicking took place on a much more local level, the surviving records bespeak recurrent skirmishes, continual disputes over water and land rights, and oaths and pacts of various kinds that were constantly being broken, renegotiated, and broken again. By c. 2700 BC, walls had gone up around the cities of the plain, showing that inter-city warfare had already become endemic (Cooper 1983: 7). And while the Neo-Assyrians and Neo-Babylonians are often cast as aggressors—think here of Lord Byron's poem *The Destruction of Sennacherib* with its lines "The Assyrian came down like the wolf on the fold, and his cohorts were gleaming in purple and gold"—the riches of Mesopotamia constantly attracted hostile incursions from all quarters, necessitating constant defence. The fact that the core kingdom of Assyria had no natural boundaries and was vulnerable to attack is often given as the reason it developed into a military power.

By the time the Neo-Assyrian Empire was at the pinnacle of its wealth and influence over a thousand years after the burials at the Royal Tombs of Ur, the center of power had shifted to the north, and to the great Assyrian cities like Nimrud, Nineveh and Khorsabad. Renowned throughout the ancient world as places where "There is no end of treasure or wealth of every precious thing" (*Book of Nahum* 2: 9–10, in Thomason 2004: 151), they were at the center of a vast network of trade, tribute and diplomacy that linked Mesopotamia to the world system of its day (Edens 1992), although under the militaristic Assyrians much of what flowed in to the great cities took the form of tribute rather than trade, and securing foreign food supplies was important as the Assyrians did not have the same irrigated agriculture base as the Sumerians. The temple retained an honored position and the pantheon endured but was now part of a state religion headed by the patron deity of the origin-city of Assur and of the Empire, the god Assur, for whom even the mightiest kings described themselves as acting as vice regent. Although beer was still consumed, red and white wine was now drunk widely, facilitated by closeness to the wine-producing Zagros Mountains, and proximity to trade routes bringing wine as commodities or tribute from places like present-day Turkey and the Lebanon. Wine was distributed through rations, and it is through the wine ration lists that a picture emerges of elite Assyrian palace society and culinary culture.

The best known of these is from Calah-Nimrud, on tablets found in the wine storeroom of the royal palace which, by the time of Adad-Nirari III and Shalmaneser IV (reigned 811–783 BC and 783–773 BC respectively), boasted a household of some 6,000 persons, from the royal family and harem to state officials, courtiers, craftspeople, soldiers, guards and menials (Mallowan 1972). The lists reveal how large rationing establishments used "messes"—places where people ate together informally—organized on the basis of occupations, with chariot teams going to one place, bowmen to another and so on—to ensure that each group received different and appropriate wine rations and food. There are references to a "king's mess," for princes, persons closely related to the king, and emirs or high officials, and separate accounts for the queen, indicating that the king and queen did not normally dine together (Kinnier Wilson 1972: 6, 82). Here too a system of redistribution operated. Formal contracts would be drawn up entitling people to eat specific royal leftovers, describing foods, drinks and quantities (Parpola 2004). The royal harems—of which Adad-nirari III had two—were separate establishments with their own rations, and the eunuchs—divided into those of the inner court and the outer court—had their own rations also. As a document from the state archives of the Assyrian king Esarheddon (reigned c. 681–669 BC) put it, "the eunuchs and the bearded courtiers eat bread under the king's protection" (Luukko and Van Buylaere 2002: 158–9).

By now, the palaces designed for splendor and statecraft, and the strategic feasting seen at Mari nearly a millennium earlier, had reached new heights. The great innovation of Neo-Assyrian palace decoration from the time of King Ashurnasirpal II (reigned c. 883–859 BC) onwards was the use of large, carved stone panels, many of which are now in the British Museum's Assyrian galleries. Considered by many to be the beginning of historical narrative in art (Winter 1985), these meticulously detailed, labor-intensive and extremely expensive stone panels show the Assyrian army on campaign, with the kings receiving the submission of vanquished kings, princes and cities, along with their booty and tribute. Other panels show the exploits of the king in the hunting field, and in the presence of divine figures. Highly decorative, they are also visualizations of the Assyrian worldview. Not solely a celebration of battle and conquest and the defeat and humiliation of foreign peoples, as they are often seen to be (Cifarelli 1998; Bonatz 2004), they are a statement of the values that had sustained Mesopotamian life for some three thousand years. These campaigns are "at the command" of the gods, rebellion and failure to send tribute voluntarily are insults to the gods, the spoils and booty are gifts to the gods, the captured harvests will be served to the gods, and at the center of all the battle scenes, overlooked by art historians, is food. In panels showing campaigns in the marshes, enemy soldiers attempt to hide in the reeds, where they crouch surrounded by shellfish, crabs and eels. Prisoners are led alongside rivers full of fish, and troops in the mountains are shown moving through stands of fruit trees. In the renowned panels devoted to the conquest of the rebel city of Lachish by Sennacherib (reigned c. 704–681 BC), the battle takes place against a background of date palms, trees laden with ripe figs, and vines heavy with grapes. What the Assyrian eye sees is not a landscape but a foodscape, and everything on the panels is perceived as the work of the gods.

To celebrate Assyria's mastery over Southwestern Asia, Ashurnasirpal II built a new capital at Calah-Nimrud, at the heart of which was a sumptuous palace— "my royal residence and for my lordly leisure" as the king put it (Grayson 1991:

289)—which included eight grand reception suites, each made of a different precious wood—boxwood, mulberry, cedar, cypress, pistachio, terebinth, tamarisk and poplar—entered through great gates of cedar bound with bands of bronze, hung in doorways of bricks glazed with lapis lazuli. The grand rooms of the palace were decorated as the king's inscription declares, "in splendid fashion ... I depicted in greenish glaze on their walls my heroic praises, in that I had gone right across highlands, lands and seas, and the conquest of all lands" (Grayson 1991: 289), themes which were repeated on the stone carvings that proliferated throughout the palace. There were also scenes of abundance including processions of servants bearing trays of small cakes and fruits arranged in high pyramids. The finest of these were installed in the throne room—"by concentrating them in the throne room ... and by placing the throne room itself at the center of the palace, the king conveyed the fundamental message that, as the throne room is the heart of the palace, so the palace is the heart of the state" (Winter 1993: 36). The king built new temples to the gods too, using cedar beams brought from faraway lands. The images of the gods were made resplendent with red gold and sparkling stones and, the king noted, "I gave to them gold jewellery and many possessions which I had captured" (Grayson 1991: 291). In Calah, Ashurnasirpal II also created a menagerie of exotic animals—tigers, lions, elephants, ostriches, panthers, bears and monkeys, which he displayed to the public. It was conventional for kings to warn their successors to care for their palaces and temples, but this warrior who oversaw some of the fiercest military campaigns in history left this strangely touching inscription—"O later prince among the kings my sons whom Assur calls, or later people, or vice-chancellor, or noble, or eunuch—you must not despise these animals. Before Assur, may these creatures live!" (Grayson 1991: 226).

Finally, when all was completed, Ashurnasirpal II gave the greatest feast yet known in history, which lasted ten days and involved 69,574 guests. It was an event of which the king was so proud that he had the list of provisions for the feast engraved on a stone stela that he set up in the palace, which shows the king beneath the symbols of his tutelary gods Sin, Assur, Samas, En-lil, Adad and the Sibetti or "The Seven Gods" signified by seven dots (Wiseman 1952: 25), surrounded by the following description of the food required for his epic festivities:

> When Ashurnasirpal, King of Assyria, consecrated the joyful palace, the palace full of wisdom in Calah and invited inside Assur, the great lord and the gods of the entire land; 100 fat oxen, 1,000 calves and sheep of the stable, 14,000 sheep which belonged to the goddess Istar my mistress, 200 oxen which belonged to Istar my mistress, 1,000 siserhu-sheep, 1,000 spring lambs, 500 aiialu-deer, 500 deer, 1,000 ducks, 500 usu ducks, 500 geese, 1,000 meskku-birds, 1,000 quribu-birds, 10,000 pigeons, 10,000 turtle doves, 10,000 small birds, 10,000 fish, 10,000 jerboa, 10,000 eggs, 10,000 loaves of bread, 10,000 jugs of beer, 10,000 skins of wine, 10,000 containers of grain and sesame, 1,000 boxes of greens, 300 containers of oil, 300 containers of malt,

300 containers of mixed *raqqatu* plants, 100 containers of *kudimmus* [a salty plant], 100 containers of parched barley, 100 containers of *ubuhsennu*-grain, 100 containers of fine *billatu*-beer, 100 containers of pomegranates, 100 containers of grapes, 100 containers of mixed *zamrus*, 100 containers of pistachios, 100 containers of onions, 100 containers of garlic, 100 containers of *kuniphus*, 100 bunches of turnips, 100 containers of *hinhinu*-seeds, 100 containers of *giddu*, 100 containers of honey, 100 containers of ghee, 100 containers of roasted *absu* seeds, 100 containers of *karkartu*-plants, 100 containers of *tiiatu*-plants, 100 containers of mustard, 100 containers of milk, 100 containers of cheese, 100 bowls of *mizu*-drink, 100 salted oxen, 10 homers of shelled *dukdu*-nuts, 10 homers of shelled pistachios, 10 homers of *habbaququ*, 10 homers of dates, 10 homers of cumin, 10 homers of *sahunu*, 10 homers of *urianu*, 10 homers of *andahsu*, 10 homers of *sisanibu*, 10 homers of *simberu*-fruit, 10 homers of *hasu*, 10 homers of fine oil, 10 homers of fine aromatics, 10 homers of *nasssabu*-gourds, 10 homers of *zinsimmu* onions, 10 homers of olives.

(Grayson 1991: 292–3)

As is usual in Mesopotamia, this is a list of provisions rather than a description of preparation and service. Although the figures are rounded, they can be seen as a fair approximation of what was consumed (Finet 1992: 38) given the number of guests who would have been fed differentially, and although there is no menu, the outlines of the feast can be drawn from other sources. As for the guests, the king had inscribed: "When I consecrated the palace of Calah, 47,074 men and women who were invited from every part of my land, 5,000 dignitaries [and] envoys of the people of the lands Suhu, Hindanu, Paninu, Hatti, Tyre, Sidon, Gurgumu, Malidu, Hubusku, Gilzanu, Kummu and Musasiru, 16,000 people of Calah and 1,500 *zariqu* of my palace, all of them—altogether 69,574 including those summoned from all lands and the people of Calah—for ten days I had them bathed, and I had them anointed. Thus did I honor them and send them back to their lands in peace and joy" (Grayson 1991: 293). Of these, most would have been fed in an expanded version of the palace "mess" system, but it is the elite level of the feast that is of interest here. Calah-Nimrud was a cosmopolitan capital, the center of a diplomatic and military network that embraced much of the then-known world, and all the social dynamics enacted through feasting in Mari took place here on a magnificent scale.

For the grand feast, the already splendid halls would have been further decorated and embellished, the air was perfumed with incense, and music would have been played. The principal guests were placed in the halls panelled in stone carved with scenes of the king's triumphs, and in the main hall the king would be seated on a dais flanked by cupbearers and servants holding torches or fans. The guests closest to him, being those to whom he wished to show particular honor, enjoyed the best of food and drink, served to them at their individual tables by attentive servants, as the ever-present cupbearers refreshed their cups. Feasting was such a key demonstration of power, arena for the display of distinction and instrument of socio-political consolidation that to deprive an enemy of the ability to feast was similar to destroying his walls, damming his irrigation channels or salting his fields. Thus the Assyrian kings, when enumerating their booty, always emphasized items like "100 bronze casseroles, 3,000 bronze receptacles, bowls and containers" (Grayson 1991: 211). These "casseroles" were not the small domestic pots known by that term today, but the large, high status vessels needed to prepare and serve feasts which, along with the other captured vessels, were then used and displayed at the celebrations of the victors.

The splendor of the clothing of the host and principal guests echoed that of their surroundings. Neo-Assyrian textiles were renowned throughout the ancient world, the particular feature of royal and elite robes being marvellous mixtures of pattern on pattern, accentuated with decorative borders and deep fringes. Among the patterns favored by the elite were palmettes, lotus flowers, vines, rosettes, concentric circles and squares, chequerboard patterns and diagonal stripes, in varying combinations, mixed with chevrons, dots and wavy lines of different widths (Guralnick 2004), further enriched with gold appliqués in the shape of rosettes, triangles, circles and stars. To the initiated, these garments would have been as expressive of hierarchy as the food and the seating arrangements—the concentric circle motif seems to have been most closely associated with royalty. The robes were enhanced by copious amounts of jewelry, the perfume and cosmetics worn by both sexes, and the hair dressed with scented pomade in which the Assyrians took pride. Thus arrayed, the feasters—as at Mari—would participate in elaborate ceremonies and rituals, obeisances that included a ritual kissing of the king's feet (Munn Rankin 1956) and hand-clasping, along with gift giving and presentations. The food and drink came and went and entertainments were staged, while intrigue and intense political negotiations took place under the guise of festive enjoyment in which intimidation and magnanimity were mixed in equal measure. Neo-Assyrian society was intensely competitive, depending "on a sense of institutional loyalty and personal relations up and down the system" (Postgate 2007: 358 in Radner 2011: 38) that would be constantly confirmed and renegotiated through feasting. As a Sumerian proverb had put it long ago, "the palace is a slippery place." And in the case of Ashurnasirpal II's great feast, this process of display, negotiation, exclusion and inclusion went on for ten days.

Unsurprisingly, the Neo-Assyrian kings often sought refuge in the more private pleasures of the royal gardens. Earlier, ornamental city gardens had been emblematic of civilized Mesopotamian life, the most elaborate being associated with temples and palaces, although there were also public gardens. In the words of a hymn to the god Ezida: "Gardens enhance the pride of the city" (Wiseman 1983: 138). Ornamental gardens were even more of a luxury than palaces, and it was here that the kings' private feasts and entertainments were held, on shaded terraces or in pavilions, early examples of aristocratic dining *en plein air*. A grand garden is shown in reliefs from the North Palace at Nineveh now in the British Museum. The central feature is a raised area supported by vaults and surmounted by a pavilion, with aqueducts and channels arranged to generate a downhill flow that would water every part of the garden. It has been suggested that this is a legacy of Sennacherib (reigned 705–681 BC), grandfather of Ashurnasirpal II, who built a 'palace without a rival' at Nineveh along with a magnificent garden that may have benefited from the use of a mechanical water-raising screw for irrigation, over five hundred years before Archimedes (287–212 BC) was supposed to have invented it (Dalley and Oleson 2003). Lavish public gardens were established by the Assyrian kings, provided with cuttings from the royal gardens. The scale can be judged by a record noting an issue of 1,200 saplings for public planting, comprising 350 pomegranate, 450 medlar and 400 fig, along with aromatic trees to support the perfume industry (Wiseman 1983: 142). The gods had their gardens too, located in proximity to the temple.

In the passage with which this chapter began, Ashurnasirpal II celebrated the garden he established, planted with trees, fruits and flowers brought back from his conquests. In the British Museum, a carved stone panel called the "Banqueting Frieze" shows Ashurnasirpal II and his wife, feasting in his garden, under a gazebo of grapevines. The occasion is the celebration of the king's victory over Te-Umman, king of Elam, whose severed head has been hung among the vines. From the point of view of feasting, the notable feature of the carving is not the trophy head, but the king himself, who is shown reclining on a couch rather than sitting, the first known depiction of the *position couché* that would become associated with the later Greeks and Romans (Dentzer 1982; Pinnock 1994). An examination of the panel suggests one possible reason for this innovation. Over the millennia, the low stools favored by the Sumerians had given way to chairs, with people of higher rank

3.1 Ashurnasirpal II and his wife feast in the garden after the battle of Elam; the head of the defeated king has been hung among the vines. This is the first known depiction of the reclining position for dining. © The Trustees of the British Museum. Museum number 1856.0909/53. Image number AN 237000

having ever more elevated seats, until the "highest of the high" were literally that, perching on the equivalent of very high barstools, their feet hanging in the air or resting precariously on high footstools, the position taken by the queen on the panel. The king—who normally sat on a high throne on a raised dais—could either go even higher, or adopt the radically different prone position, an inversion that further marked his superior status.

After the fall of Assyria in 609 BC, the Neo-Babylonians continued elaborate feasting practices. Seen through the disapproving eyes of Hebrew writers, all pagan feasts were occasions for idolatry, the Babylonian examples being exacerbated by the sufferings of the Israelites during their Babylonian exile (Josephus 2006). From their perspective, these feasts were the trope of the decadent Orient (Said 1978), cast as arenas for the public display of opulence, sensuality and excessive consumption that ultimately bring about their own destruction, a moral discourse. All of these are suggested in Rembrandt van Rijn's painting *Belshazzar's Feast* painted in about AD 1686, which portrays a scene from the *Book of Daniel*, set in the royal palace of Babylon on the eve of a great battle. There King Belshazzar holds a grand feast for a thousand of his nobles along with his wives and concubines. While drinking wine with his guests, Belshazzar gave orders to bring in the sacred goblets of gold and silver that had been seized from the temple of Jerusalem by his predecessor, King Nebuchadnezzar, when the Israelites were taken into captivity. This would have been seen as sacrilege by the Israelites, and as an act of symbolic domination by the king. Belshazzar and those present then drank wine from the temple vessels while praising their "gods of gold and silver, of bronze, iron, wood and stone." Rembrandt shows Belshazzar in rich robes and jewels, surrounded by drunken courtiers, at the moment when a ghostly hand appears and writes upon the wall the mysterious words MENE, MENE, TEKEL, UPHARSIN. This was interpreted as a warning to Belshazzar that the days of his kingdom were numbered: "You have been weighed in the balances and found wanting; your kingdom is to be given to the Medes and Persians." Belshazzar jumps to his feet in alarm, upsetting the feast goblets before him, while his terrified guests shrink away in a room gone dark with foreboding.

Achaemenid Persia—The Empire of the Gift

The enemy at the gates of Babylon that night was Cyrus II (reigned c. 559–530 BC), the first of the Great Kings of Achaemenid Persia, men whose voracious appetite for conquest was popularly believed to be matched by that for food, as seen in their rumored daily diet of gargantuan meals involving the consumption of hundreds of animals and vast amounts of other edibles at a single sitting, a misapprehension of the kind of provision list seen earlier at Calah-Nimrud. The capture of Babylon with the help of Mede allies and subsequent conquest of Mesopotamia was but the initial phase in the formation of the first world empire, the wealthiest and most powerful before the rise of Rome, with a royal court which was a byword for luxury and magnificence in antiquity. In its time, "Achaemenid power was unrivalled. Nothing directly comparable to the Achaemenid royal court existed. It was simply *the* court – the emblem of what kingship could and should be" (Kuhrt 2010: 902). That court was splendid, but it was built on a foundation of high social control, separation and surveillance:

> The king himself, they say, lived in Susa or Ecbatana, invisible to all, in a marvellous palace with a surrounding wall flashing with gold, electrum and ivory; it had a succession of many gate towers and the gateways, separated by many *stades* [unit of distance] from one another, were fortified with brazened doors and high walls; outside these the leaders and most eminent men were drawn up in order, some as personal bodyguards and attendants to the king himself, some as guardians of each outer wall, called Guards and Listening-Watch, so that the king himself ... might see everything and hear everything.
>
> (Pseudo-Aristotle in Brosius 2007: 29)

The Achaemenid Empire stretched from the Aegean Sea to the Indus Valley and from Central Asia to the Nile. This is territory usually associated with Alexander III, the Great, of Macedon (356–323 BC) and his successors, but in the view of an increasing number of historians, Alexander did not so much forge an empire as take over one that had already been created, leading to him being called "Alexander, last of the Achaemenids" (Briant 2002: 2). However, the Achaemenids themselves benefited from their Mesopotamian predecessors and especially from the Assyrian model, which they appropriated, of central administration through a system of provinces and vassal states, with economic networks based on tribute and taxes. On the ground, the mechanics of food production in the various parts of the empire remained largely the same, but the ideology changed. In Mesopotamia, as described in Chapter Two, food was perceived in terms of obligation and service rendered to the gods and latterly to the kings as the stewards of the gods. In the official Achaemenid worldview, "gift" rather than "service" was the dominant ideology. All good things were a gift from the ruler albeit with divine approval, with the king receiving the gifts of his grateful people in the form of loyalty, service and produce in return (Sancisi-Weerdenberg 1989). This found expression in elaborate displays of gifting, in strategic royal feasting, and in the institution known as "the King's Table." Elements of these had been seen in Mesopotamia and Assyria, but under the Achaemenids they were elaborated to an unprecedented degree, adapted to the needs of a new dynasty, a changing social order and a court on the move.

The Persian court has come down through the ages as the embodiment of the corrosive relationship between wealth, power and decadence. This image of the Persians is based on largely hostile accounts by their enemies the Greeks, who came under Persian domination when Cyrus II invaded Ionia in 547 BC. The Greek city-states subsequently revolted in the series of conflicts now known as the Persian or the Greco-Persian Wars which lasted from 499 to 449 BC. For much of this time, although you would not know it from Greek sources, they were heavily outnumbered by the Persian forces, often overwhelmed by the resources the Persians brought to bear, and ultimately the conflict ended inconclusively. It was Alexander the Great, not the Greeks, who finally defeated the Persians although it would later be said that Persian culture conquered Alexander, for he took up Persian luxury after he had triumphed over them.

To the Persians, the wars with the Greeks were little more than a skirmish on the periphery of their great empire, and were hardly mentioned in their sources. As will be seen, the Persians perceived their campaigns as a divine mission to bring the benefits of Persian order to all (Lincoln 2007: 69–70). By contrast, the Greeks considered the wars as nothing less than a battle "between freedom and democracy on the one hand and tyranny and despotism on the other" (Curtis and Tallis 2005: 9). Throughout the conflict and long afterwards, the Greeks—from a position of military disadvantage—deployed their developing literary forms and nascent narrative history in a propaganda campaign in which the Persians were cast as barbaric Other to the "civilized" Greeks, and food was one of their main weapons.

Persians, Greeks and Tryphé

To the Greeks, the difference between themselves and the Persians could be summed up in a single Greek word—*tryphé*—softness, effeminacy, wantonness, luxurious living or simply "luxury," which was seen as the catalyst for a chain of moral causation in which excessive prosperity and indulgence led inevitably to personal and social decadence and destruction (Gorman and Gorman 2007). The Greeks of the period therefore feared *tryphé*, which they masked with the lofty disdain seen in the funeral oration for dead warriors delivered by the Athenian statesman and general Pericles and recorded by Thucydides, which is widely considered to be a defining statement of Greek values and virtues—"Our love of what is beautiful does not lead to extravagance; our love of the things of the mind does not make us soft. We regard wealth as something to be properly used, rather than as something to boast about." Persian ways were perceived and represented by the Greeks as the very opposite of their own. These differences rapidly became stereotypical, acting to vilify the enemy while consolidating "Greek-ness" when the Greeks were far from homogenous. To give one of many examples, this account by the Greek writer Xenophon (c. 430–354 BC) is taken from the *Cyropedia* (8.8.15–6), his idealized account of the life of Cyrus II, the Great. Of the Persians of his own time, Xenophon wrote:

> Furthermore, they are much more effeminate now than they were in Cyrus's day. For at that time they still adhered to the old discipline and the old abstinence that they received from the Persians, but [then] adopted the Median garb and Median luxury ... I should like to explain their effeminacy in more detail. In the first place, they are

not satisfied with only having their couches upholstered with down, but they actually set the posts of their beds upon carpets, so that the floor may offer no resistance, but that the carpets may yield. Again, whatever sorts of bread and pastry for the table had been discovered before, none of all those have fallen into disuse, but they keep on always inventing something new besides; and it is the same way with meats; for in both branches of cookery they actually have artists to invent new dishes.

Gastronomically, this says more about the Greeks than about the Persians. Greece was not a land of abundance, the early Greeks were not gourmets, and despite the idealized meat consumption of their Homeric heroes (see Chapter Four), of necessity the daily diet of the ordinary people tended to the frugal and monotonous. Sir Alfred Zimmern famously summed up the classic Attic meal as consisting of two courses, of which the first was "a kind of porridge, and the second a kind of porridge" (in Kitto 1957: 33), and the Persians were contemptuous of Greek food. The comic playwright Aristophanes has a Persian character say, "But what could leaf-chewing Greeks, scant of table, accomplish? Among them, you can get only four little pieces of meat for a ha'penny. But among our ancestors they used to roast whole oxen, swine, deer and lambs. Lately our cook roasted a monster entire and served the Great King with a hot camel" (Athenaeus IV: 130–1). In the Greek way of eating, there were two kinds of food: *sitos* or staple grains such as barley and wheat, and *opson* or fancy dishes and sauces; they thought the ideal diet should consist mainly of *sitos*, with *opson* used only as an occasional relish. The Greeks found the large quantities of meat and the variety of dishes consumed by the Persian court—a diet which in their terms was primarily *opson*—deeply foreign, and did not hesitate to turn the dietary differences into moral parables at every opportunity, as in this passage from Herodotus's *Histories* (IX: 82). In it, soldiers under the command of the Spartan general Pausanias capture the abandoned war-tent of the Persian King Xerxes at Plataea:

> ... when Pausanias, therefore, saw the tent with its adornments of gold and silver, and its hangings of diverse colours, he gave commandment to the bakers and the cooks to make him ready a banquet in such a fashion as was their wont ... Then they made ready as they were bidden; and Pausanias, beholding the couches of gold and silver daintily decked out with their rich covertures, and the tables of gold and silver laid, and the feast itself prepared with all magnificence, was astonished at the good things which were set before him, and, being in a pleasant mood, gave commandment to his own followers to make ready a Spartan supper. When the suppers were both served, and it was apparent how vast a difference lay between the two, Pausanias laughed and sent his servants to call to him the Greek generals. On their coming, he pointed to the two boards, and said: "I sent for you, O Greeks, to show you the folly of this Median captain who, when he enjoyed such fare as this, must needs come here to rob us of our penury".

Even when the Greek city-states were no more, the negative images of the Persians persisted, embedded in the literature and perpetuated in later periods, providing a paradigm example of the power of food stereotypes (Sancisi-Weerdenberg 1995), how they come into being and endure over time.

Anthropologists prize *emic* or native accounts of self and society, but the Persians—like the early Mesopotamians—did not have a tradition of narrative descriptive writing, and left little documentation of court life apart from a few administrative records, so their past lay largely in the hands of the Greek writers until the advent of archaeology. Both Xenophon and Herodotus traveled in Persia and, although much of what they wrote was gathered from informants rather than observed at first hand, their work has an ethnographic quality—a sense of "being there" (see Lincoln 2007: 27–8)—that would otherwise be absent from the Achaemenid narrative. This applies to another writer on food and feasting, Athenaeus of Naucratis, whose multi-volume work *The Deipnosophists* or *The Learned Banqueters* written at the end of the second and the start of the third centuries AD incorporates quotations from some 1,000 earlier authors and 10,000 quotations the originals of which are now lost. Even these sources offer only tantalizing glimpses of court life, of which Greek descriptions tend to be laconic, as though they feared to even write of *tryphé* lest they be polluted by it, although they are happy to describe Achaemenid military and political matters in great detail. As noted in Chapter One, while past historians and archaeologists approached these sources and others with reluctance, considering them "unreliable," the cultural turn in history and ongoing scholarship has enhanced their status, particularly that of Herodotus, who is now seen by many as not only the first historian but also the first anthropologist. As for the texts themselves, to anthropologists all sources are the imperfect products of particular times and places, their truth is relative and contextual, and what is important are the patterns and dynamics they reveal, in this case the different ways people see themselves and each other through food and feasting.

The Realm of the Wise Lord

Between c. 550 and 330 BC, the rulers of the Achaemenid Persian Empire were Cyrus II (the Great); Cambyses; Bardiya; Darius I; Xerxes I; Artaxerxes I; Xerxes II; Darius II; Artaxerxes II; Artaxerxes III; Artaxerxes IV; Darius III and Artaxerxes V. The reign names suggest a continuity that was continually contested by the dynamics of family and empire. The Achaemenid rulers were patriarchal and polygamous, with several wives and numerous concubines, which inevitably led to succession crises and internal family rivalries, exacerbated by contending factions in a highly competitive court. Because of its size and its constantly changing boundaries, which embraced an increasingly cosmopolitan and multi-lingual population, the empire had deeply centrifugal tendencies. On the ground, these forces were counteracted by rigorous rule through a system of satrapies or large provinces which numbered some twenty at the empire's height, administered by provincial governors (satraps) or local rulers appointed by the Great Kings, through satrapal courts run on the lines of the royal court in the heartland. There was no attempt, as later under the Romans, to remake the world in the Persian image, and none of the conformity demanded by "democratic" Athens. Under the Achaemenids, conquered peoples were largely allowed to keep their customs and beliefs, as long as they submitted to Persian order, respected the court religion and provided substantial tribute to the central administration. This diversity increased the need for mechanisms of social cohesion which, beyond a highly efficient intelligence service known as "the eyes and ears of the King" and the threat of swift and stern reprisals for dissention and revolt, included a court religion that supported unity through the ideologies of magnificence, gifting and kingship.

The court religion of the Achaemenid kings has been described broadly as "Mazdean," devoted to the worship of the "Wise Lord" Ahura Mazda, a pan-Iranian deity believed to have created the world and happiness for mankind. In the early Achaemenid period there were no temples; rituals and sacrifices centered on fire, water and the sun were performed outdoors or privately within the palace (de Jong 2010: 543). In their analyses of Mazdean religion, Lincoln (2007) and Herrenschmidt (Herrenschmidt and Lincoln 2004) portray Achaemenid cosmology as dominated by the opposition of Truth (*Arta*) and the Lie (*Drauga*), the latter a demonic force that corrupted all before it, constantly threatening the happiness and unity originally bestowed by the Wise Lord on all peoples. The weapons of the Lie were the Three Great Menaces: enemy armies, famine or scarcity of food, and untruth. The king was portrayed as having been chosen by the Wise Lord to protect the land and people from all three, with the ultimate aim of eradicating the Lie and restoring perfect happiness over all the world through reuniting its peoples, scattered by Drauga. As the Persians saw it, their conquests were not aggrandizing but an attempt to restore the world to proper order, to the ultimate benefit of "those fortunate enough to be encompassed, whether by voluntary submission or by conquest, [who] were assisted in making the transition from lawlessness to law and from the Lie to truth" (Lincoln 2007: 26). It is easy to dismiss this *emic* view as self-serving and cynical but "cynicism is not the only possibility, for it is often the case that those who would persuade others are themselves most persuaded of all … rather than simply providing an apologia *ex post facto*, they constitute an indigenous metaphysic of power and an ideological precondition for the confident, relatively guilt-free use of same" (Lincoln 2007: xv). While not a god himself, having had the kingship bestowed upon him by the Wise Lord, the king became the ultimate mediator of all dealings between humans and the divine. During state processions and when massing for battle, a splendidly decorated but empty chariot drawn by white horses accompanied the king, representing the invisible and omniscient presence of Ahura Mazda. It was the duty of the king and court to display their magnificence and grandeur, a sign that they enjoyed the approval of Ahura Mazda, and a manifestation of the Wise

Lord's power. And in all he did, the king invoked the image of gifting and bestowal, reenacting Ahura Mazda's original creation of the world and its people. Thus, at the Persian court, luxury was both religious practice and political instrument, deployed in ritual and symbolic display, the deeper "significance of which was utterly lost on outsiders" (Lincoln 2007: 14).

Haoma

Among the finds at Persepolis, see below, were two hundred and sixty-nine mortars, pestles, plates and trays made of a distinctive green stone. Discovered in the Treasury they were not kitchen implements but objects used in the ritual preparation of *haoma* or *soma*, a plant central to early Indo-Iranian worship. The plant itself was considered to be a god, and by ingesting it one acquired some of the god's divinity, thus making the consumption of *haoma* a form of divine communion and ritual feast, whether on its own or accompanied by food. Herodotus (I.132) describes sacrifices in which, after the dedicated animal is blessed and dispatched, it is dismembered and boiled, then laid out on tender herbage, especially trefoil, which may have been *haoma*, after which the Magi chant and sing hymns over the meat, which the participants are then allowed to take away with them. *Haoma* was also regarded as a substance consumed by the gods themselves to ensure their own immortality, and to increase their strength against their enemies (Bowman 1970: 8). *Haoma* produced exhilaration and altered states of consciousness, and was believed to be health-giving, to provide protection in battle, increase potency and fertility, stimulate the mind, enhance eloquence and bestow supernatural power. It was said to be the first thing given to a newborn, and the last to one who was dying. It is much-debated as to whether *haoma* was a hallucinogen or merely a strong intoxicant. The *haoma* plant has not been identified; ephedra is a candidate along with ginseng, hemp, wild garlic, wild rhubarb and *amanita muscaria*. There are other possibilities, but in any case it is thought that the original *haoma* plant, like the herb silphium, became extinct in antiquity, and others were then used. At the Achaemenid court, the use of *haoma* was regulated by the officiating priests or Magi, who alone were allowed to prepare it. *Haoma* was crushed and pounded in a stone mortar, strained through a sieve of bull's hair, then mixed with pomegranate juice, water and milk, possibly fermented and then drunk by the Magi and by other participants in the ritual. The purification of ingredients and implements, the correct hand to be used at each point in the ritual, the direction in which the plant was ground and the rhythm in which the pounding took place, were all prescribed, as were the position and number of participating Magi, who are sometimes described as being eight in number, standing aligned according to the cardinal directions. A fire altar was involved. Among the later Achaemenids, *haoma* became associated with Mithra, the god of war. According to Athenaeus (X: 470), "at the festival of Mithra alone, of all the festivals celebrated by the Persians, the King gets drunk and dances 'the Persian dance.'" This is a rare glimpse of the divine intoxication and ecstatic dancing of the *haoma* rituals that were a feature of the court religion of the early Achaemenid kings, but of which little is known. As a form of formal devotion, *haoma* consumption was later opposed by Zoroaster or Zarathustra, founder of Zoroastrianism (Burkert 2004: 114), but the practice continued covertly in the empire, and elsewhere, for long afterwards.

Kingship at Persepolis

The Achaemenid court had no single permanent home—it was where the person of the king was. At its height in the latter reigns, the court consisted of the extended royal family, the courtiers and the military guards, along with full administrative and support staff numbered in their thousands. In the course of a year, this large cohort moved between royal residences in the heartlands of the empire. The Greek writers Xenophon and Strabo claimed that Cyrus II divided his year, spending the seven winter months in Babylon, the next three months in Susa and then two months in Ecbatana, choosing the times when the climate of each destination was such that he could enjoy the warmth and coolness of perpetual springtime in yet another example of *tryphé*. State matters and surveillance, military campaigns and the need for fresh resources to feed the large court lay behind Achaemenid movement, and it is no longer thought that these were the only royal residences, or that the nomadic progresses were as regular as suggested

The great testament to Achaemenid kingship is carved in stone at Parsa, or Persepolis as the Greeks called it, on the plains north of Shiraz in present-day Iran begun by Darius I, the Great (reigned 522–486 BC) and completed by his successors. Persepolis was not a city in the Mesopotamian sense of a permanent and varied urban center, but a complex of palaces and buildings of state with satellite settlements that have yet to be excavated, which served periodically as a grand ceremonial center and stage for the performance and promotion of kingship when the court was in residence. Achaemenid art "is the art of kings" (Root 1979: 1), commissioned in the service of kings and intended to project images of power and hierarchical order, underlain by the cosmological scheme outlined above. The distinctive features of Achaemenid formal architecture were grand columned halls or *apadanas* boasting corner towers and upper floors, with the buildings sometimes situated on raised stone terraces approached by monumental staircases. The lavish decoration of the palaces bespoke the ability of the rulers to command riches from all corners of the empire—silver, gold, precious stones, exotic woods, marble and ivory. To the Persians, this was not just a display of luxury for its own sake, but a symbolic statement of the Mazdean imperative to reunite the peoples and wealth of the world as they had been when first created by the Wise Lord.

At Persepolis, the largest chamber, the so-called Hall of a Hundred Columns, "could hold up to 10,000 guests at ground level alone, not including other levels in the building" (Curtis and Razmjou 2005: 54); there were smaller halls where guests could also be received. The nature of these receptions is suggested by the "Persepolis reliefs," carved on the staircases and stone platform on which the Apadana is built. The carvings summon up a vision of a gathering on a scale of unprecedented grandeur, with massed delegations summoned from all parts of the empire supplemented by the nobility of the Persian court and the royal guards, consisting of the famed Immortals, the king's personal bodyguards. So-called because it was said their number was never allowed to fall below 10,000, they were ranked within themselves; the higher rank closest to the king having golden pomegranates or apples on the ends of their spears, the others silver fruits (Herodotus VII.41, 83). The central panel showed the enthroned Persian king, approached from both sides by the representatives of twenty-three different subject peoples in their national dress, bearing tribute, including goods, animals and foodstuffs. It has been claimed that the scenes on the Persepolis reliefs represent *No Ruz* or *Nowruz*, the Zoroastrian New Year festival marking the first day of spring, still celebrated across Eurasia, or possibly the annual celebration of the king's official birthday, but these are unproven. Instead, the reliefs are generally taken to be an idealized celebration of kingship, empire and the Mazdean mission, incorporating elements of ceremonies held at various times at Persepolis and other places in the Persian dominions. There are resonances here with the Assyrian stone reliefs of military triumphs and booty, but whereas they showed conquered peoples in postures of abject submission, on the Persian reliefs the relationship is "consistently expressed as a cooperative effort of voluntary support of the king by his subject peoples" (Root 1979: 130). This harmonious vision is consistent with the Mazdean world view, as is the attention lavished on the details of costume and tribute, represented here in symbolic form as gifts for the king, rather than as the obligatory governmental tax revenues that flowed in from the satrapies and were then redistributed. Babylon, the richest of the satrapies in terms of agricultural produce, was the most heavily taxed. On the reliefs, Lydians in capes and beehive-shaped hats offer bowls and bracelets; Cappadocians in trousers and cloaks fastened at the shoulder lead in a fine horse; Ionians wearing fringed cloaks bring bowls, cloth and balls of wool; Parthians in belted tunics with trousers tucked into high boots follow, carrying more bowls and leading a Bactrian camel, and so on. Also portrayed are royal guards, officials and courtiers in rich robes and jewelry, differences in rank marked by differences in dress and adornment. Flanked by the royal guards and led by court ushers, the delegates would have mounted the steps in order, led ever upwards towards the majesty of the king. Inside the reception halls, the high columns were topped with carved bulls, eagles and lions, and the walls were embellished with carved stone reliefs and polychrome glazed tiles. In the palaces of Darius and of Xerxes at Persepolis, additional carved reliefs on the staircases show processions of servants bearing food, wine, skins and animals assumed to be for a banquet. With the royal guards, officials and staff, the size of the court even in the early days of empire numbered in the thousands. By the time of Darius III, the king's traveling entourage including military support would include some fifty thousand individuals. Billeted in suites in the palace complex or camped on the plains around Persepolis, the Persian elite, foreign and colonial delegates and military corps were placed in ranked order corresponding to their importance. Once assembled, they performed the rituals of homage and loyalty and engaged in feasting over many days. That the feast foods were drawn from all over the empire symbolized the king's domination. According to Plutarch, Xerxes refused to eat choice Attic figs until he had conquered the country that produced them: in consuming the food of the country, the king consumed the country itself.

It was at Persepolis that a defining document of Achaemenid feasting was discovered—and destroyed—by Alexander the Great, after he had defeated the Persians. According to the Macedonian writer Polyaenus (*Strategems* 4.3.32):

In the palace of the Persian monarch Alexander read a bill of fare for the king's dinner and supper, that was engraved on a column of brass: on which were also other regulations, which Cyrus had directed. It ran thus. "Of fine wheat flour four hundred *artabae* [a Median *artaba* is an Attic bushel]. Of second flour three hundred *artabae*, and of third flour the same: in the whole one thousand *artabae* of wheat flour for supper. Of the finest barley flour two hundred *artabae*, of the second four hundred, and four hundred of the third: in all one thousand *artabae* of barley flour. Of oatmeal two hundred *artabae*. Of paste mixed for pastry of different kinds ten *artabae*. Of cresses chopped small, and sifted, ten *artabae*. Of mustard-seed the third of an *artaba*. Male sheep four hundred. Oxen a hundred. Horses thirty. Fat geese four hundred. Three hundred turtles. Small birds of different kinds six hundred. Lambs three hundred. Goslings a hundred. Thirty head of deer. Of new milk ten *marises* [a *maris* contains ten Attic *choas*]. Of milk whey sweetened ten *marises*. Of garlick a talent's worth. Of strong onions half a talent's worth. Of knot grass an *artaba*. Of the juice of benzoin two *minae*. Of cumin an *artaba*. Of benzoin a talent worth. Of rich cider the fourth of an *artaba*. Of millet seed three talents worth. Of anise flowers three *minae*. Of coriander seed the third of an *artaba*. Of melon seed two *capises*. Of parsnips ten *artabae*. Of sweet wine five *marises*. Of salted gongylis five *marises*. Of pickled capers five *marises*. Of salt ten *artabae*. Of Ethiopian [Aethiopian] cumin six *capises* [a *capise* is an Attic *chaenix*]. Of dried anise thirty *minae*. Of parsley feed four *capises*. Oil of Sisamin ten *marises*. Cream five *marises*. Oil of cinnamon five *marises*. Oil of acanthus five *marises*. Oil of sweet almonds three *marises*. Of dried sweet almonds three *artabae*. Of wine five hundred *marises*. [And if he supped at Babylon or Susa, one half was palm wine, and the other half wine expressed from grapes.] Two hundred load of dry wood, and one hundred load of green. Of fluid honey a hundred square *palathae*, containing the weight of about ten *minae*. When he was in Media, there were added—of bastard saffron feed three *artabae*: of saffron two *minae*. This was the appointment for dinner and supper. He also expended in largesses five hundred *artabae* of fine wheat flour. Of fine barley flour a thousand *artabae*: and of other kinds of flour a thousand *artabae*. Of rice five hundred *artabae*. Of corn five hundred *marises*. Of corn for the horses twenty thousand *artabae*. Of straw ten thousand load. Of vetches five thousand load. Of oil of

Sisamin two hundred *marises*. Of vinegar a hundred *marises*. Of cresses chopped small thirty *artabae*. All, that is here enumerated, was distributed among the forces, that attended him. In dinner, and supper, and in largesses, the above was the king's daily expenditure. While the Macedonians read this appointment of the Persian monarch's table, with admiration of the happiness of a prince, who displayed such affluence; Alexander ridiculed him, as an unfortunate man, who could wantonly involve himself in so many cares; and ordered the pillar, on which these articles were engraved, to be demolished: observing to his friends, that it was no advantage to a king to live in so luxurious a manner; for cowardice and dastardly were the certain consequences of luxury and dissipation. Accordingly, added he, you have experienced that those, who have been used to such revels, never knew how to face danger in the field.

Here again the fear of *tryphé* is apparent, but Alexander misunderstood the significance of the column, an error that echoed down the centuries. This was no personal menu or record of regular gluttony as Alexander and others thought. Like the Assyrian Ashurnasirpal's record of his palace feast in Chapter Two, which had been lost by Alexander's time, it was a political and symbolic statement expressed through food. The quantities are sufficient to feed large numbers of people and support animals, on the occasion of special large gatherings like those shown on the Persepolis reliefs but also more generally when the court was in residence, as part of the ration system described in Chapter Two for the Mesopotamians and adopted by the Achaemenids. The exotic ingredients all figure in the lists of tax and tribute demanded of various satrapies. Both quantities and commodities bespeak the power of the king, in the service of Mazdean religion. The dishes sought for the king's table from all over the empire must be seen in the same light, as should the royal paradise gardens which, like those of the Assyrian kings, included rare plants and animals from all parts of the royal dominions.

The Achaemenid Court and the King's Table

The kings visited Persepolis intermittently, but the administrative documents called the *Persepolis Fortification Texts*, which cover the period 509–493 BC, include lists like those on the monument destroyed by Alexander that give insight into royal consumption and feasting while the court was in residence. The *Persepolis Fortification Texts* make clear that "everyone in the state sphere of the Persian economy was on a fixed ration-scale ... or rather a fixed salary expressed in terms of commodities" (Lewis 1997: 226). These consisted of foodstuffs and supplies that were distributed from the royal stores to all, from the royal family down to the lowest minions, the quantity and quality depending on social rank. As in Mesopotamia, the infrastructure of the court is revealed through their food allocations which show many grades of courtiers and military, administrative and civilian personnel, supported by small armies of servants and specialists including musicians, chaplet-weavers, wine-filterers, perfume-makers and the "butlers and cooks and confectioners and cupbearers and bathmen and flunkeys to serve at table or remove the dishes," mentioned by Xenophon (*Cyropedia* Epilogue 20). Always an important part of the lists were the military, care being taken that they should be well fed, and fed equally within their ranks, to promote solidarity and avoid conflict. In the ancient world before the rise of Rome, no one understood better than the Achaemenids that an army marches on its stomach, and the Persian armies went on campaign with a full quartermaster division and brigades of cooks and other culinary specialists. This was much remarked on by the Greeks, who saw battlefields as a place for warriors only, and the ability to withstand hunger as heroic.

"Consumed before the King," and "poured before the king," phrases that recur in the *Persepolis Fortification Texts* and elsewhere in connection with large amounts of food and supplies like those listed on the column, did not necessarily mean eaten or drunk in the king's immediate presence, nor did the phrase "the King's Table" mean literally the piece of furniture off which the king dined. All were metaphors for the institutionalized redistribution or ration system that supported all levels of society. This was the case within the central royal court, and in the peripheral satrapal courts, that were responsible for sending tribute and the finest specialities of their region to the great king, while redistributing the remaining produce and other supplies locally. Disbursed by administrators acting in the name of the king, rations were represented explicitly or implicitly as gifts from the ruler. The "king's great banquet table was simultaneously a means of redistribution, a display of royal generosity and a microcosmic image of the empire at large" (Lincoln 2007: 14). At least one of the Greek writers, Heracleides of Cumae, appreciated some of how the system worked in principle:

> ... the king's dinner, as it is called, will appear prodigal to one who merely hears about it, but when one examines it carefully it will be found to have been got up with economy and even with parsimony; and the same is true of the dinners among other Persians in high station. For one thousand animals are slaughtered daily for the king ... And of all these only moderate portions are served to each of the king's guests, and each of them may carry home whatever he leaves untouched at the meal. But the greater part of these meats and other foods are taken out into the courtyard for the body-guard and light-armed troopers maintained by the king; there they divide all the half-eaten remnants of meat and bread and share them in equal portions. Just as hired soldiers in Greece receive their wages in money, so these men receive food from the king in requital for services. Similarly, among other Persians of high rank ... when their guests have done eating, whatever is left from the table, consisting chiefly of meat and bread, is given by the officer in charge of the table to each of the slaves; this they take and so obtain their daily food.
>
> (Athenaeus IV: 145–6)

By the time Heracleides wrote in the fourth century BC, the institution of the King's Dinner or the King's Table had already undergone considerable modification since the time of Cyrus, reflecting changes in Achaemenid social organization. The Achaemenids were originally a tribal federation of some six large clans, among whom the Pasargadae had been the preeminent for generations before Cyrus, a Pasargadae scion, became the federation's leader and embarked on the formation of the empire. In this warrior society Cyrus was *primus inter pares*, first among equals, legitimating his position by being able to provide for the others, and gaining support from them through his generosity. In the early days of campaigning, "before he could confer benefits by wealth," as Xenophon wrote (VIII.2), Cyrus habitually dined with many guests who all shared the same food that was set before him:

> ... after he and his guests had dined, he would send out food to his absent friends, in token of affection and remembrance. He would include those who had won his approval by their work on guard, or in attendance on himself, or in any other service, letting them see that no desire to please him could ever escape his eyes. He would show the same honour to any servant he wished to praise; and he had all the food for them placed at his own board, believing this would win their fidelity, as it would a dog's. Or, if he wished some friend of his to be courted by the people, he would single him out for such gifts; even to this day the world will pay court to those who have dishes sent them from the Great King's table, thinking they must be in high favour at the palace and can get things done for others. But no doubt there was another reason for the pleasure in such gifts, and that was the sheer delicious taste of the royal meats.

At this stage, Cyrus used the simple inclusions of commensal dining, either face-to-face or more indirectly, to create and consolidate social solidarity, but as the empire took shape, new social distinctions emerged and dining with the king became more complex. Xenophon is among the most functionalist of the Greek writers, always seeing the iron hand in the velvet glove. Unconcerned with the fine details of food and drink—he glosses over the royal dinner of the Median king Astyages as "dainty side-dishes and all sorts of sauces and meats"—he focuses instead on the social dynamics of Achaemenid feasting and the significance of seating, in the early days of the empire:

> Now Cyrus offered sacrifice and held high festival for his victories, and he summoned to the feast those of his friends who bore him most affection and had shown most desire to exalt him ... Gadatas was the chief of the mace-bearers, and the whole household was arranged as he advised. When there were guests at dinner, Gadatas would not sit down, but saw to everything ... As the guests entered, Gadatas would show each man to his seat, and the places were chosen with care: the friend whom Cyrus honoured most was placed on his left hand (for that was the side most open to attack), the second on his right, the third next to the left-hand guest, and the fourth next to the right, and so on, whatever the number of guests might be. Cyrus thought it well it should be known how much each man was honoured, for he saw that where the world believes merit will win no crown and receive no proclamation, there the spirit of emulation dies, but if all see that the best man gains most, then the rivalry grows keen.

Thus it was that Cyrus marked out the men he favoured by the seat of honour and the order of precedence. Nor did he assign the honourable place to one friend for all time; he made it a law that by good deeds a man might rise into a higher seat or through sloth descend into a lower; and he would have felt ashamed if it were not known that the guest most honoured at his table received most favours at his hands. These customs that arose in the reign of Cyrus continue to our time, as we can testify.

Cyrus did not invent these practices, which are universal and timeless, but he deployed them to advantage as the Persian military elite emerged from tribalism. Indeed, the changes in Cyrus's feasting practices as reflective and constitutive of sociopolitical change are reminiscent of the pattern seen long before in Ur, as noted in Chapter Two. The next stage in the development of the Persian Empire and feasting came with the adoption of the ration system, the emergence of exalted Achaemenid kingship and the formation of a royal court in which a meritocratic courtier class replaced the hereditary militaristic elite and balanced the power of the king's own extended family and clan. Distance was an essential part of the new enchantment of kingship that Cyrus sought to create. No longer *primus inter pares* but now king over all, Cyrus withdrew from daily public engagement, creating an inner court consisting of members of his immediate family, and an outer court comprised of the king's extended family, the satraps or provincial governors, and members of the "old guard" or hereditary Persian nobility drawn from the original tribes and ranked among themselves. For the king, the court functioned "as a theatre of power which emphasized his unique position through pomp and court ceremony" (Brosius 2007: 59). Increasingly, the court was joined by meritocrats, often commoners, who won their place through actions that benefited or pleased the king (Brosius 2007). The newcomers were also ranked among themselves, the highest status being held by those upon whom the ruler had bestowed the formal title of King's Friend. As Xenophon put it of Cyrus in the *Cyropedia*—"There is no one indeed in all the world whose friends are seen to be as wealthy as the friends of the Persian monarch; no one adorns his followers in such splendor of rich attire, no gifts are so well known as his, the bracelets and the necklaces and the chargers with the golden bridles. For in that country no one can have such treasures unless the king has given them." Position at court—even among the king's relatives—was not fixed, but was subject to the king's continued approval, which had to be renewed constantly, creating a highly competitive social milieu in which the fear of loss of status was pervasive.

In the *Cyropedia,* Xenophon describes how Cyrus used ritual and display to establish and enhance the image and power of majesty, using techniques described by Kertzer in Chapter One. Adopting techniques of self-presentation in common use today— dismissed by Xenophon as "deception and artifice"—he had his courtiers dress in rich Median robes "which concealed any bodily defect, enhancing the beauty and stature of the wearer" and in Median shoes, which were designed so that a sole could be added, to make a man seem taller than he was. The courtiers were encouraged to use ointments to make the eyes look more brilliant and pigments to make the skin look fairer. He trained his courtiers never to "turn aside to stare at anything. They were to keep the stately air of persons whom nothing can surprise. These were all means to one end, to make it impossible for the subjects to despise their ruler." Progresses in which the magnificence of the king and court were on public display were a feature of Achaemenid kingship. In his first public progress in order to offer sacrifice, Cyrus had the courtiers and generals dress in splendid Median robes of purple, scarlet, crimson and glowing red, with the captains of the guard, cavalry and charioteers also richly dressed. Four thousand imperial lancers flanked the palace gates, and the road was lined with Persians on the right and allies on the left. When the gates opened, the bulls intended for sacrifice were led out, followed by the sacred chariots—that of Ahura Mazda, white with a golden yoke, followed by the white chariot of the Sun, and the red draped chariot of the sacred Fire:

> And then at last Cyrus himself was seen, coming forth from the gates in his chariot, wearing his tiara on his head, and a purple tunic shot with white, such as none but the king may wear, and trousers of scarlet, and a cloak of purple. Round his tiara he wore a diadem, and his kinsmen wore the same, even as the custom is to this day. At the sight of the king, the whole company fell on their faces. Perhaps some had been ordered to do this and so set the fashion, or perhaps the multitude was really overcome by the splendour of the pageant and the sight of Cyrus himself, stately and tall and fair. For hitherto none of the Persians had done obeisance to Cyrus. (Xenophon, *Cyropedia*)

This obeisance, later known as *proskynesis*, apparently more like a curtsey than full prostration, became formalized as a part of court etiquette, and all those approaching the king were required to perform it.

As the royal wealth increased, so did royal gifting, expanding the network of obligation, intensifying the dynamics of inclusion and exclusion and setting a template for future reigns. The very careful attention given to details of dress and adornment in the Persepolis reliefs can be seen as an explicit statement of social hierarchy; these were either gifts from the king or only worn with his approval, and recipients would have felt obliged to wear them, to honor the king and as a mark of favor and distinction in the competitive social displays of the court. Gifts also flowed out to the satrapies, to foreign allies and rulers, and to visiting delegations, each receiving items appropriate to their rank. The negative aspect of these royal gifts did not go unremarked, for to accept them was to acknowledge the superiority of the king, and to signify a relationship of dependence. For this reason, the Greeks dealt harshly with any of their envoys who accepted Persian largesse, as did Timagoras from Artaxerxes, while according to Herodotus (III: 20) the king of Ethiopia refused the presents of a purple robe, a golden neck chain and armlets, an alabaster box of myrrh and a cask of palm wine that came from Cambyses, saying to the royal envoys "The king of the Persians sent you not with these gifts because

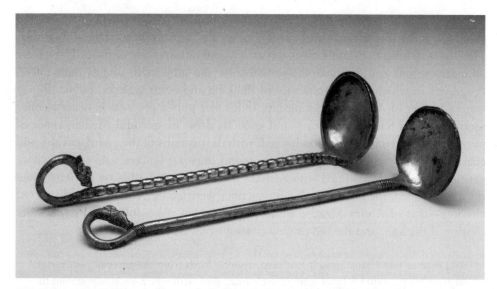

3.2 Achaemenid silver ladles with bull's head terminals. Fifth to fourth centuries BC. © The Trustees of the British Museum. Museum number AOC1. Image number AN 20536

he much desired to become my sworn friend ... for you are come to search out my kingdom." For the most part, however, those on all levels to whom royal gifts were offered found themselves unable to refuse. Loyalty and service were the gifts the king expected in return.

As the wealth and extent of empire increased, court feasting became more elaborate and social competition between the courtiers more intense. In addition to being ritualized celebrations of the benevolence of the king through eating and drinking, feasts were sites in which inclusion, exclusion and the dynamics of distinction were enacted. There were different kinds of royal feasts—from the great annual celebration of the king's birthday and official banquets to smaller gatherings when on campaign—along with the meals that followed sacrifices, victory celebrations, and the normal round of the King's Dinner. Whatever their size and setting, because the food and drink were in the gift of the king, all these commensal meals can be considered feasts and were controlled by protocol and ritual in which etiquette and degrees of distance were deployed strategically. Courtiers were expected to be present at court for much if not all of the time, and to attend feasts like that described by Heracleides of Cumae (Athenaeus IV: 135):

All who attend upon the Persian kings when they dine first bathe themselves and then serve in white clothes, and spend half the day on preparations for dinner. Of those who are invited to eat with the king, some dine outdoors, in full sight of anyone who wishes to look on; others dine indoors in the king's company. Yet even those do not dine in his presence, for there are two rooms opposite each other, in one of which the king has his meal, in the other the invited guests. The king can see them through the curtain at the door, but they cannot see him. Sometimes, however, on the occasion of a public holiday, all dine in a single room with the king, in the great hall. And whenever the king commands a symposium (which he does often), he has about a dozen companions at the drinking. When they have finished dinner, that is, the king by himself, the guests in the other room, these fellow-drinkers are summoned by one of the eunuchs; and entering they drink with him though even they do not have the same wine; moreover, they sit on the floor while he reclines on a couch supported by feet of gold; and they depart having drunk to excess ...

In Heracleides's account, the drinking party is a feast within a feast, adding yet another level of inclusion and exclusion. Those present would have dressed, bejeweled and groomed themselves according to court requirements, the magnificence of their appearance reflecting their standing in the king's favor, as did where and on what articles of furniture they were seated. Different ranks were served different foods on different kinds of tableware (Athenaeus XI: 464a); those who were judged to have been worthy of reward were served on silver and gold, those who did not merit the kings gratitude were given earthenware. The food was served in courses; when Greeks, accustomed to simple and frugal fare, dined with elite Persians, they disgraced themselves by falling upon the first offerings and eating until they were full, not realizing there was much more to follow. By contrast, the Persians took small helpings, in order to enjoy all that was set before them (Briant 2002: 291; Sancisi-Weerdenberg 1997). Variety was as important as the look or taste of the dishes, for in its sumptuousness and variety the king's table "was emblematic of the political and material might of the Great King" (Briant 2002: 200). The Greek writers mention— but do not describe—hundreds of dishes, although not every one of them was enjoyed by every guest. The King would order choice items to be offered to particular guests as a mark of favor, in the full view of all, adding further social *frisson* to the proceedings. Far from being events of careless and companionable self-indulgence, the competitive element in Achaemenid feasting and the hierarchy manifested through food and drink would have overshadowed the enjoyment of all those present except the king's favorites, and even they were mindful that their position was precarious. Also, by sometimes choosing to sit behind a veil, the King introduced distance; he could see, but not be seen, the ultimate demonstration of hierarchy and power.

No Achaemenid recipes have yet been discovered, but the culinary specialists revealed in the allocation texts indicate that courtly cuisine was much like that described by Bottéro (see Chapter Two) for the Mesopotamians, supplemented by the novelties and new techniques an expanding empire had to offer. The records indicate that honey and poultry—ducks, game and wildfowl—were reserved for the court, which also received the lion's share of cattle, sheep and goats. Certain items, like the "royal" dates from Bagoas near Babylon, were reserved for the king alone. We are to think

3.3 Achaemenid gold jug with a lion head handle, from the Oxus Treasure. Fifth to fourth centuries BC. © *The Trustees of the British Museum. Museum number 1897 1231.17. Image number AN 23330*

of the elite eating a great deal of meat, including roasts, fowl with sweet or savory stuffings and the rich slow-cooked stews favored by the Assyrians, the cooking wares for which the Achaemenids carried to their satrapal courts (Dusinberre 1999). Records give tantalizing glimpses of delicacies such as pomegranate possets, candied peaches and plums, grape jelly and apricots stuffed with walnuts that were relished (Henkelman 2010); Herodotus noted that they enjoyed many different kinds of dessert, and Polyarchus praised the "many kinds of cakes" invented by the Persians (Athenaeus XII: 545e). Breads are mentioned often, and the range would have been as wide as that enjoyed by the Assyrians. Knives, ladles, spoons and fingers were used, forks only coming into use in the later Sassanian period (Simpson 2005: 110). The hands were washed with perfumed water before commencing, and frequently wiped on a napkin as the meal proceeded, while cupbearers stood by to replenish the drinking cup and bowls of the king and his guests.

For these cupbearers to kings perform their business very cleverly; they pour in the wine without spilling it and give the cup, holding it on three fingers, and presenting it in such a manner as to put it most conveniently into the hand of the person who is to drink ... For these cupbearers to kings, when they give the cup, dip a little out with a smaller cup, which they pour into their left hand and swallow; so that, in case they mix poison in the cup, it may be of no profit to them.

(Xenophon, *Cyropedia* 1.3.8–9)

As to what was in the vessels, there could be new and aged grape wine, fruit wine, local beers, juices, syrup and yoghurt drinks and, for the king, the royal water. According to Herodotus (I. 188), the kings only drank water from the river Choaspes, said to be especially clear and tasty. A supply, ready boiled for use, accompanied him on his travels, contained in silver jars and carried in a long train of four-wheeled mule wagons. Wine, however, was the most esteemed elite drink, Herodotus (I. 133) noting:

They are very fond of wine, and drink it in large quantities. To vomit or obey natural calls in the presence of another is forbidden among them ... It is also their general practice to deliberate upon affairs of weight when they are drunk; and then on the morrow, when they are sober, the decision to which they came the night before is put before them ... and if it is approved of, they act on it; if not, they set it aside. Sometimes, however, they are sober at their first deliberation, but in this case they always reconsider the matter under the influence of wine.

Music was an integral part of royal feasting and pleasure: flutists, harpists and singers performed during the meal, stopping when the king drank and resuming when the guests' drinks were poured (Briant 2002: 294). On the occasions when the king ate in private, Heracleides reported, "sometimes his wife and some of his sons dine with him. And throughout the dinner his concubines sing and play the lyre; one of them is the soloist, the others sing in chorus ..." (in Athenaeus 4.145). When the kings wished to be merry and get drunk, Plutarch reported, they sent their wives away, but the music girls and concubines remained. As in Assyria, the principal royal women had their own households, their own chefs and confectioners and their own musicians and banquets, and concubines had their own quarters, as revealed through the food allocation records.

Just as guests were allowed to take unfinished food with them, those whom the king wished to favor were sometimes allowed to take the tableware as well. Two kinds of ware are particularly associated with the Achaemenid court; *rhyta* or decorative drinking horns, and *phialai* or handle-less cups or bowls apparently used for drinking wine (Dusinberre 1999), in shallow or deep styles. It was a mark of distinction to possess as many *phialai* as possible. The Greeks wondered at the Persian penchant for cups; it was not, as they thought, because of an inordinate fondness for drink but because they were objects of high status, gifts of the king directly or indirectly. Rank could be reckoned in terms of the cups and plates one possessed, especially those inscribed as royal gifts. One of the Achaemenid kings was reported to have given a favored individual a hundred large *phialai* of silver and silver mixing bowls, along with twenty gold *phialai* set with jewels (Athenaeus II: 48fn).

Herodotus and other Greeks were fascinated by the magnificence of Achaemenid tableware—gold and silver goblets, cups, dishes and bowls for drinking from and for mixing wine in, wonderfully ornate and sometimes set with jewels or cloisonné work. Elite vessels were also made of marble, granite, colored diorite, agate and onyx, as well as blue and grey lapis lazuli, rock crystal, glass and creamy alabaster. Plates were plain or footed, the latter suitable for displaying pyramids of fruit or small cakes, as seen in Assyria. Few of the most splendid pieces in precious metal

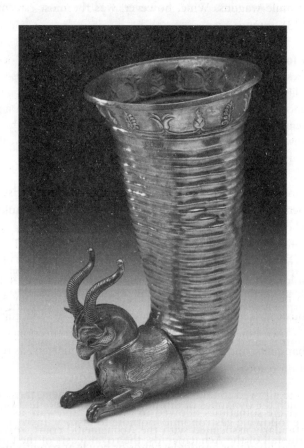

3.4 Achaemenid silver gilt rhyton for wine, consisting of a silver fluted horn on a winged griffon base. The griffon originally wore a necklace set with a gem. Fifth century BC. © The Trustees of the British Museum. Museum number 1897.1231. 1.78. Image number AN 20550

have survived. When Alexander sacked and burned Persepolis in 330 BC, Plutarch claimed that 10,000 mules and 5,000 camels were needed to transport the royal treasure, most of which was subsequently melted down, but the glories of the royal table are attested to by discoveries from the periphery of empire, like the Oxus Treasure in the British Museum, a hoard of gold and silver Achaemenid tableware, jewelry and other items, which evoke rich feasts served off gleaming dishes, and wine poured into glowing cups.

In sum, in this empire of the gift, food was the ultimate benefaction of the king and the Wise Lord, used to create and perpetuate the network of favor, patronage and military power on which Achaemenid kingship rested. The culinary myth perpetuated by the Greeks—that of gluttonous royal feasts and presided over by a king who ate many animals at a single sitting—was a misunderstanding of a mechanism that was simultaneously, as Lincoln (2007) put it, a means of redistribution, a display of royal generosity and a microcosmic image of the empire at large, as well as a powerful means of social control. Similarly, luxury and display were not *tryphé*, but a manifestation of the majesty that was central to Achaemenid kingship and the Mazdean imperative. At the Achaemenid court, the role of the feast as arena for the display of hierarchy, the enacting of competition and conflict, the forging of alliances and allegiances, and the creation and consolidation of identity through exclusion and inclusion can be clearly seen. The degree of attention and fine detail lavished on dress, adornment and gifts in the Persepolis reliefs are not aesthetic flourishes, but a record of the Achaemenid social distinctions that were so important, turning each courtier into what the artist Antonin Artaud called a "living hieroglyph." The expression of social distinctions reached its acme in differentiated food, drink, seating and tableware, the emphasis varying at different stages of the empire's development. In the early, emergent phase under Cyrus II and his warrior elite, the focus was on building solidarity, as seen in egalitarian dining and sharing the same food. At the empire's height, the emphasis was on distinctions of hierarchy, status and power, displayed through the complex dining and drinking of the socially competitive court. There was Achaemenid coinage, but it was not used as money inside Persia; the royal control of food through tax and tribute paid in kind and the ideology of the gift created a far more effective dependency on all levels.

Achaemenid Feasting Redux

The extent to which the dynamics of dining depend on the context of time and place are shown by the following gastronomic footnote to history. In AD 1971, nearly two millennia after the fall of the Achaemenids, the royal feasts of the Great Kings were re-enacted at Persepolis as part of the celebration of what was called the 2,500th anniversary of the Persian Empire. The host was Mohammed Reza Pahlavi, King of Kings, known to the world as the Shah of Iran or Shah of Persia. Only the second member of his family to occupy the throne, the Shah sought to establish oil-rich Iran as a modern nation and full member of the international community. He also wished to draw attention to Persia's ancient might and heritage, and to legitimize his own young dynasty through association with the Great Kings of old. With these aims, he invoked the power of the feast to link past and present, by holding the greatest banquet of modern times to which the world's royalty, heads of state and their representatives were invited. These included the Emperor of Ethiopia; Prince Philip, Duke of Edinburgh, and Princess Anne of Great Britain, the kings and queens of Denmark, Belgium, the Hellenes and Nepal, the Crown Prince of Sweden, the King of Jordan, Prince Rainier and Princess Grace of Monaco, the Emir of Bahrain, Prince and Princess Mikasa of Japan, the Vice President of the United States and the First Lady of the Philippines, Imelda Marcos.

Held at Persepolis, the Shah's feast recreated the great celebrations of Darius I with the ruins of the palace providing a backdrop for events. Guests were driven about, not in chariots, but in a fleet of two hundred and fifty red Mercedes cars. The opening ceremonies were held at the tomb of Cyrus I at Pasargadae, followed by a great parade at Persepolis that reproduced the royal processions carved there in stone, with four thousand men from the Iranian army dressed in ancient Persian costumes marching and riding in review on horses or camels to the sound of drums and trumpets, followed by full-scale models of a siege tower pulled by oxen, and three oared warships filled with archers. To accommodate the guests a grand encampment called the Golden City was built around the palace, as had been the case in the days of the Great Kings, although these were prefabricated luxury apartments concealed beneath tents of gold and blue. Around them, the fabled royal gardens of old were recreated with trees imported from France and lavish plantings of flowers. At the tent city's heart was the grand banqueting hall decorated in gold-embroidered blue velvet and lit with chandeliers of Bohemian crystal. For the state banquet, the glassware was by Baccarat, the linen by Porthault and the table was set with specially created Limoges china with the Pahlavi arms painted in the center. With the emphasis on elite community and inclusion, a special table fifty-seven meters long was built, curved like a serpent so that the sixty principal guests could eat at the same table, avoiding problems of precedence and protocol, and allowing all to see and be seen equally by the other guests who sat at round tables around them. On this occasion, everyone was served the same food and drink. Although the celebrations harked back to the past, the food was not traditional Persian but French, the elite diplomatic cuisine of the day, to signify Iran's full entitlement to sit at the world's top table. Catered by the renowned French restaurant Maxim's in Paris, the menu and wines for the state banquet included: quail eggs stuffed with Iranian golden caviar (Chateau de Saran), crayfish mousse (Chateau de Haut Brion Blanc 1969), roast lamb with truffles (Chateau Lafitte Rothschild 1945), Champagne sorbet (Moët 1911), roast peacock stuffed with *foie gras* (Musigny Comte de Vogue 1945), and port-glazed figs and raspberries. A hundred and sixty chefs, waiters and bakers attended to the guests, who numbered six hundred in all, at a feast that lasted five and a half hours. It was followed by a *son et lumière* display of the story of Persepolis, culminating in its sacking by Alexander. On this occasion, feasting did not produce lasting solidarity, and magnificence did not make the positive impression intended. The lavishness and expense of the event which was estimated to cost up to twenty-two million dollars, worth at least three times that in today's currency, was widely criticized both inside and outside Iran, drawing unwelcome attention to the regime. Within a few years the Shah had fallen from power—a victim, the ancient Greeks would have said, of *tryphé*.

CHAPTER FOUR

The Greeks: Now Let Us Hasten to the Feast

I myself feel that there is nothing more delightful than when the festive mood reigns in the hearts of all the people and the banqueters listen to a minstrel from their seats in the hall, while the tables before them are laden with bread and meat, and a steward carries round the wine he has drawn from the bowl and fills their cups. This, to my way of thinking, is perfection.

(*Odyssey* 9: 5–10)

This passage, spoken by Odysseus in the *Odyssey*, is the earliest Greek description of the pleasures of eating and drinking together. The mythic world of the Homeric epics was structured around rites of commensality (Murray 1995: 221). Adapted by the Romans, then "inherited by the post-Roman West and given new life at the Reformation" (Sherratt 2004: 330), Greek commensality provided models for formal and informal feasting and drinking in Western culture that continue down to the present day, so embedded and familiar that we take them for granted. In the popular imagination, early "Greek feasting" conjures up the romantic world of "Classical Antiquity" as painted by Sir Lawrence Alma-Tadema and Sir Frederick Leighton, and beloved of the Victorians. Here alluring women dressed in flowing chitons disport themselves among young men garlanded with laurel and as handsome as gods, sharing cups of wine in palatial marble halls under a cerulean sky. This is a beautiful fantasy.

Dominant figures in the cultural history of the West and Western feasting though the Greeks later became, in the eyes of the great powers of antiquity in the eras dealt with so far they were largely invisible. From the Persian viewpoint, between the eighth and third centuries BC the Greeks were "a disparate, remote people living on the edge of the world" (Kuhrt 2002: 27), far from the centers of power. Indeed, "Greece" and "Greek" in the sense of a united territory and homogeneous people are inventions of later times—as expressed in the artistic convention of "Classical Antiquity"—conflating different groups, periods, places and cultures. The geographical area involved was vast and varied, comprising the mainland of present-day Greece, the Aegean islands and the western coast of Asia Minor, part of present-day Turkey and Sicily, parts of southernmost Italy, Macedonia and possibly parts of Thrace. This inevitably resulted in regionalism, exacerbated by the diversity of the peoples who passed through or settled during the so-called Dark Ages, as attested to by different origin narratives embedded in myths and early literature, and by the distinct identities of groups such as the "Achaeans," "Ionians," "Dorians" and others whose origins remain uncertain and contested. The later *poleis* or city-states varied in their policies and practices; much of what we think of as "typically Greek" is strictly representative only of Athens, and even there the record is far from complete. The study of ancient Greece has generated an immense body of specialized scholarship. As Burkert (1985: 7) said of Greek religion, in a caveat that applies equally to Greek feasting which is so closely linked to it—"the evidence is beyond the command of any one individual, methodology is hotly contested and the subject itself is far from well defined." But before Greece, there was the Mycenaean period.

The Mycenaean Prelude

"Mycenaean" is a contested term, but here it refers to the "palace economies" and "palatial civilizations" that emerged on the Greek mainland c. 1600–1400 BC, later spreading to Crete and the Aegean islands. The best known sites today are Tiryns, Pylos, Thebes, post-Minoan Knossos and the eponymous Mycenae, ironically the least systematically excavated of the sites. At its height, Mycenaean Greece was comprised of independent kingdoms of different sizes, ruled from palaces that were the administrative centers of redistributive economies, which controlled large territories and participated in long-distance trade. There are parallels between Mycenaean social organization and that of Mesopotamia, seen in Chapter Two. Wright (2006: 37) describes the Mycenaean palaces as "a cultural cloak the elite wrap around themselves, and in which they symbolically envelop their retinue, clients and commoners," with the palace serving as "the focus of political, economic, social, ideological, historic and myth-historic practices and beliefs," engines for promoting the legitimacy of the ruler and creating Mycenaean identity. The exterior architecture of Mycenaean palaces was intended to impress a wide audience, while lavish schemes of interior decoration, intended for viewing by a restricted elite, celebrated the power of the ruler (Kilian 1988). Painted frescoes show long-haired men and women dressed in a style reminiscent of Minoan Crete, the men in kilts or loincloths and the women in tight fitted jackets and long skirts of colorful patterned textiles. There were columns and colonnades, richly decorated reception rooms and grand courtyards for receptions, and palace inventories list furniture such as a throne of rock crystal embellished with jewel-colored glass and gold, and tables of ebony inlaid with ivory (Palaima 2004: 235).

This was a hierarchical society comprised of the ruler (*wanax*) who was also the paramount spiritual leader, supported by an aristocratic warrior caste who enriched the state through conquest, and by administrators, priests, craftspeople, serfs and slaves. The workforce deployed by the palace was considerable, and the workers were highly specialized, producing both basic and luxury goods including fine textiles and perfumed unguents in palace workshops (Killen 2006). Duties and work were specified, rations issued, payments made, seeds distributed and land appor- tioned, all listed in records in Linear B script, in a bureaucratic style reminiscent of Mesopotamia and Egypt. The origins of the people are unclear, but it appears that over time different elements came together to form a supra-regional "Mycenaean" elite culture and identity in which feasting played a central and consolidating role.

For Bronze Age feasting in the Aegean, much of the evidence is visual and artifactual, relying on archaeology rather than on text. Frescoes on the palace walls show proces- sions of men and women bearing food and drink, hunters with game, men boiling what appears to be meat in large pots, and men carrying large vessels thought to have contained wine. Abundant deposits of cups, chalices and other vessels suggest an emphasis on drinking, with a preference for distinctive styles of ware emerging, made in ceramic, bronze, silver and gold, which were used according to social status. The distribution of remains indicates hierarchical seating, with feasters seated in different areas, also depending on status (Bendall 2004, 2008). At Pylos, there was a feasting site divided into three contiguous seating areas separated by doors. The seating areas corresponded to high, medium and low status, as evidenced by metal drinking cups in the first area, and more ordinary cups of descending quality in the other two areas. The doors between areas could be closed, with the middle group having access to both, but with the high group not having to see the low and the low group not being able to see the high, emphasizing hierarchy.

The contents of early elite graves consist largely of tripods, cauldrons, bowls, basins, pans and sets of drinking vessels, indicating that feasting and drinking were so significant that aristocrats took all the necessary equipment for it into the afterlife. Archaeological remains indicate that in the bigger centers "a large quantity of beef was distributed at Mycenaean feasts, but while it was roasted over an open flame, meat from the hunt was boiled and distributed to a more exclusive audience" (Wright 2004a: 160). On smaller sites, goat and sheep were the main feast meats. As in Mesopotamia, palace inventories specify commodities —wheat, spelt, cheese, figs, sheep, pig-boar—but no recipes or descriptions of dishes from the period have yet been found. Burnt sacrifice was practiced, with neonatal pigs as a common offering (Hamilakis and Konsolaki 2004), and there was a bull cult. Little is known of Mycenaean religion. Although several of the deities named in Linear B inscriptions, including Poseidon, Zeus, and Hera, appear in the later Greek pantheon, it is not possible to say to what extent they correspond to their later incarnations. These same inscriptions enumerate offerings of vessels, sacrificial animals and slaves to the deities: "to Poseidon, gold bowl 1, woman 1 ... to Hermes Areias gold chalice 1, man 1" (Palaima 2004: 240–1), but descriptions of the rites and feasts are not given. The question of whether this dedication of people refers to service to the deity or human sacrifice has been much debated, but is unresolved.

More generally, the remains suggest a familiar trajectory for feasting as Mycenaean society developed. In the earlier periods, there is evidence for intensive feasting among the elite to establish positions of dominance and build social networks among kin, retainers and peers. As Mycenaean society became more complex and social divisions became more marked, feasting was extended to the non-elite, mobilizing and consolidating the wider community that now supported the political and economic needs of the palaces (Wright 2004a: 170–1). Here we see the grand state-sponsored feasts, in which large numbers of animals were sacrificed and consumed, and banquets for a thousand people and more, who periodically participated in the activities of the elite. Wealthy and powerful, Mycenaean civilization flourished until, around 1200 BC, it collapsed suddenly. One of the mysteries of cultural history, the causes and precise details of the fall of Mycenae as part of a more general collapse that affected the eastern Mediterranean as a whole—to the East, the Hittite Empire and the Egyptian Empire in Syria fell at the same time—are unknown. It was once believed that Mycenaean culture was entirely destroyed and there was a complete break with the past, but ongoing archaeological excavations in Greece have revealed sites where hierarchical social organization persisted. It is now thought that the centuries following the destruction of the palace system—once called the Dark Ages—were actually a period when Mycenaean culture creatively transformed itself in response to changed circumstances and the inward migration of new peoples.

In the post-palatial period, agonistic motifs and "heroic male" designs (Deger-Jalkotzy 2006: 174) on the painted vases of the period reflect social instability and conflict as leaders competed to establish themselves. In an environment no longer dominated by the palace, there were new opportunities for social mobility, based on the accumulation of wealth and personal achievement in hunting, war, and competitions. Generally, in the post-palatial period, the emerging new upper class combined "two conflicting principles for the justification of rulership, one based on individual accomplishments and the other on the proof of descent from the former elite" (Maran 2006: 143). The latter point was attested by the finding in post-fall elite tombs of heirlooms from the Mycenaean period, clearly treasured for their links to the past. The discovery of large decorated open mixing bowls used for wine and many deposits of drinking vessels indicate that the old drinking activities continued. However, palatial culture never reasserted itself, and in the following centuries leadership was exercised on the level of local community chiefdoms which sprang up in the territories formerly controlled by the palace systems, each led by a chief or *basileus*, whose authority was subject to constant challenge. Substantial deposits of animal bones adjacent to the dwellings of the ruling classes indicate that large scale feasts continued to be held, now even more important in providing *basileis* with a competitive medium for displaying and increasing influence, the basis of their power along with prowess in war and the possession of arable land (Ainian 2006: 206) or other wealth. Although much of what happened in the "Dark Ages" has yet to be revealed, it is clear that the "Greek" people who emerged at their end were "a very different society, one that had its links with the past, but lived a much simpler life" (Dickenson 2006: 111) with fewer skills and more limited horizons, but still retaining a distant memory of a palatial past, reflected in the *Iliad* and the *Odyssey* (Maran 2006: 144). Instead of dining in splendid palaces from dishes of gold and silver, as imagined by Alma-Tadema and Leighton, or engaging in great temple feasts, they sit like Homer's Odysseus, in humble surroundings, eating simple food in fellowship.

The post-Mycenaean Greek past is today conventionally divided into several overlapping and contested periods—the Homeric or Heroic, formerly known as the Dark Ages (c. 1200–800 BC); the Geometric (c. 900–700 BC) and the Archaic (c. 800–480 BC) which are sometimes combined as the Archaic period (900 BC–480 BC); the Classical (c. 508–322 BC); and the Hellenistic (c. 323–31 BC), each with its distinctive forms of feasting and drinking. The account that follows focuses on the social dynamics of all-male public sacrifice feasts, private banquets and the *symposion* and institutionalized misogyny that were key features of the Greek never-ending feast.

"Heroic" or "Homeric" Feasts

The difference between Mycenaean and Homeric feasts is that the former were real and the latter were not. It was once thought that the Homeric epics which tell of the battle for Troy (the *Iliad)*, and of the homeward journey of Odysseus from Troy (the *Odyssey*), along with other works now lost or of which only fragments remain, were accurate if distant accounts of the Mycenaean period. For example, Agamemnon, who led the forces of the Greeks at Troy in the *Iliad,* was described by Homer as the king of Mycenae. However, it is now generally agreed that neither of these works, which were first written down in the eighth or early seventh century BC, some four centuries after their fall, describes the world of the Mycenaean palaces (Raaflaub 2006: 451). Instead, they appear to describe a social group in Greece in about the eighth century BC, a crucial period in Greek social and political evolution, which saw the emergence of the city-state or *polis*. Whether Homer was an historical person has been much debated (see Morris 1986) and it is no longer thought that the works were written by a single hand. However, their social, literary and artistic influence was profound, and of the original Greek writings that have survived from antiquity, the vast majority are copies of the works of Homer. The Homeric epics enshrine values and practices materialized through feasting and drinking that were perpetuated in later periods down to the present day. But how accurately were these practices first portrayed? To what extent were they an invented tradition from the outset?

In the Homeric epics, "feasting is ubiquitous and constant—it is what Homeric heroes do in company at every opportunity" (Sherratt 2004: 303). It is the most frequent activity along with fighting, and in the epics the protagonists go from feast to fight to feast until, as Sherratt put it, "a sense of realism is sometimes lost" (Sherratt 2004: 302), even allowing for literary license. Indeed, every meal seems to be a feast. In the past, the precise details of the feasts portrayed were often glossed over, the assumption being that they approximated to the romantic repasts glimpsed through the rosy lens of "Classical Antiquity," or that they were plot devices that gave no insight into past social life and processes. A close reading reveals a different picture, to be considered below, but the thing to bear in mind is this: the later Greeks believed Homer existed, and saw themselves in and through the Homeric epics and the myths associated with them. In the Homeric narrative, mythic and historic time are one and the same. Mythically, it was a time when the gods walked the earth, and involved themselves in human affairs. For anthropologists, as Burkert (1985: 8) put it, "the importance of the myths of the gods lies in their connection with the sacred rituals for which they frequently provide a reason," serving as the metaphor for and vehicle of social practice. For a *cultural* understanding of a society, it is necessary to *not* separate history and myth. To an exceptional degree, in Greece "history and politics merged with the suggestive power of religion" (Kotaridi 2011: 9). So why did the Greeks embrace the portrayal of feasting in the Homeric epics, and seek to reenact it down the centuries?

The society portrayed in the *Iliad* and *Odyssey* was not that of Mycenaean Greece. Homer describes a rural landscape of scattered self-sufficient holdings of varying sizes and levels of prosperity that appears to correspond roughly to what is now known of the social organization of the post-palatial period. Among them are eminent "households" or *oikoi* led by a senior male and comprised of his extended kin, supporters, servants and slaves who sought to improve their position by allying with or subordinating other *oikoi*, while remaining autonomous themselves. Wealth was reckoned in pigs, cattle and sheep, and cattle-raiding was endemic, considered an honorable peacetime activity, the counterpart to war. In anthropological terms, "a household's wealth, land, warriors and workers formed an interlinked system of production. Wealth and land supported and attracted people. People produced more goods, and warriors not only defended what one possessed, but allowed one to seize more" (Beidelman 1989: 230). *Oikoi* were held together through kinship, formal political alliance, personal loyalty, fictive kinship or "brotherhood" in which close friendship was as strong as the ties of blood, and *"xenia"* or "guest friendship," an aristocratic tradition of hospitality in which strangers were invited to share a meal, effectively giving them the opportunity to join or ally with the social group. Large *oikoi* were inherently unstable and volatile. The position of the leader was precarious and constantly challenged, with membership of the *oikoi* expanding and contracting to reflect kinship rivalries and realignments and the shifting loyalties of supporters (Donlan 1985: 304). In societies like these, reciprocal gift exchange—of armor, horses, garments, women, booty and prestigious objects like drinking bowls—flourishes as a way of building mutual obligation, but the greatest gift was the feast.

In societies of this kind, only aristocratic leaders and warriors (*aristoi*) had the resources to give large formal feasts and the sacrifices, contests, games and races that often accompanied them, and only *aristoi* participated in them. Feasts were used by leaders to demonstrate their wealth and power, gain prestige, enhance their authority, build loyalty and forge alliances that would benefit their *oikoi* and win divine approval and patronage, while on an individual level the giving of feasts enhanced a warrior's reputation. Most importantly from an *emic* point of view, feasting created and perpetuated community and identity. There were feasts on a smaller scale, and contributory feasts to which everyone brought provisions, but in all cases food and drink played a sacramental role, generating the fellowship and joint participation that marked the feasters as members of the group in which, notionally or at least for the duration, all were equal, although, as will be seen, some were more equal than others. Feasts were not only given, but returned, becoming part of a system of reciprocal exchange that further consolidated community. Yet in the Homeric epic, the hierarchical role and power of the *aristoi* as feast givers is veiled.

As portrayed in the epics, the key components of Homeric feasting were "meat-eating, wine-drinking and inclusion of the gods by a ritual sacrifice and libation" (Sherratt 2004: 303). In times of peace or war, the Homeric leader is shown in his hall, tent or out of doors with his chosen male companions, sitting upright—for the reclining position for meals had not yet been introduced—and drinking wine served from a common mixing-bowl. Even making allowances for the fact that the protagonists are often on the move or in battle, there is no suggestion of the elaborate cuisine implied by the Mycenaean finds—roasted meat, bread and wine are the only foods mentioned, with very few exceptions. Also unlike Mycenae, there is little or no differentiation of the vessels and baskets in which the food is served, or hierarchical seating, or mention of a variety of foods, although an occasional reference is made to the kind of cauldrons used for boiling seen at Mycenae, which implies the existence of different kinds of food for people of different status—a distinction which is passed over. Despite the passage from the *Odyssey* with which this chapter began, a "festive mood" is not the dominant theme that emerges from the Homeric feast narrative. Instead, the preoccupation is with the division and distribution of meat, of the kind familiar to anthropologists as a feature of simple societies (Borecky 1965). The contrast with the hierarchical feasts of Mycenae is striking. The emphasis is on equality which is facilitated by the fact that the Homeric feasting group tends to be small. Food placed upon a common table, for people to divide among themselves in equal shares, or distributed in equal portions by a servant, reflected and created community, but at the same time the *basileus* or most honored person present had the right to carve and divide the meat and to take a choice part of the meat during a feast, which he could eat himself or give to another as a mark of special favor. Beef and pork back ribs are mentioned as especially esteemed portions. He could assert these rights in order to emphasize hierarchy, or make a show of disregarding them in order to promote solidarity, as the semi-divine hero Achilles does at a feast he gives to celebrate the arrival of Odysseus on a mission of conciliation, serving the food and sitting as an equal among those who are in awe of him (*Iliad* 9: 195–220).

> Achilles spoke ... "Welcome, you are my friends who have come, and I greatly need you ... set up a mixing-bowl that is bigger and mix us stronger drink and make ready a cup for each man" ... Patroclus ... tossed down a great chopping-block into the firelight, and laid upon it the back of a sheep, and one of a fat goat with the chine of a fatted pig edged thick with lard, and brilliant Achilles carved them, and cut it well into pieces and spitted them, as meanwhile [Patroclus] ... made the fire blaze greatly. But when the fire had burned itself out, and the flames had died down, he scattered the embers apart, and extended the spits across them, lifting them to the andirons, and sprinkled the meats with divine salt. Then when he had roasted all, and spread the food on the platters, Patroclus took the bread and set it out on a table in fair baskets, while Achilles served the meats ... and told his companion, to sacrifice to the gods, and he threw the firstlings in the fire. They then put their hands to the good things that lay ready before them.

These are the sons of gods and of kings, great heroes and warriors, but the official Homeric image constructed in the epics and perpetuated thereafter was of a simple band of brothers joined in the equal fellowship of feasting and of something more. With the battlefield, the feast was one of the twin arenas of power in the Homeric epic, the site of events that mark and move social action. As Homer put it in the *Iliad,* "Now let us hasten to the feast, that we may plan the movements of the war." Here the talking and the oratory which the Greeks valued as highly as combat skills took place. It was, in modern parlance, where the business was done.

Sacrifice and Cuisine

The mythic roots of the sacrifice that was part of Greek feasting are found in the early poet Hesiod (c. 750–650 BC), whose *Works and Days* (II: 109–20) sets out an origin narrative in which there were several ages and races beginning with "a golden race of mortal men" who lived like gods, free from toil and grief, and "made merry with feasting beyond the reach of all evils … for the fruitful earth unforced bore them fruit abundantly and without stint." So, from the outset, feasting was established in the Greek worldview as the fundamental and defining social activity, and one approved of by the gods. The Titan Prometheus then tricked Zeus into choosing between two sacrificial meat offerings. The larger, which Zeus selected, turned out to be merely bones wrapped in fat, while the smaller comprised all the choice edible meat, which went to man. Prometheus also stole the gods' eternal fire to give to man. In punishment, the gods brought the Golden Age to an end. Zeus hid food beneath the earth, so it could only be obtained through cultivation. While the food of the Golden Age required no cooking, man now had to cook using mortal fire which, unlike the fire of the gods, had to be kept alight through constant effort. As a final punishment for stealing fire, Zeus gave man the first woman. As the French anthropologist Jean-Pierre Vernant (1989: 65–6) put it, "woman is the counter-gift to fire in the banal sense that, if Zeus brought her to men, it is to make them pay for the fire that Prometheus had stolen from him … women can compensate for fire and provide the balance because she herself is a kind of fire, which will burn men alive by consuming their strength day by day."

Myths provide a cultural rationale of "why we do things the way we do," in this case giving insight into the primarily male nature of Greek sociality and into the misogynistic cast of Greek culture. Only men could be full members of the Greek political community. Women were excluded from performing blood sacrifice, from taking part in the great public feasts, and from playing a part in formal civic life, although they had their own rites and celebrations (see Burton 1998). Women were enjoined to stay at home, could not leave the home unchaperoned, were discouraged from drinking wine; and "respectable" women—the wives and daughters of citizens— were excluded from the private drinking feasts or *symposia* (see below) held in their own homes, Athens being the most extreme in the restrictions placed on females. The myths also give a precedent for the unusual form taken by Greek sacrifices. Although other cultures offered their gods the best foods, formal sacrificial offerings to the Olympian gods consisted of bones wrapped in fat, as in this episode from the *Iliad* (I: 455–70), in which sacrifice is made to propitiate Apollo, followed by a feast on the remaining meat, a procedure that was repeated in formal sacrifices down the centuries:

After praying [to Apollo] and sprinkling the barley-meal, they drew back the heads of the victims and killed and flayed them. They cut out the thigh-bones, wrapped them round in two layers of fat, set some pieces of raw meat on the top of them, and then Chryses laid them on the wood fire and poured wine over them, while the young men stood near him with five-pronged spits in their hands. When the thigh-bones were burned and they had tasted the inward meats, they cut the rest up small, put the pieces upon the spits, roasted them till they were done, and drew them off: then, when they had finished their work and the feast was ready, they ate it, and every man had his full share, so that all were satisfied. As soon as they had had enough to eat and drink, pages filled the mixing-bowl with wine and water and handed it round, after giving every man his drink-offering.

By repeating the original offence, Vernant suggested, the Greeks commemorated their fall from grace, acknowledged their fallibility and confirmed their subservience to the gods, in so doing courting their favor. The bone sacrifice also emphasizes human mortality, and the distance between god and man. The gods do not require mortal food and drink; the smoke may honor them, but it does not provide divine nourishment as they only eat a heavenly substance called ambrosia. And nor do they require wine, for they drink nectar. Men, by contrast, eat and drink because they must. It is a human weakness: as the Greek poet Alexis later put it, "all the difficulties of life occur to satisfy the belly" (Athenaeus X: 421–2).

Enshrined in myth, the rules of Greek sacrifice were as follows. First, frequent sacrifice was obligatory, for reasons of self-interest as much as piety. As Hesiod put it in *Works and Days*: "sacrifice to the deathless gods purely and cleanly, and burn rich meats also, and at other times propitiate them with libations and incense, both when you go to bed and when the holy light has come back, that they may be gracious to you in heart and spirit, and so you may buy another's holding and not another yours." Second, blood sacrifice could only be performed by men. Third, the animals for formal blood sacrifice had to be domesticated beasts and poultry whose rearing required human labor—not wild animals and game birds, which were seen as having been raised by the gods. The most prestigious sacrificial animal was the ox, especially the bull, followed by sheep, then goat, then pig and finally piglet (Burkert 1985: 55), the last often used in rituals associated with women, like the Thesmophoria fertility rite. Fourth, all domesticated meat eaten by humans must first have been sacrificed to the gods or killed in a ritually approved manner. Fifth, cereal—which required human cultivation—was also a part of sacrifice, ritual and feasting, as was wine. The Greeks distinguished three kinds of victuals: *sitos* (the staple, usually bread), *opson* (whatever one eats with the staple) and *poton* (drink) (Davidson 1999: 205). Meat, bread and wine were both symbol and sustenance, nourishment that embodied man's origins and relationship to the gods—but there the Homeric feast menu ends. The only other dish that Homer describes in detail is a restorative preparation of wine, barley and grated goat's cheese, a combination many antiquarians considered doubtful until archaeologists found miniature cheese graters among early drinking wares (Ridgway 1997). But is this all there was?

Athenaeus of Naucratis, the grammarian and author of the fifteen-volume *The Deipnosophists* (*The Learned Banqueters*) asked this question. Writing around the end of the second to early third century AD, when Greek gastronomy had become very elaborate, he complains with the irritation of a frustrated gourmet that, in Homer, the only food that is eaten is bread and platters of meat:

> Now this meat, too, was roasted, and was for the most part beef. Excepting this he never places before them anything, whether at a festival or a wedding or any other gathering. And yet he often makes Agamemnon entertain his chieftains at dinner; no *entreés* served in fig-leaves, no rare titbit or milk-cakes, or honey-cakes, does Homer serve as choice dainties for his kings, but only viands by which body and soul might enjoy strength ... Even the suitors [in the *Odyssey*], insolent though they were, and recklessly given over to pleasure, are not represented as eating fish or birds or honey-cakes, for Homer strenuously excludes the tricks of the culinary art, the viands which Menander calls aphrodisiac ... Although Homer describes the Hellespont as teeming with fish, and pictures the Phaeacians as devoted to the sea, and although he knows that in Ithaca there are several harbours and many islands near the shore abounding in fish and wild fowl, and moreover counts the sea's bounty in supplying fish as an element of prosperity, he nevertheless never represents anyone as eating any of these creatures. What is more, he does not place fruit upon the board either, though it was abundant.
>
> (Athenaeus I: 39)

With anthropological insight, Athenaeus (I: 38) concluded that the sparse Homeric menus were not an accurate description of the dietary practices of antiquity, but a retrospective moral narrative and statement of social values expressed through simple food and restrained consumption:

> Homer saw that moderation is the first and most appropriate virtue of the young, harmoniously joining together and enhancing all that is fair; and since he wished to implant it anew from beginning to end so that his heroes might spend their leisure and their endeavour on noble deeds and be helpful to each other and share their goods with one another, he made their way of living frugal and contented ... they who abide resolutely in frugality are well-disciplined and self-controlled in all the exigencies of life. He has, therefore, ascribed a simple manner of life to all.

By Athenaeus's time, food had indeed become a moral dialogue, with the simplicity of the past contrasted with the destructive luxury of the present, but there was more. As always in anthropology and the best history, the invisible is as important as the visible, the immaterial as significant as the material. What is missing from the feast narrative in the epics?

Just as the emblematic meat, bread and wine are the only foods on the Homeric feast table, so elite heroes and warriors are the only fully drawn figures on the

Homeric landscape. This is a man's world of fighting and feasting. In Homer, feasts are virtually the only meals mentioned. We are only shown "a life divided between a public sphere where men display themselves in the service of communal values and private space about which, perhaps, the less said the better, a 'space of disappearance' where babies are born and other things happen, beneath the notice of the polity" (Redfield 1995: 169). In Homer, servants, entertainers, captives, women and others are sketchily drawn and appear fleetingly in supporting roles, while the wider society is simply invisible, although the power of the elite was based on the labor, "gifts" and service of the unseen common people. Heroes are shown feasting as equals with their fellow diners, even though glimpses of the cauldrons, and of social differentiation seen elsewhere in the epics and in varying burial rites and kinds of armor, and a knowledge of the food available during the period, indicate that the picture of Homeric feasting has been oversimplified, even misrepresented. From what is known of the social organization of the period, Homeric feasting should have been more hierarchical. Instead the epics showed *aristoi* fraternizing as equals, in a landscape free of hierarchy because other figures had been removed from the narrative. This portrayal would have far reaching consequences.

In sum, the Homeric feast as portrayed in the epics was a structured social event that began with the meat sacrifice which linked the sacred and the secular, bestowing divine approval on the proceedings. The sequence continued with the drinking of wine served from a common bowl, eating equal portions from a shared table, and carrying on with the drinking after the food has been finished. There were speeches and recitations—the main form of cultural transmission in a preliterate age—and discussion about matters such as the conduct of hostilities and diplomatic initiatives, the making and breaking of alliances, the division of spoils, the resolution of quarrels, and future plans. Feasting, talking, fighting and politics were inseparable, and to be barred from the table was to be excluded from power. Then the Homeric world began to change.

Feasting in the Geometric and Archaic Periods

The Homeric epics may have been an invented tradition (Hobsbawm and Ranger 1992), but later generations saw in it a template for social relations in a period of change that saw a sharp rise in population and diversity, an increase in wealth and the emergence of a radical new form of sociopolitical organization—the *polis* —that challenged the old elite. Or rather *poleis*, because they were not uniform at the time nor is there agreement about them today (see Hall 2007; Fisher and van Wees 1998). It was once thought that—rather like the birth of Athena fully-fledged from the forehead of Zeus—all *poleis* emerged as self-sufficient, self-governing communities of citizens (*polites,* collectively *demos*) with new democratic ways of thinking, occupying an urban center and surrounding territory and defended by a new kind of military organization: standing armies consisting of hoplites or citizen-soldiers who were trained to carry out a more disciplined form of group warfare in phalanx formation rather than the individual heroic exploits of the mythic period. It is now clear that there was considerable variation between *poleis*, and that they changed over time, from the early rudimentary polities of the Geometric era to the highly developed city-states of the Classical period. The transition was far from orderly, for the strife within *poleis* was as contentious as the warfare between them.

Whatever their differences, all *poleis* had one thing in common, which remained constant in the face of change: "from Homer onward the Greek political community was conceived of as a self-governing band of warriors ... the political community consisted of men" (Redfield 1995: 165), specifically those freeborn men recognized by their peers as being entitled to participate in communal public activities such as hunting, attending assemblies, taking part in games, and engaging in sacrifices and feasting. The *aristoi* initially dominated the *polis* and its public communal activities and strove to retain their mastery, with the tensions between them and the developing *demos* continuing down the centuries, as did the warfare between *poleis*. Also during the Geometric period, the Olympian deities—Zeus, Hera, Poseidon, Demeter, Athena, Apollo, Artemis, Ares, Aphrodite, Hephaestus, Hermes and Dionysius—and others to whom the *aristoi* had previously controlled access through sacrifice, and from whom some *aristoi* claimed descent, were established as the gods of the *poleis*. Now each *polis* had its own patron gods, goddesses or semi-divine founders for whom temples and sanctuaries were created. Henceforth, "with the possible (and by no means certain) exception of some philosophers, being a member of a *polis* was for a Greek inseparable from worshipping the gods of that *polis*" (Crawford and Whitehead 1983: 1). The "*polis* anchored, legitimated and mediated all religious activity" (Sourvinou-Inwood 1990); the *polis* articulated religion and vice versa, with the sacrifice feast being the arena for both. Meat was so closely associated with political and religious practice that vegetarianism, later practiced by Pythagoras and his followers, was seen as radical dissent and refusal.

Taken together, the changes were profound, and it is no accident that this was also a period of intense symbolic production in the form of literary and material culture, the latter including the ceramics that gave the Geometric era its name. It has been suggested that these social changes were inseparable from the popularity of the epics: responding to the challenges posed by the emergence of the *poleis*, the *aristoi* supported and promoted heroic narratives that enshrined their elite values. "Poetry was being exploited to serve as an ideological tool to legitimize elite domination, presenting it as natural and unchangeable. This, the poet is saying, is how it was in the Heroic Age; this, he is implying, is how it should be now" (Morris 1986: 123). This would explain why the epics "seem consciously to promote the illusion of describing an ancient society" (Raaflaub 2006: 455). However, what is striking in the Greek case is how the same Homeric traditions appealed to two groups with fundamentally opposed views and objectives—the *aristoi* and the emerging *demos*. Still compelling today, the heroic narratives became common culture, providing a mythic "Panhellenic" past (Sherratt 2004) that drew disparate peoples together, even as the relationship between the *aristoi* and the *demos* was undergoing transformation.

The anthropologist Mary Douglas (1970) identified a pattern in which periods of pervasive social change are often accompanied by periods of cultural "effervescence" which see the emergence of new values, groups and social relations. Equally, old symbols and rites may persist in new guises, or in outwardly similar modes but with different purposes to those they once had. This is what happened to the Homeric rituals of eating and drinking. As Schmitt-Pantel (1989: 199) rightly says, "we cannot appreciate collective practices such as banquets while separating them from their historical context ... as well as from the particular political system (in this case the *polis* or city-state) that created and developed them."

In the Geometric and Archaic periods, the feasting and drinking seen in the Homeric epics emerged as social practice, used by competing factions to establish their position in the emerging *poleis*. The simple eating, drinking, listening and talking praised by Homer's Odysseus developed into three forms of commensal practice, although the distinction between them was not entirely clear in antiquity and is still contested today. They were the sacrificial feast, the private banquet and the *symposion*, the all-male drinking parties for which the Greeks became renowned. On the Homeric model, the sacrificial meal consisted of a sacrifice and the offering of their portion to the gods, followed by the cooking and dividing of the meats, and its consumption by those present. The banquet was a shared private meal not necessarily tied to an act of public sacrifice, although any domesticated meat eaten would have to have been dispatched in a religiously approved manner, like *halal* and kosher butchery today. There were no such restrictions on wild game or fish, which appear more frequently than domesticated meat and fowl on private banquet tables. The *symposion,* as noted, was a formalized version of the drinking and discussion that took place at feasts in the heroic narratives. In all cases, the consumption created the community that generated the all-important talk and social dynamics that held society together, linking the sacred and the secular by the invocation of the gods throughout the event. In the feasting and drinking, social and sacred technology were combined.

At first, as depictions on pottery reveal, little distinction was made between the meal and the drinking that followed, one segueing into another (Schmitt-Pantel 1994) as in the Homeric epics. However, the postprandial drinking—the *symposion*— developed its own rituals and character. What actually happened at early Archaic symposia is not altogether clear. This is partly because of the scarcity of early textual sources and partly because symposia changed over time with the fuller accounts coming from later periods and primarily Athenian settings. This chapter focuses on Athens because of the sources, and because it is Athenian commensal practices that

4.1 ΣΨΜΠΟΣΙΟΝ *by the English Edwardian artist, Charles Ricketts. This unpublished woodcut was intended to illustrate an edition of Plato's* Symposium. *C. 1895–1910. © The Trustees of the British Museum. Museum number 1917.0623.1. Image number AN 391681*

continue to influence us today. Mainly, however, the problem has been the later "development of a philosophical literature of commensality in the classical and postclassical world" that produced "an idealized vision" (Murray 1995: 220–1) of the commensal practices of old, rather than an accurate one.

Symposia are known to us today mainly through the later "*sympotic*" literature and art they gave rise to. Very broadly, the former includes works such as odes, poems and riddles performed at *symposia*, as well as dramatic, comedic, lyrical, poetic, historical and philosophical works by Aristotle, Aristophanes, Epicurus, Xenophon and many others in which the *symposion* and banquet serve as setting or metaphor (see Wilkins 2000; Bowie 1997; Klotz and Oikonomopoulou 2011; Putz 2007). A special genre of *sympotic* literature was the *scolia* or drinking songs, with refrains like this:

> Drink with me, sport with me, love with me, wear wreaths with me, rage with me when I am raging, be sober when I am sober.
>
> (Athenaeus XV: 695)

The art, which in addition to heroic and mythic themes depicts *symposia*, sacrifices and banquets, is found on the many pottery cups, vessels, bowls and pitchers used at them that survive in museums around the world. The British Museum has a particularly fine collection on which the never-ending feast plays itself out in lively merriment. In their quantity and quality, both literature and art attest to the *symposion* as "a nodal point of Greek social life" (Neer 2002: 4). There has been so much scholarly emphasis on idealized behavior and the artistic and literary aspects of *sympotic* culture, that the social dynamics underlying *symposia* and banqueting have often been lost sight of.

From an anthropological perspective, the early Greek warriors—either active combatants or those who saw themselves as warriors in any sense—are neither more nor less than an example of a universal and fundamental organization of power—the men's group. In all societies, men's groups establish a private space in which the culture and practices of their particular group can be perpetuated. Men's groups usually have "men's houses," club houses or other places where the younger men are initiated and trained, the older men pass on their knowledge, and all share in the private culture and traditions of the group, which will be tested against those of other competing groups through contests of skill or through open warfare. The group engages in confrontational displays to intimidate or provoke other groups. The dynamics of inclusion and exclusion are in force; women, uninitiated children and strangers are strictly excluded, and the proceedings are kept secret. Male superiority and the exploits of the group and its members are celebrated, with a view to informing and inspiring initiates. Groups may embrace the whole society, with all males being divided among the clubs, or membership may be more selective with only the elect included as in the Homeric epics. The emphasis is on intense bonding among group members, which may involve pain through trials of strength and endurance and ritual violence, or pleasure of various sorts, sometimes sexual and often including the altering of consciousness through intoxication which will intensify the bonding experience and create a heightened level of group consciousness. The gods and ancestors will be invited to join the proceedings, or invoked to give their approval. There will be feasting, often on symbolic foods, and music, chants, dances, contests and speeches. Proceedings often involve the use of a private language or words and formulae whose meaning is known only to group members. The objective is to build solidarity and identity through the

4.2 Kylix or cup used for drinking wine. Black glazed pottery, Attic. © The Trustees of the British Museum. Museum number 1864.1007.152. Image number AN 966448

transmission of sentiments and values to successive generations, the education of new members, and the fostering of a sense of "belonging" and "togetherness." In these groups, "'the power of society itself' is manifested in microcosm" (Read 1952 in Langness 1977). This model applies to the sacrifice feast, the private banquet and the *symposion*.

Archaic Symposia

Often thought of as a Greek invention, the *symposion* was simply the Greek version of the drinking party that had long flourished in the ancient Near East, as seen in Chapters Two and Three. The Greek refinement was the addition of a distinctive kind of institutionalized pederasty (relationships between older and younger men, originally conceived as one of mentoring, see Percy 1996), homosexual bonding, "free love" (Murray 1994), and a highly developed form of ritualized drinking. The Archaic *symposion* of the *aristoi* has been described as the Homeric warrior associations "transformed into a leisure group under the impact of the changed position of the aristocracy, in a world where their military function had been taken over by the hoplite army of the *polis*" (Murray 1983 in Bremmer 1994). These groups met regularly in each other's houses, in the *andron*, the men's room set aside for eating and drinking. Once the remains of the meal had been cleared and the room cleaned, the *andron* became a "sympotic space" which had three dimensions: physical, metaphysical and alcoholic. The *symposion* is treated here at some length because of the scholarly attention it has received, and because it represents an elaborate form of what Mary Douglas (1987a: 8) called "constructive drinking," referring to the way in which alcohol makes the structure of social life apparent, and, through the ceremonials of drinking, constructs an ideal world. What follows is a retrospective description, constructed from accounts of the Archaic *symposion* by later writers. Athenaeus, as noted, is a very late source (third century AD) but his *The Deipnosophists* incorporates many earlier works which have since been lost.

The physical arrangement and dynamics of the formal *symposion*, as of the meal that preceded it, were dictated by the introduction from the East, in about the seventh century BC, of the reclining mode of dining and drinking on couches, portable or fixed to the floor. Instead of sitting, participants lay on couches on their left sides, leaving the right hand free. Couches were identical so that everyone was on the same level as his companions, positioned so everyone could see each other, and within easy range of sight and hearing so conversation would flow. Each couch could hold one or two men, in arrangements of seven, eleven or fifteen couches, giving a maximum of thirty principal participants, not counting musicians, entertainers and wine-pourers. This was considered the maximum ideal number for generating the *eusebia* (respect for the gods) *euergesia* (respect for the equality of those present), *heyschia* (tranquility and harmony of the group) and *pistis* (trust) that were essential to sympotic proceedings. In the Archaic period, seven couches was the usual number, indicating the more intimate and confidential nature of early *symposia*. Physical seclusion was reflected in metaphysical separation. "The *symposion* became in many respects a place apart from the normal rules of society with its own strict code of honor in the *pistis* there created, and its own willingness to establish conventions fundamentally opposed to those within the *polis* as a whole. It developed ... its own sense of occasion" (Murray 1994: 7).

Xenophanes of Colophon's (c. 570–470 BC) description of the *andron* prepared for the *symposion* brims with anticipation:

> Now at last the floor is swept, and clean are the hands of all guests, and their cups as well. One slave puts plaited wreaths on their heads, another offers sweet smelling perfume in a saucer; the mixing-bowl stands full of good cheer; and other wine is ready, which promises never to give out—mellow wine in jars, redolent of its bouquet, and in the midst the frankincense sends forth its sacred fragrance; and there is water, cool and fresh. The yellow loaves lie ready at hand, and a lordly table groans with the weight of cheese and luscious honey; an altar in the middle is banked all round with flowers, and singing and dancing and bounty pervade the house.
>
> (Athenaeus XI: 462–3)

In the middle, next to the altar used for libations, stood the *krater,* a large ornamental bowl for mixing wine. The *krater* was an iconic object of prestige, power and desire, signifying that its possessor was wealthy enough to fill the *krater*, and influential enough to summon a group of his elite peers to drink from it (Luke 1994). To be without a *krater*—to be *akratos*—was to be powerless. The Kerameikos cemetery in Athens, used in Archaic times, contained *kraters* several feet high, used as early grave markers. The Greeks may not have invented wine-making or the drinking party, but in the *symposion* they developed the most elaborate wine consumption rituals known in the ancient world, which orchestrated the social dynamics in the group through controlling levels of alcohol-induced consciousness.

The proceedings were directed by a Symposiarch selected by the participants who chose the music, performances topics of conversation and managed the social inter-action. Anyone who disobeyed the Symposiarch was made to leave and excluded from the group. The Greeks distinguished three colors of wine—red (*melas*), white (*leukos*) and amber (*kirrhos*)—and they loved all three, distinguishing bouquets such as "earthy" and "fruity," and appreciating the relative merits of wine from particular regions, sweetness being particularly appreciated. Far more important than taste were wine's psychotropic properties, for the Greeks well knew that Dionysius's gift could be bane or boon, as these proverbs and exhortations show:

> Do not get drunk and revel in order that you may not be recognized as the sort of man you happen to be, instead of the sort you pretend to be.
>
> (Pittacus in Athenaeus X: 427)

> As bronze is the mirror of the outward form, wine is the mirror of the mind.
>
> (Aeschylus in Athenaeus X: 427)

> For wine in fact nourishes souls, lulling to sleep its pains, as mandragora lulls men to sleep, and on the other hand it stirs feelings of friendship, as oil stirs flames.
>
> (Socrates, in Athenaeus XI: 504)

> When wine goes down into the body, evil words float on top.
>
> (Herodotus in Athenaeus IV: 303)

There is also a legend that Dionysius showed a farmer how to make wine; the farmer shared the drink with others and they, thinking they had been poisoned, murdered him. Confronted with such a potent substance, the Greeks sought to control it. As always there was a myth. It was said that when wine was first brought to Greece from the Red Sea by the god Dionysius, men drank it unmixed and became delirious or fell into stupors. A fortuitous rainstorm filled a wine bowl with water, and men discovered that the mixture of wine and water was both pleasant and painless (Athenaeus XV: 675). For this reason, one of the libations that opened the *symposion* was always dedicated to Zeus Sotor, Zeus Saviour, who saved mankind from the dangers of unmixed wine by sending the rain.

4.3 Krater, used for mixing wine and water, showing Herakles and Apollo. Attic, 390–370 BC. © The Trustees of the British Museum. Museum number 1924.0716.1. Image number AN 38346

In mixing, the custom was to put the water into the *krater* first, and then add the wine. Wines were mixed with water in proportions that could vary widely—two parts wine to five of water, five parts wine to ten parts water, or water to wine in proportions of "3:1 to 5:3 or 3:2 depending on the desired strength of the mixture ... with proportions thought of as harmonic balances, almost like music" (Lissarrague 1990: 8). It was considered that only a fool would drink a half-and-half mixture, and only a barbarian or madman would drink wine neat. In *Philebus*, Plato spoke of the art of mixing in this way: "we have two fountains beside us one of which, the fountain of pleasure, one might liken to honey; the other, the sobering and wine-less fountain of wisdom, like to a well of homely and healthful water; these we must mix in the best possible way" (in Athenaeus X: 423). The Symposiarch decreed the number of *kraters* that would be drunk in the course of the evening, and the proportions in which the wine and water would be mixed. The objective was to achieve a finely judged balance of decorum and impropriety, order and disorder, introspection and gaiety, and to reveal truths and grasp the essence of things, in order to generate discussion and debate of the highest quality. The mixtures were also supposed to sustain a receptiveness to the singing of drinking songs, poetry, plays, music, games and speeches that constituted the formal entertainment, in which pedagogy and pleasure were combined. As the poet Alexis had Solon say in *Aesop*: "This you see is the Greek way of drinking; by using cups in moderation, they can talk and fool with each other pleasantly" (Athenaeus X: 431–2). Once mixed, the wine was dipped from the common bowl into a pitcher and poured into the guests' cups by servants, moving from left to right around the central space. The size of the *krater* depended on the occasion and number of guests.

So far, this synchronic account of the *symposion* corresponds in principle to both the mythic model of the Homeric narrative, and the universal dynamics of men's groups. At the outset of the Geometric period, the *aristoi*'s position was still displayed and consolidated through public sacrifice, feast and drinking in a mode that re-enacted the heroic epics and the ritualistic feast meal of meat, bread and wine, with older men mentoring younger ones in the warrior tradition. The smaller numbers of couches used in the early period—usually seven—testifies to the select and probably secretive nature of the group, as do the riddles, puns and puzzles which bespeak an origin in the private language of a group. At first, *aristoi* feasting consisted of eating accompanied by drink, followed by further drinking, but social change modified this sequence. As time went on, the *aristoi* found their prerogatives eroded in the developing *poleis*, which began to appropriate the practices that allowed the elite to display hierarchy, status and power. Sport and organized athletic games sponsored by the *polis* displaced single-handed aristocratic warrior combat as primary tournaments of value, the hero tales and performances once staged by the *aristoi* began to be mounted as civic performances for the public and access to the gods, once led by the *aristoi*, was now increasingly democratized through city shrines, which held sacrifices to the gods on behalf of the city and its people.

These changes were reflected in the aristocratic *symposion*. As challenges to aristocratic hegemony mounted, the drinking part of the feast where cultural production was at its most intense took on greater importance as the primary arena for the affirmation and transmission of *aristoi* values and warrior ways. The images of feasting and drinking on *symposion* wares—which were themselves a form of material culture, meant to embody and perpetuate the values and practices they portrayed and facilitated—reveal a trajectory in which moderation was replaced by excess. Elders, the former fonts of wisdom, were now infrequently depicted, and younger men are shown dominating the proceedings. Feasting was no longer shown, only drinking, and the *komos* or ritualized violence that had always been part of *symposia* became more extreme. The *symposion* became the setting for a party game that swept the ancient world like a craze in the fourth and fifth centuries BC. Called *kottabos*, it combined drinking and skill—the wine left at the bottom of a cup was flicked at a target, with the throw meant to be as graceful as possible. At the height of the craze, circular rooms were constructed in order that, when the target was set up in the center, all might compete at an equal distance and from similar positions. According to Athenaeus (XI: 479–80):

4.4 The youth on the right holds a kylix by one handle, ready to flick it in a game of kottabos. *Red figured cup, Attic, 490–480* BC. © *The Trustees of the British Museum. Museum number 1836.0224.212. Image number AN 760033*

> They made it a point not merely to hit the mark, but also to carry through each motion in the correct form. For the player, leaning on his left elbow (on the couch), was obliged to swing his right arm with supple motion and so toss the *latax*; that is what they called the liquid which fell from the cup. Consequently some persons took greater pride in playing *kottabos* well than do persons who pride themselves on hurling the javelin".

There was also an erotic element. Throws were often dedicated to the beloved, with kisses as prizes, and the game frequently became riotous (see Putz 2007: 175–92).

All were *aristoi* reactions to social and political developments and the increasing and unaccustomed degree of social control and restrictions being placed on them in the *poleis*. This corresponds to the anthropological model in which conflict and reaction play out in scenes of social and sexual abandon which, though shocking at first, then become ritualized and institutionalized (Douglas 1970). The ease with which this appropriation of *aristoi* prerogatives took place can be traced back to the Homeric epics, and the people and things that were excluded from the narrative. The mythic age of aristocratic heroes now provided a template for the new forms of society, and ironically, this was easily done. By leaving the common people out of the epics and making them invisible, the heroic myths of the *aristoi* had described a society of equals to which the new men of the *poleis* felt entitled. In the heroic equals of old, the new men had a template in which they could realize the revolutionary idea that the people—the *demos*—could rule themselves, using commensality to consolidate democratic community and further their collective aims. The mythic precedent for the *aristoi*'s own future struggles had been written into the Homeric feast.

Feasting in the Classical Period

In the Classical period (c. 508–322 BC), also known as the Golden Age, the *poleis* continued to develop across Greece, with Athens being the center of radical participatory democracy. *Poleis* took different forms—democracies, oligarchies in which power was held by an elite, monarchies, and *poleis* ruled by tyrants who had seized power—but in all of them, commensality was at the center of the sociopolitical processes. Although private *aristoi symposia* had changed their character as described above and their direct influence had lessened, they continued to be held, becoming a space in which to explore and "negotiate new political categories" (Neer 2002: 6), as well as an arena for the expression of feelings of being threatened, wronged, and on the verge of being marginalized (Steiner 2002: 354). An unrestrained *aristoi symposion* of the Classical period was described in this way by the comic poet Eubulus:

> Three *kraters* only do I mix for the temperate—one for health, which they empty first, the second to love and pleasure, the third to sleep. When this is drunk up wise guests go home. The fourth *krater* is ours no longer but belongs to *hybris* (arrogance and pride), the fifth to uproar, the sixth to drunken revel, the seventh to black eyes. The eighth is the policeman's, the ninth belongs to biliousness and the tenth to madness and hurling the furniture.
>
> (Athenaeus II: 36)

This gives insight into how the same event could be described as a forum for serious discussion and as a debauch. The tight kinship and alliance groups on which *aristoi* power was once based could no longer operate effectively in *poleis* where civic roles were increasingly awarded by lot or popular election, and *symposia* became larger, with more couches, to widen and strengthen *aristoi* solidarity under pressure, and acculturate newcomers who might swell their ranks. But the politics of commensality were now playing out in other arenas—private banquets and public feasts.

So much scholarly attention has been focused on the heroic warrior tradition and the aristocratic *symposia* of the Archaic period—reflecting a preoccupation in the original sources—that the private banquets of the Classical period and other communal meals seem to suddenly appear from nowhere. They had, of course, been there all along, in the "space of disappearance" alluded to above. To the historian's question "where is the evidence?" the anthropologist's response is, "the people themselves." The *aristoi* cannot have survived only on roasted meat and a great deal of wine for centuries, nor can the *demos* have been without their own commensal practices. Within *aristoi* circles, the *symposion* might have split off from the Homeric feast–banquet–drinking sequence and developed its own character, but more generally the old integrated practice continued, as seen in the following account of the philosopher Menedemus (c. 345–261 BC), being a rare description of more humble and restrained dining and drinking:

> But Antigonus of Carystus, in his Life of Menedemus, relating the way in which the banquets of that philosopher were managed, says that he used to dine with one or two companions at most; and that all the rest of his guests used to come after they had supped. For in fact, Menedemus' supper and dinner were only one meal, and after that was over they called in all who chose to come; and if any of them, as would be the case, came before the time, they would walk up and down before the doors, and inquire of the servants who came out what was being now served up, and how far on the dinner had proceeded. And if they heard that it was only the vegetables or the cured fish that was being served up, they went away; but if they were told that the meat was put on the table, then they went into the room which had been prepared for that purpose. And in the summer a rush mat was spread over each couch, and in the winter a fleece. But everyone was expected to bring his own pillow; and the cup, which was brought round to each person, did not hold more than one *cotyla* (nearly half a pint). And the dessert was lupins or beans as a general rule; but sometimes some fruits, such as were in season, were brought in; in summer, pears or pomegranates; and in spring, pulse; and in winter, figs.
>
> (Athenaeus X: 419–20)

As *aristoi symposia* became more extreme, it was this integrated practice that reasserted itself in public and private life, serving as it had always done as a forum for social and political life, where things of importance were discussed and debated, including *demokratia*, the power of the people, and sentiments orchestrated with the help of wine. And there were other forms of commensality known to the ancients and practiced widely in all periods, but never dealt with in the *aristoi* narratives. There were "basket dinners," "when a man gets up a dinner for himself, and putting it into a basket goes to somebody's house to eat it" (Athenaeus VIII: 364–5), and dinners called *eranoi* in which the repast consisted of food contributed by the diners, a kind of pot luck supper (Athenaeus VIII: 362). As shared meals, these forms of commensality were ideal for furthering the democratic project, and for discussing ideas in a non-hierarchical context.

The difference between public and private in ancient Greece has always been problematic because of the cultural attitude to private life noted previously. Public life was glorified while the domestic sphere was insignificant and invisible, "as if the city state wished away the private life of families so that it could get on with its self-representation as a self-sufficient society organized around the competition of identically qualified peers" (Redfield 1995: 169–70). An additional factor is the partial Homeric landscape referred to above. Just as heroes and *aristoi* are the only people shown, so only "public" events are described, although in practice many of these were private, restricted to the *aristoi*. Setting aside the drinking *symposion*, in the Classical period three main kinds of commensal eating can be identified:

> Domestic family meals (private/private)
> All-male banquets and dinners (private/public)
> All-male sacrificial feasts (public/public)

The fact that only one extended description of a family meal has come down in the literature of the Classical period, compared to the many references to the private all-male banquets of the era, reflects the fact that the domestic meal was considered culturally and socially insignificant. However, the remaining two commensal practices—"private" banquets and "public" feasts—were central to the political process, and were paradigms of different kinds of inclusion/exclusion.

Returning to the Homeric template, feasting was a defining and inherently political social activity. No less than the battlefield, the feast was an arena of combat where men could display wealth and status, forge solidarity and compete in oratory, games and singing. The Greeks "generally took the view that only by participating in such a community of competing peers could one become a human being in the full sense" (Redfield 1995: 164). Eloquence of speech was as valued as skill at arms—as Telemachus says to his mother Penelope in the Odyssey, "speech is for men," and in this sense the sacrificial feast and the private banquet always acted as a political forum for the *aristoi*. To be included was therefore highly significant, while to be excluded from the feast and banquet was to be barred from full participation in society. For this reason, Schmitt-Pantel (1994: 25) argued that the *aristoi symposion* and, by extension, banquet were not strictly private because "the groups practicing this form of sociability are the very groups which comprise the civic body" of the city. The difference between feast and banquet, never clarified in the original sources, appears to be this. Just as Homer showed his warriors eating heroic fare with restraint in public, although presumably eating other foods in private, so cultural values continued to dictate that consumption must not be conspicuous, and that indulgence of any kind should be concealed, if practiced at all. Thus, at the top of the social hierarchy, was the public feast (public/public), the ritual consumption of sacred foods—and alongside it the private banquet (public/private) where more latitude was allowed, both in foods eaten and in behavior. These were paralleled by the humbler shared meals of the emerging *demos,* also (public/private) as the civic influence of the participants increased.

The elite Athenian private banquets are the best known. With the establishment of its empire and navy, Athens became rich and powerful, increasing the range of foods and luxury goods available, while the number of people—not only *aristoi*—who could afford them grew. The comic playwright Hermippus captures the excitement of these new cargos—silphium stalks from Cyrene, salted fish from the Hellespont, sides of beef from Thessaly, pigs and cheese from Syracuse and from Rhodes, raisins and figs for sweet dreams (in Miller 1997: 63–4), along with many delicacies out of season. These were the ornaments of the feast, and what feasts they were. Military and diplomatic contact with Persia in the late sixth and fifth centuries introduced the Athenians and other Greeks to Achaemenid opulence, as seen in Chapter Three. New ways of prolonging and enhancing pleasure were devised. Instead of mixing wine with plain water, water in which myrrh, aromatics, anise, saffron, costmary, cardamon and cinnamon had been steeped was used, believed to arrest intoxication by "softening the spirits," allowing more to be drunk. The wreaths worn by feasters were chosen with great care—the astringent scent of myrtle was thought to dispel the fumes of wine, roses were thought to have sedative power against headaches, and carnations, lavender, apple blossom, saffron crocus, violets and lilies were esteemed, but marjoram which was thought stupefying was avoided (Athenaeus XV: 675). As for the banquets themselves, this description by Philoxenus of Cythera (435–380 BC)—known for his fondness for seafood—is representative of the more extravagant:

The tables glistened in the rays of the high-swinging lamps, freighted with trenchers and condiments delectable ... to pleasure life, tempting lures of the spirit. Some slaves set beside us snowy-topped barley cakes in baskets, while others brought in loaves of wheat. After them first came not an ordinary tureen ... but a riveted vessel of huge size ... a glistening dish of eels to break our fast, full of conger-faced morsels that would delight a god ... After this ... a soused ray of perfect roundness. There were small kettles, one containing some meat of a shark, another a sting-ray. Another rich dish there was, made of squid and sepia-polyps with soft tentacles. After this came a grey mullet, hot from its contact with fire, the whole as large as the table, exhaling spirals of steam. After it came breaded squid ... and cooked prawns done brown. Following these we had flower-leaved cakes and fresh confections spiced, puff-cakes of wheat with frosting ... Last there came ... a monstrous slice of tunny, baked hot ... carved with knives from the meatiest part of the belly ... I nearly missed a hot entrail, after which came in the intestine of a home-bred pig, a chine, and a rump with hot dumplings. And the slave set before us the head, boiled whole, and split in two, of a milk-fed kid, all steaming; then boiled meat-ends, and with them skin-white ribs, snouts, heads, feet and a tenderloin spiced with silphium. And other meats there were, of kid and lamb, boiled and roast ... afterwards there was jugged hare, and young cockerels, and many hot portions of partridges and ring-doves were now lavishly laid beside us. Loaves of bread there were, light and nicely folded; and companioning these there came in also yellow honey and curds, and as for the cheese—everyone would avow that it was tender, and I too thought so. And when by this time we comrades had reached our fill of food and drink, the thralls removed the viands, and boys poured water over our hands.

(Athenaeus IV: 147–8)

The critique of luxury became a central theme in philosophical discourse, partly because the growing inequalities of wealth were seen as inimical to egalitarianism, partly because if luxury became available to all, the masses could no longer be controlled by an elite. And partly because luxury—the feared *tryphé*—posed a threat to the good order of the physical as well as the social body. This fear became more pronounced after the Greeks' defeat by the luxurious Persians of Chapter Three. In *The Republic*, Plato fulminated against the "luxurious State," peopled by those who were no longer satisfied with the simpler way of life, but insisted on embellishing their dinners, "adding sofas and tables, and other furniture, also dainties, and perfumes and incense, and courtesans, and cakes, all these not of one sort only, but in every variety." In the comedies performed in Athens, food, drink and luxury become metaphor and medium for exploring social issues, satirizing consumption while satisfying a growing public appetite for it. Periodic attempts were made to restrain private consumption and the display of wealth through civic regulation, while in public the Heroic Age and its restrained commensal practices were idealized, valorized and perpetuated through social ritual which involved feasting on the plain food of the past, not on the luxurious food of the present. Amid excess, the simple symbolic consumption of the mythic age, laden with social values, was always present—the ghost at the feast. And it was a troublesome ghost, for from the beginning Greek feasting embodied and epitomized the conflicting tendencies of exclusion/inclusion, egalitarianism/hierarchy, public/private and simplicity/luxury.

In Athens and many other *poleis*, despite the emergence in Greece of civic institutions like assemblies, law courts and magistracies (Schmitt-Pantel 1990) to deal with issues that used to be decided by the *aristoi* when dining or drinking, and the development of alternative fora like gymnasia and agoras for debate, public commensality continued. Because of the later scholarly preoccupation with aristocratic *symposia*, along with the tendency to relegate sacrifice to the status of a "mere" religious rite and the assumption that non-sacrificial eating and drinking were part of the private domestic sphere, as well as the fascination with banquets *de luxe*, the public commensal practices of the Classical period and their social dynamics have tended to be underappreciated and overlooked. For although "business" of various sorts was no doubt done in private banquets, it was in public commensality that social values writ large were displayed and contested.

As noted above, the heroic myths and the commensal practices embedded in them were as empowering to the *demos* as to the *aristoi*. Instead of seeing commensal practices in Classical Athens as an egalitarian appropriation of *aristoi* ways, they should be seen as democratic re-enactments of mythic practices, which coexisted alongside the surviving *aristoi* versions of the same practices. One of the prized privileges of public life in Athens, awarded to a select number of people, was the right to dine as a guest of the *polis*. One dining hall on the Athenian Agora, the Prytaneion, catered for "those with hereditary rights to eat at state expense, envoys and dignitaries, overall ... elites in Athenian society (Steiner 2002: 348). Here the *aristoi* tradition of dining among peers and extending *xenia*, guest friendship, to distinguished strangers, persisted. The meal consisted of a repast of roasted meat and plain fare such as "cheese and a barley-puff, ripe olives and leeks in memory of their ancient discipline" according to Chionides (Athenaeus IV: 137–8): a sharp contrast to luxurious private banquets. Another dining hall on the Agora, the Tholos, catered to citizens selected by lot for a limited amount of time, drawn from a broad spectrum of the citizens involved in the affairs of the *polis*, mixing common people and the elite, but excluding strangers. Food was not provided as it was at the Prytaneion. Instead, diners were given an allowance and brought their own food, which they ate together off wares that were stamped with the symbol for *demosion*, or "public property." Seating in the Tholos was also democratic: diners did not recline as at private banquets, but sat upright in a round structure that could not conveniently accommodate couches (Luke 1994: 28). In the ostentatious simplicity of the fare and the sober conduct of the repasts, both Prytaneion and Tholos offered a public challenge to the upstart luxury and *tryphé* of the private banquets, using dining to build community and claim legitimacy using "equality" in different and contesting ways, yet both harking back to the Homeric tradition. And in these competing forms of public commensality can be seen the contradiction at the heart of Greek "democracy" and "equality."

Public feasting also took place around the many sacrifices connected to temples, shrines and festivals which were often linked to a particular *polis*. There were some one hundred and twenty official festivals on the Athenian state calendar, headed by the Panathenaia, dedicated to the city's founder-goddess. The festival had four main features: the gathering together of the male citizens of Athens; the procession which brings the sacrificial victims to the altar; and the sacrifice of animals; all depicted on the Parthenon friezes in the British Museum. Not shown is the fourth, the all-male public feasting which followed the sacrifice, held in tents and on platforms built for the occasion on the Acropolis, replicating the feasts of the Heroic Age. The Panathenaia was of some antiquity, but it was reorganized with an enlarged festival programme in the early sixth century BC by the tyrant Peisistratus, who sought to replace local group allegiances with a loyalty to the *polis* enshrined in new/old rituals, a well-known anthropological strategy of power. By the fourth century BC, the Panathenaia procession began at dawn and the feasting that followed went on through the night. The fortunes of the *polis* for the coming year were thought to depend on the sacrifice and rituals being carried out correctly, including the distribution of meat which—after the god's portion—consisted of the old "share of honor" for dignitaries and a more or less equal distribution of the rest.

Today the democracy that was embedded in the Homeric epic and embodied in the Homeric feast is the dominant political form in the West, as are two contesting forms of feasting with their roots in ancient Greece—aristocratic and exclusive private dining and drinking clubs and fraternities on the one hand, and the ideal of democratic dining—non-hierarchical seating, equal and identical food and good fellowship on the other. However, vanguard archaeological work in Greece is beginning to question both the hegemony of democracy and its nature. Outside of Athens, democracy was by no means universal or consistent, and the ongoing struggle between hierarchy and equality, *aristoi* and *demos* seen in Athens and played out through feasting, drinking and *symposia* are repeated *ad infinitum*, in those places where democracy took hold. Democracy and equality are compelling ideals, but do they work in practice? Political events in our own times continue to pose this question. The portrayal of the social landscape and feasting in the Homeric epics was not accurate—was it written as an idealized myth, or retrospectively when the *poleis* began to emerge? This is not clear, and may never be known, but it is possible that of all the Greek myths, the greatest has been democracy. In 338 BC, Philip of Macedon defeated the armies of Athens and Thebes, ushering in the Hellenistic Period. It is said that the buildings that embody Greek culture are the gymnasium, the agora and the temple, but the most important institutions of all were the Greek versions of the never-ending feast.

CHAPTER FIVE

Eurasia: The Mongols—An Empire Built on Drinking

At the entrance to the Palace of Mangu Khan at Caracarum ... there was ... a great silver tree at the foot of which are four silver lions having a spout and all pouring forth mare's white milk. Four spouts are introduced in the tree at its top, and from there they pour out their milk from the mouths of gilded serpents whose tails twine around the trunk of the tree. From one of these channels flows the wine, from another karakumiss or purified mare's milk, from the third honey-drink and from the fourth rice-mead, and each liquor is received at the foot of the tree in a special vase ... then the cupbearers draw off that liquor and carry it to the men and women of the palace ...

(in Komroff 1929, pp. 170–1)

Lying between the Atlantic and Pacific Oceans, Eurasia is the world's largest continental landmass. Although it is a single geographical entity, Eurasia has long been divided—culturally, historically and conceptually—into Europe and Asia, with the borders between them shifting and contested. This division is reflected in mapping. Until recently, standard world maps centered on the Atlantic Ocean, with Europe and Africa on one side, and North and South America on the other. On these maps, Eurasia is cut in half, the divided continent making up "Eastern Europe" on the extreme right hand of the map, and "Asia" on the extreme left. This projection reflects a mindset in which East and West, Europe and Asia, are seen as being on

5.1 *The Eurasian Continent, c.* AD *1500, from Jacques Joosten's "De Kleyne Wonderlijcke Werelt," Amsterdam 1649. © The Trustees of the British Museum. Museum number 1972,U.40.3. Image number AN 1101136*

opposite ends of the earth, entirely separate and with little or no contact between them. It also emphasizes Atlantic sea trade with the New World, and the long ocean routes between Europe and the Far East established during the early modern period, a perspective that has been critiqued as "modernocentric" (Bentley 2006) as well as Eurocentric.

By contrast, other world maps like the Dutch map (Figure 5.1) place Eurasia at the center. In this version, Europe and Asia are contiguous, and it is the land rather than the sea that provides the main means of trade, travel and communication. Lying in a belt across this greatest of continents is the Eurasian steppe, a terrain that includes savannah, shrublands and desert with forests to the north, much of it forbidding, inhospitable to strangers and unsuitable for agriculture. The steppe's chief feature is the wide grasslands, stretching from present-day Manchuria to Hungary, once likened to a sea of grass. Once seen as a barrier and impediment, it is becoming apparent that the steppe was a natural corridor for cultural interchange, and the stage for early globalization. The steppe was also the place where a distinctive diet, way of life and drinking feasts emerged, which changed much of the then known world, leaving a culinary legacy that remains to this day.

The steppe demanded a special form of human exploitation—nomadism—moving herds across the steppe in search of grass and water in response to the seasons and other factors. Domesticated on the steppe around 3500 BC, the horse was central to the nomads' mastery of their environment, and equestrian expertise led to the development of mounted archery, using the bow while at full gallop, which gave the nomads a huge tactical advantage in hunting and in warfare. There were no margins for error. Failure resulted in starvation and death, while success brought its own problems, because "nomads experience constant population surpluses vis-à-vis their environment ... that drives a centrifugal movement" (Bylkova 2005: 141).

There was always intense competition for pasturage and water, and if a group and their herds grew larger, it became necessary to expand their territory through movement, alliance and conquest. Nomads also needed or desired to obtain from sedentary peoples goods, including foods, they could not produce themselves, which was a further spur to migration and conquest. Thus the nomadic life of the steppe was inherently unstable, with groups constantly on the move, expanding and contracting, enmeshed in changing webs of loyalty and conflict, seeking to acquire goods and opportunistic in outlook.

Driven from Inner Asia, it is now thought, by a combination of environmental and social factors (Noonan 1994), nomads from the inner Eurasian steppe were a threatening presence on the periphery of many of the peoples (Levi 1994) seen in earlier chapters. The early steppe peoples were not literate—although petroglyphs and what might be a runic script of uncertain meaning have been found in the modern era—so surviving written descriptions of the nomads have been drawn up by others, invariably enemies. In the east, Chinese texts indicate their presence during the Shang period and probably earlier, and for millennia the relationship with the steppe people was uneasy, alternating between Chinese attempts to appease the nomads—and acquire good steppe horses—and outright conflict. The *Shih Chi* describes the nomads as "a source of constant worry and harm to China." Alliances were built through the marriage of high-ranking Chinese women to leading nomads, the subject of the *Lament of Hsi Chun*, a classic of Chinese poetry. In about 110 BC, during the Han Dynasty, a Chinese princess was sent to be the bride of the nomad king K'un Mo, an unhappy arrangement memorialized in this poem (Waley 1918: 75):

My people have married me
In a far corner of Earth
Sent away to a strange land
To the King of the Wu-Sun.
A tent is my house,
Of felt are its walls;
Raw flesh my food
With mare's milk to drink.

Always thinking of my own country
My heart sad within.
Would I were a yellow stork
And could fly to my old home.

To the south, nomadic steppe peoples were recorded by the Assyrians and bedeviled the Achaemenids, even defeating their Great King Darius. And they were well known to the Greeks, who first encountered them in the Pontic/Black Sea region, as well as to the Romans. The Greeks called them "Scythians," although it is now known that this term embraced several different nomadic peoples whose history before they emerged from the deep steppes is presently unclear. To the Greeks, to be non-Greek was to be a barbarian to a greater or lesser degree and therefore a figure of comedy, ridicule and fear. The nomadic Scythians were seen by the Greeks as the very epitome of Otherness, even more Other than peoples like the Persians and, later, the Gauls who were also cast in this role (Bonfante 2011). To the Greeks, the very term "Scythian" meant "solitary and completely wild places," "people who, being in control of no land, constantly change the place where they live" and "abandoned people" (in Hartog 1988: 13).

The nomads were believed by the Greeks to be descended from a mythical ancestress who was part woman and part snake (Ustinova 2005), an ancestry of which the Greeks were reminded when confronted by one of the Scythians' most fearsome weapons—the poison they put on their arrowheads. Known as *sythicon*, it was a toxic mixture of putrefied blood and decomposed snakes, left to mature in sealed jars buried in dung, which gave off a slow heat that accelerated decomposition. Sythicon delivered what Ovid called a "double-death," for if the arrow alone was not fatal, the poison would be (Rolle 1989: 65). To the Greeks, the use of poisoned arrows offended their beliefs about the honorable way to engage in battle, giving further evidence of Scythian barbarism. And the nomads' equestrian expertise may have given rise to the legends of half-man half-horse centaurs, for as the Roman historian Ammianus (XXXI) wrote "they are almost glued to their horses ... from their horses by night or day every one of that nation buys and sells, eat and drinks, and bowed over the narrow neck of the animal relaxes into a sleep so deep as to be accompanied by many dreams."

For the Greeks to whom cities were the hallmarks of civilized life, nomadic habitations posed another challenge, as the Scythians had no proper houses or permanent settlements. Instead, they lived in wagons or large carts with four, six or more wheels, drawn by oxen and surmounted by tents made of felt or hide stretched over a frame similar to present-day yurts or gers. When on the move, the women and children traveled in the wagons and the men rode on horseback, with the flocks and herds following alongside. When they stopped, the wagons were drawn up together to form encampments. According to Ammianus (XXXI), "They are all without fixed abode, without hearth, or law, or settled mode of life, and keep roaming from place to place, like fugitives, accompanied by the wagons in which they live." While most early writers were contemptuous of these dwellings and way of life, the Greek Herodotus saw their tactical advantage in that they freed the Scythians from the constraints of land-holding and agriculture. He wrote:

> Since they have no towns or strongholds, but carry their homes around with them on wagons, since they are all expert at using their bows from horseback and since they depend on cattle for food rather than on cultivated land, how could they fail to be invincible and elusive?
>
> (Herodotus Book IV: 46)

Herodotus is considered the first anthropologist, and his work stands apart from other Greek accounts, introducing complexity where others over-simplified, giving context when others gave none, and always attempting to see things from the Others' point of view as well as from that of the Greeks, who he was not above criticizing. This was seen by other Greeks as a betrayal, and Herodotus was condemned by Plutarch as *"philobarbaros"*—lover of barbarians—a label that has stuck to anthropologists ever since. But even to Herodotus, the inner dynamics of nomadic life remained something of a mystery.

The Greeks and Romans considered agriculture another marker of the civilized life, but the cultivated grains esteemed by them as emblematic of the superiority of culture over nature, seemed to play little part in the Scythian diet. As had happened with the Persians and *tryphé*, food was used to emphasize the Otherness of the Scythians. According to Pseudo-Hippocrates, Scythian viands consisted primarily of the meat from their flocks, usually boiled, and hippace or mare's milk cheese. Ammianus (XXXI: 2) claimed that "No one in their country ever plows a field or touches a plow handle," going on to assert that "they are so hardy in their way of life they have no need of fire or of savory food but eat the roots of wild plants and the half-raw flesh of any kind of animal whatever, which they put between their thighs and the backs of their horses and thus warm it a little." This is the first reference to a dish that became known as "steak tartare," raw beef said to have developed from the steaks the Tartar nomads of later times put beneath their saddles to tenderize as they rode, although this shows that it was of much earlier origin. It has also been claimed that the steaks were put under saddles to ease sores on a horse's back (Jack 2010). Herodotus, always alert to cultural specialities, noted an ingenious method of cookery that has been called the "self-cooking ox," an innovation arising from the scarcity of trees on the steppe. The animal was killed, flayed and deboned, and the flesh put into cauldrons with water or sewn into the animal's paunch or stomach, to which water was added. Then, the animal's bones were used instead of firewood, burning under the cauldrons or paunch until the meat was done. In this way, as Herodotus (IV: 61) put it, the ox or other animal was made to cook itself.

The Greeks left no descriptions of Scythian feasts, but they were fascinated by Scythian drinking, which seemed to them the essence of barbarism. In Greek plays and prose, Scythians are depicted as noisy, loud and, especially, drunk. To the Greeks, "drinking in the Scythian fashion" meant drinking to excess, for unlike the Greeks, the Scythians drank wine unmixed with water. In the *Laws*, Plato noted with distaste that they drank with such abandon that they let the wine pour down on their clothes, while Anacreon wrote:

> Let's not fall
> Into riot and disorder
> With our wine, like the Scythians
> But let us drink in moderation
> Listening to the lovely hymns.
>   (Anacreon 76, in Athenaeus 11.427a, in Lissarrague 1990: 91)

Chamaeleon of Heracleia, in his lost work *On Drunkenness*, claimed that King Cleomanes of Sparta went mad after learning to drink unmixed wine from the Scythians, and when people wanted to switch from a watery drink to a strong one they would say—"make it Scythian" (Athenaeus: X).

Wine was not a native Scythian drink, for grapes did not grow on the steppe and the nomadic lifestyle would not accommodate viticulture, so they could only obtain wine through contact or trade. Their own intoxicating drink was fermented mare's milk which they also imbibed in large quantities. Yet beneath what others saw as barbaric excess, Herodotus detected the social dynamics of Scythian commensality based on drink rather than on food. According to Herodotus, annual public ceremonies were held in which a large bowl of wine was prepared, from which all who had killed an enemy in that year were given a cup to drink. Those who had killed many men were given two cups to drink from, while those who had killed no one were excluded, and had to sit to one side in disgrace: "No greater shame than this can happen to them" (Herodotus IV: 66). Here the inclusion/exclusion mechanism of commensality is seen in operation. Full exclusion does not mean to be absent, it means to be present but visibly marginalized, for all to see.

But wine and mare's milk were not the only things the Scythians drank. Most early writers were preoccupied with Scythian bloodshed. It was said that in battle, Scythian warriors drank the blood of the first man they killed, while according to Ammianus (XXXI), "there is nothing in which they take more pride than in killing any man whatever: as glorious spoils of the slain they tear off their heads, then strip off their skins and hang them upon their war-horses as trappings." By contrast, Herodotus noted the symbolic value the Scythians set on blood, which they used in sacrifice and rituals. He reported that the Scythians sacrificed one captive in every ten they took, first pouring libations of wine over their heads, then slaughtering them over a vessel in which was collected their blood that was then offered to the gods. He also described how Scythian oaths were sworn (Herodotus IV: 70). A large earthenware bowl was filled with wine and the parties to the oath wounded themselves slightly with a knife or awl and dropped some of their blood into the wine. Then they plunged into the mixture a scimitar, some arrows, a battle-axe and a javelin, all the while repeating prayers. Then the two main contracting parties drank from the bowl of wine and blood, as did the chief men among their followers. This was the Scythian ritual of blood brotherhood, emblematic of the close friendships between men for which the Scythians were noted, their bonds often closer than those of siblings. Drinking from one cup in which their blood was joined signified they were as one person. Dipping the weapons into the blood and wine denoted that they were loyal to each other in battle unto death, and the bond was further affirmed by binding the community of witnesses together through drinking from the same bowl as the sworn pair. Another Scythian practice described by Herodotus (IV: 75) was part of the purification rites that followed a funeral. After making a small tent whose only furnishing was a dish on the ground filled with hot stones, "the Scythians take hemp seeds (cannabis), crawl in under the felt blankets, and throw the seeds on to the glowing stones. The seeds then emit dense smoke and fumes, much more than any vapour-bath in Greece. The Scythians shriek with delight at the fumes." Or, as another translation has it, they "howled like wolves."

Although sparse, the details of Scythian food and drinking are consistent—a restricted diet dictated by demanding environmental and social factors, food that is often described as "raw," basic cooking techniques consisting primarily of boiling, and a predilection for drinking to excess, all bespeaking an "uncivilized" state to the Greeks and other observers. Embedded in the Greek world view, enshrined in literature and art, the stereotypical image of savage barbarians from the steppe became part of Western culture. As Aeschylus warned in *Prometheus Bound* (707–12 in Hartog 1988: 193):

> First turn to the sun's rising and walk on
> Over the fields no plough has broken: then
> You will come to the nomadic Scythians
> Who live in wicker houses built above
> Their well-wheeled wagons; they are an armed people,
> Armed with the bow that strikes from far away:
> Do not draw near them.

This view is now being challenged by the new field of steppe archaeology. Long overshadowed by classical archaeology and that of the ancient Near East, steppe archaeology has been given momentum by contemporary political developments, and shaped by national boundaries and political and disciplinary barriers (Mair 2006). In the early twentieth century, the archaeology of the western steppe came within the territory of the former Soviet Union, and that of the eastern steppe within that of the People's Republic of China, both of whom discouraged foreign involvement. The southern steppe began to draw archaeological interest when favored fieldwork sites in Iran and Afghanistan became conflict zones, and the subject as a whole received new impetus when the collapse of the former Soviet Union opened up channels of scholarly communication.

The conventional opposition drawn between the "the steppe" and "the sown," with agriculture bespeaking the sedentary life and great civilizations, while the steppe was associated with nomadism and "cultures barely worth speaking about" (Genito 1994: xvii) is now being discredited. Excavations have revealed previously unappreciated environmental, cultural, economic and ethnic complexity, one result of which has been the development of specialist subfields devoted to the study of different early steppe peoples such as Pazyryk and Sarmatian studies. Instead of living independently and in isolation as was once thought, the grave goods of steppe peoples have revealed substantial wealth and extensive trade and intercultural contact, with metallurgy, the use of the spoked wheel, animal-keeping, mastery of the horse and associated horse technology including stirrups and trousers spreading across Eurasia (Sherratt 2006). The vessels that are ubiquitous, appearing across the steppe in all periods, in huge numbers and in a large range of sizes are the cauldrons mentioned by Herodotus. Some are large enough to take a whole sheep which— along with the known scarcity of firewood for roasting—indicates the predominance of large meat stews and broths in everyday eating. The frequent discovery of Greek amphorae and golden drinking horns in the deep steppe far from Greece confirms the Scythians' reported fondness for wine. Above all, nomadism itself has been re-evaluated. Instead of being merely a "profound state of undevelopment" dictated by the physical conditions of the steppe, or an evolutionary stage between hunting and gathering and settled farming, it is now possible to see nomadic pastoralism as an elective way of life and as "one of the most complex and exceptional processes of human specialization and economic adaptation" (Genito 1994: vii).

However, the questions remain—how exactly did this specialized way of life function, how was it possible to live on such a restricted diet, and what role was played on the steppe by feasting and drinking? In the Scythian case, these remain unclear. The rhythm of nomadic life is one of ebb and flow. The steppe peoples of the classical period withdrew into their heartland and faded away, for reasons that have not yet been fully established. Then, nearly a thousand years later, it seemed as if they had returned.

The Mongols

"Like dense clouds," went one account of events in Russia in AD 1240:

> the Tartars (Mongols) pushed themselves forward towards Kiev, investing the city on all sides. The rattling of their innumerable carts, the bellowing of camels and cattle, the neighing of horses, and the wild battle-cry, were so whelming as to render inaudible the conversation of the people inside the city.
>
> (Karamsin 1826, v. IV in Komroff 1929: 11)

5.2 A Scythian and his horse, from a sixteenth-century German cosmographia. In this image, the Scythians of antiquity have been conflated with the European Wildman and the Mongols, but the message is clear: all the nomad requires is his horse. © The Trustees of the British Museum. Museum number 1982.U.2331. Image number AN 614960

Kiev itself was razed and, according to Russian accounts, most of those who survived the siege and battle were put to death by the victors. In an earlier engagement on the banks of the Dnieper River, it was reported that captured Russian princes were "tied to planks upon which the Mongols sat to eat and drink and celebrate their victory" (Komroff 1929: 10), and were pressed to death. As the medieval chronicler Matthew Paris wrote in *Chronica Majora*:

> They are inhuman and beastly, rather monsters than men, thirsting for and drinking blood … dressed in ox-hides … drinking with delight the pure blood of their flocks … They are without human laws, know no comforts, are more ferocious than lions or bears … are wonderful archers, sparing neither age, nor sex, nor condition … They wander about with their flocks and their wives, who are taught to fight like men.

This account might have been written by Ammianus, but these were not the steppe peoples of old. Unlike the Scythians whose ethnic origins are a matter of contention, the Tartars or Mongols were an Asiatic people, but they shared with their predecessors nomadism, dependence on the horse and mounted archery—to such an extent that it is possible to speak of a *longue durée of* steppe culture (Antonini 1994: 287). And there is a further parallel, because just as the early nomads are now seen as sophisticated rather than as simple, and as agents of early contact and exchange, so specialists in Mongol studies such as Paul Buell argue that the Mongol age is a critical period in world history and the Mongol conquerors the creators of the first globalization, and thus the inventors of the modern world, and the first world cuisine (Buell 2001; Allsen 2001).

By the time the Mongols appeared on the borders of Europe, great changes had recently taken place on the Eurasian steppe. As Herodotus had noted of the Scythians long before, unencumbered by the need to defend sown fields or permanent settlements, the Mongols had been free to develop a warrior culture in which stealing each others' flocks and horses, competing for the best grass and water, hunting, "war and raiding—and the 'vengeance' (*os*) that justified them—were the glory of the tribe" (Fletcher 1986. 14). Then social change—sometimes described as a shift from tribal to feudal—took place in the relatively short time of two generations, a transition captured in a document called *The Secret History of the Mongols*. Although the Mongols were not literate, they had access to peoples who were, and at some time between 1228 and 1294, with AD 1240 being the generally agreed date (de Rachewiltz 2004), they caused to have written in Uighur script what anthropologists call an "origin myth" or mythologized history, which sets out the beginnings of the dynasty that transformed the fortunes of the Mongols and chronicles their rise to power, describing the basic steppe diet and culinary practices in the process.

Like many such narratives, it begins with semi-divine origins, in this case the mating of a blue-grey wolf and a fallow doe, whose offspring was the ancestor figure of the core Mongol tribe, but the history very quickly progresses to the boyhood of Temujin, later known as Chinggiz Qan or Genghis Khan. Temujin began life as a member of a branch of the ruling Borjigid lineage of the Mongol tribe and its associated confederation (Fletcher 1986), and *The Secret History* describes the seasonal round of migration and raiding, with the group engaging in pastoralism and hunting, pursuing deer, antelope, wild goats, wild ducks and geese, sometimes with the aid of hawks and falcons.

At first, references to food are infrequent, drink being mentioned more often. Wine does not appear, only *kumiss*, large pitchers of which are always placed on a bench near the entrance to the tent (de Rachewiltz 2004: 800). In *The Secret History*, the two primary categories of things consumed are *umdan*, "drink" and *shülen*, soup. The categories were flexible, with *umdan* being anything from a light broth to mare's milk, while the *shülen* could be a thickened broth or, in later periods, an elaborate banquet soup (Buell 2007: 24), but in any case, the Mongol preference was for a liquid diet. Boiling was the main method of cookery for a number of reasons. First, Eurasian ideas regarding the importance of boiled food, as boiling was thought to concentrate the essence of the animal. Second, practical considerations such as the need for liquid in a dry environment "as well as the need to share meat to the maximum" (Buell 2007: 27). Third, boiling is more fuel-efficient than roasting, and an easier method of cooking for peoples on the move. Fourth, an easily digestible liquid diet was probably more suitable for an equestrian life than solid foods. *The Secret History* suggests cooperative cooking using communal provisions provided by the leader directly or indirectly, from which people take their shares. The diet was simple, but supplies travelled with them, on the hoof. What emerges clearly—usually when there have been transgressions—are the importance of precedence, exclusion and inclusion. Even with the simplest fare, there were rules about the order in which food or drink should be distributed, who should offer the first toasts when it came to drinking, who should or should not be invited to participate in sacrifices and partake of special meals, and who had the right to sit in the seat of honor at the back of the tent, facing the door, and who sat closest to them. These were watched closely, and etiquette was used to make strong social statements. In *The Secret History*, many key events turn on the consequences of perceived insults during communal eating and drinking, when certain people are served before others, or excluded altogether.

After the early death of Temujin's father, rival factions in the confederation strove to increase their influence and in the process expelled the young Temujin, his siblings, his mother and their remaining supporters from the band, signalling their intent by excluding his mother from a sacrifice and the feast that followed. Food—or rather its lack—now assumes a central role in the narrative, highlighting the perils of being excluded from the group in a nomadic society on the steppe. The main band moves off, leaving the outcasts behind without proper weapons, shelter or flocks to live off, and just a few horses. Here we gain insight into what Ammianus described as living off wild roots and the meat of any animal whatsoever. Relying on the knowledge of his mother, Temujin and his brothers are forced to forage, gathering crab apples and bird cherries in season; using pointed sticks to dig edible roots; finding wild garlic, onion, lily bulb and leek; fishing in the streams for salmon, grayling and dace; shooting small birds with blunt-headed arrows and catching marmots and field mice (de Rachewiltz 2004: 19). The description reveals specialized gender roles, with the women gathering and men hunting. After a successful expedition, one of the men returned with his horse so laden down with marmot carcasses that it staggered (de Rachewiltz 2004: 26), but they were poor food. As *The Secret History* put it, their bellies hungered in the wild land, and they craved fat. The predicament of the outcasts bespeaks physical danger and the cultural shock of separation from the way of life and values embodied in the core Mongol foods of herd meat and milk and their communal consumption, as glimpsed in the narrative. It also throws up what might be called the official and unofficial versions of "proper Mongol food." From the beginning—and still today—the Mongols foraged and hunted in the wild, as well as living off their herds. But "milk and meat"—milk and herd meat—were the ideal foods, emblematic of success and the foods they liked to be seen as eating, whatever else their everyday diet may have included. Marooned in the landscape, the outcast group draws the unwelcome attention of enemies, and the young Temujin is forced to flee for his life, beginning a series of heroic exploits in which, fugitive though he is, his future greatness is signalled by the divine signs, as *The Secret History* puts it, of "fire in his eyes and light in his face" (de Rachewiltz 2004: 327).

Like all such documents written after the fact, *The Secret History* justifies hierarchies and events in retrospect, presenting outcomes as inevitable and legitimizing those individuals and clans who later rose to power, but beneath the personalities and inevitable questions of accuracy on certain points, a social transformation .can be discerned. As *The Secret History* makes clear, the tribal system into which Temujin was born was fundamentally unstable. This was partly due to the kinship system, which was patrilineal with agnatic ties complicated by polygamy, meaning a man could have several wives and concubines, leading to children and kin groups with competing claims. As noted previously, instability was also due to ongoing inter-tribal competition over the best territory. The tribal chief had to provide leadership, assign pasture, determine the migration routes, keep the band in order and above all ensure the food supply. On his death, the position was supposed to pass to his brothers in turn, only reverting back to the son of the original leader when the brothers were dead. In practice, the leadership went to whoever in the chiefly lineage was strongest and most competent. Factionalism and rivalry were endemic, with potential candidates jockeying for position and courting the favor of the shaman who was responsible for revealing which candidate had divine approval. The smaller the tribe and the stronger the leader, the fewer disruptions, but this brought its own problems, for small tribes could more easily fall prey to large ones who coveted their flocks and herds, migration routes and "grass and water." And the larger the herds the more the group was obliged to keep on the move, in search of fresh pasturage, exposing themselves to greater likelihood of attack. Temporary alliances between groups for mutual support were fragile, and internal dynamics and the high value placed on independence and autonomy among tribal chiefs meant that groups both large and small often dispersed under pressure, to reform in different combinations. The underlying political process was one of consultation. It could involve meetings for deliberation of the leaders and warriors of a tribal confederation or, during the imperial era, huge gatherings of the Mongol hordes for the great *kuriltais* or assemblies, where strategy was debated and leaders chosen, for "in a pastoral economy and society in which a wide dispersal of people and herds was ecologically necessary, it is not surprising to find the existence of a consultative institution which brought together people from great distances" (Endicott-West 1986: 526), a counterbalance to the tendency to fission referred to above.

The expulsion of young Temujin and his mother from the group was the outcome of internal rivalries that ultimately tore their tribal confederation apart. Under these conditions, in which much of the tribe's energies were directed inward, the focus of daily life from season to season was on exploiting the steppe habitat to the maximum, maintaining their prized mobility and tribal independence, rather than on extending outward beyond the steppes or building a larger supratribal polity (Fletcher 1986). But whether intentional or not at the beginning, ultimately Temujin's campaign to establish himself in a leadership role and to restore his confederation transformed the social organization of the steppe people, driving them outwards to dominate the known world of his time.

In his exile, Temujin began by forming a close band of blood-brothers, progressing to the making of strategic alliances and then to the conduct of ever more successful campaigns against rival groups, acquiring the name Chinggiz Qan or "Universal Qan" along the way. *The Secret History* shows him exercising the strong personal control and cultivating the loyalties that were central to the success of any steppe leader, consolidating the group and establishing and displaying hierarchy through food, involving himself personally in the matter, directing his newly appointed stewards as follows:

> When you two stewards, Onggur and Boro'ul,
> Distribute food to the right and left sides,
> Do not let it fall short
> For those who stand or sit
> On the right side
> Do not let it fall short
> For those who are placed in a row

Or who are not
On the left side.
If you distribute the food in this way my mind will be at rest.

(De Rachewiltz 2004: 145)

Chingghiz also ordered the stewards to be present and attentive throughout the meal: "when you take your seats, you must sit so as to look after the food on the right and left sides of the two large *kumiss* pitchers [i.e. of the wine table] [...] sit with Tulun and the others in the center of the tent facing north." In addition, he established a special cadre of night guards, saying (de Rachewiltz 2004: 146):

> ... the nightguards shall be in charge of the female attendants of the palace, the "sons of the household," the camel keeper and the cowherds and they shall take care of the tent carts of the palace. The nightguards shall take care of the standards and drums and the spears arranged beneath them. The nightguards shall supervise our drink and food. The nightguards shall supervise and cook the uncut meat and food as well; if drink and food are lacking we shall seek them from the nightguards who have been entrusted with their supervision." And he said, "when the quiverbearers distribute drink and food they must not distribute them without permission from the supervising nightguards. When they distribute food, they shall first distribute it beginning with the nightguards.

The inclusion of these details in the great national narrative makes clear the extent to which nomadic organization relied upon efficient centralized food supply and control. It has been claimed (Manz in de Rachewiltz 2004; and see Mote 1999) that Chingghiz's success lay as much in his organizational and administrative ability and astute use of steppe traditions as in his military prowess. The elite troops were served first and special attention was always paid to the preparation and consumption of the *kumiss* and the positioning of pitchers of it in places of honor inside the tent. Food was guarded carefully at all times day and night, and distributed equally between right and left sides of those gathered, whatever the significance of the division might have been. Further culinary and ceremonial details were not given as they were familiar to the people for whom *The Secret History* was written.

Chingghiz's aims ultimately went beyond re-establishing his tribal confederation, and then placing it in a position of supremacy on the steppe. He succeeded in uniting groups who had long been enemies, forming a mounted army of unprecedented size, and the dynamics of kinship, politics and nomadism as well as a growing awareness of the wealth that lay beyond the steppe dictated continued expansion. Mongol armies pressed into Iran, Afghanistan and raided as far as India. Bukhara and Samarkand were captured, campaigns against China were instigated, and the reconnaissance of eastern Europe begun. Ultimately, the Mongols "were able to unite more of the earth's surface under a contiguous political authority than has any other empire, before or since" (Buell, Anderson and Perry 2000: 20). After his death in AD 1227, Chingghiz's successor as Great Qan was his third son Ogedei (AD 1186–1241), who continued his father's conquests', focusing first on China and then on Europe. As literate lands were drawn into the Mongol orbit and travellers entered their territory, written accounts of the Mongols began to emerge. Herodotus had travelled in the Pontic region a thousand years before, but no early Greek writers had penetrated deep into the Eurasian steppe to observe the nomads in peace as well as in war, or to describe their way of life. These new accounts revealed much that was previously unknown or only partly understood, and supplied details that had been left out of the *emic* narrative of *The Secret History*. What is striking are the broad similarities to the material culture of the Scythians, indicating a consistent adaptation to the conditions of the steppe, although it is impossible to say at present to what extent the socio-political life of the Scythians corresponded to that of the Mongols.

After the fall of Kiev in AD 1241 and the subsequent Mongol invasion of Eastern Europe, two Franciscan friars made separate journeys to the Court of the Great Qan of the new Mongol Empire. The first journey (AD 1245–1247) was made by Friar John of Pian de Carpini, as an envoy of Pope Innocent IV, the second (AD 1253–1255) by Friar William of Rubrick, on behalf of King Louis IX of France. Their mission was to protest at the depredations and ask that they should cease; to see if the Mongols might be converted to Christianity; and to observe the way the nomads lived, in order to assess future threats. In the process, they also recorded the early phases of the social and culinary changes that were beginning to spread over the steppe.

Before heading into the deep steppe, Carpini was received at the Mongols' western outpost, the encampment of Prince Batu the grandson of Chingghiz and head of the Golden Horde or Kipchack Khanate, near the Volga River. The mightiest prince among the Mongols save the Great Qan, Batu lived in considerable magnificence, surrounded by the spoils of the Mongols' European campaigns. The tents in which Batu received visitors—fair, large and made of linen—had once belonged to the King of Hungary. Attended by a full panoply of door-keepers and officials, Batu received the friar in his tent where he sat on a raised seat or throne together with one of his wives. The rest, Carpini reported, "both his brothers and sons and others less noble, sit lower down on a bench in the middle; as for the rest they sit beyond them on the ground, the men on the right and the women on the left (Carpini in Dawson 1955: 57). On this occasion—because he had not yet visited the Great Qan—the friar was seated on the left or subordinate side of the tent. Later, after he had been presented to the Great Qan, he was seated on the right in audiences and assemblies. Apart from the throne and the benches on which the princes and nobles sat, the only other piece of furniture in the tent occupied a central position in the middle near the door—a table on which drinks were placed in gold and silver vessels. The division of the tent into right and left, male and female sides, with status showed by elevation and placement, and a table of drink in a central and mediating position would prove a constant throughout the steppe, at all levels.

Almost immediately, Carpini was given permission by Batu to visit the Great Qan far to the east, and now his privations began in earnest. Although they traveled eight years apart, visited different Qans and approached from different directions, Carpini from Russia and Rubruck from Acre, the accounts by the two friars are consistent. On their long journeys to the Great Qan, lasting several months each way, the friars shared the regimen of their guides, living as the nomads lived. The Mongols were strange to European eyes. As Rubruck put it (Jackson and Morgan 1990: 71): "When I came among them, I really felt as if I was entering some other world." Carpini described them as "unlike to all other people" with "flat and small noses, little eyes and eyelids standing straight upright"—a reference to the epicanthic fold typical of Asiatic peoples. They let their hair "grow long like woman's hair," wearing it in two plaits, bound up behind each ear and wore tunics with hair on the outside, and tails that hung down to their thighs (in Komroff 1929: 28–9). The Mongols, they reported, rode on steeds that were smaller, faster and hardier than European horses, each man having several, a minimum of five, to ensure that a fresh mount was always available. In addition to their use in warfare, raiding and transportation, the friars remarked on the use of the horse as a food source, providing milk, meat and blood (Levine 1998). It was initially as food that the horse was domesticated, and it was central to the Mongol diet, in addition to providing hides and horsehair for wear and use. The horse was the keystone species of the steppe, essential to social, economic and culinary life. As the national epic *The Secret History of the Mongols* put it, "what is a Mongol without his horse?"

As with the Scythians, there were no lasting cities on the steppe. The Mongols were mobile, moving for pasturage between the warmer regions in winter and the colder ones in summer (Rubruck in Jackson and Morgan 1990), living in round felt tents. The small ones could be dismantled quickly and carried on baggage animals while the larger fixed tents—some thirty feet across—were carried on ox-drawn wagons with axles as large as a ship's mast, according to Rubruck. Riding on horseback, the friars could appreciate the relative comfort of the Mongol wagons. In addition there were smaller wagons which carried possessions in chests, and carts piled with supplies. The friars observed that when on campaign or migration, the mounted men would be in the vanguard of the group, followed by the women, children and goods in ox-drawn covered wagons, accompanied by their flocks and herds of oxen, sheep, goats and horses and sometimes Mongolian camels. In the management of the wagons, the friars noted the gendered social roles apparent in *The Secret History* that marked all aspects of Mongol society. The wagons were driven by the women. One woman was sufficient to drive twenty or thirty wagons which were lashed together. The woman sat in the lead wagon driving the oxen, and the tied wagons and oxen followed behind at a walking pace, a speed that was convenient for the flocks who were driven along beside. In addition to driving the wagons, the women put up and took down the portable tents, milked the cows, churned butter, foraged and made all the articles required for daily life—a division of labour that freed the men for hunting, raiding and warfare, a highly efficient form of environmental exploitation and social organization. Women could also ride and shoot, and children were taught to do both from a very early age.

The country through which the friars traveled was unfruitful for agriculture but, Carpini wrote, good for cattle, though bedeviled by "intemperate air" and "astonishingly irregular" weather. In summer, there was extreme heat and outbreaks of thunder, lightning and hail. At other times there were "such mighty tempests of cold wind that sometimes men are not able to sit on horseback … [and] we were often constrained to lie grovelling on the earth and could not see by reason of the dust" (Carpini in Komroff 1929: 28). Under these climate conditions, with a population on the move, food was often uncertain of supply and feeding opportunistic rather than regular, as borne out by the friars' experience.

As Carpini described it, "rising early, we travelled until night without eating anything, and oftentimes we came so late to our lodgings that we had no time to eat the same night, but that which we should have eaten at night was given us in the morning. Often changing our mounts, for there was no lack of horses, we rode swiftly and without intermission, as fast as our steeds could trot." Rubruck endured a similar regime. "We were given food only in the evening", he wrote (in Jackson and Morgan 1990: 141). "In the morning they gave us something to drink or millet (broth to sip) while at night we were given meat—shoulder and ribs of mutton—and as much broth as we could manage to drink." Yet on what seemed a meager diet—and ominously for Westerners who feared an imminent invasion from the steppes—Carpini (in Komroff 1929: 30) reported that the Mongols "are very hardy, and when they have fasted a day or two, they sing and are merry as if they had eaten their bellies full. In riding, they endure much cold and extreme heat." And Rubruk found that "when we had enough meat broth to fill us, we were completely reinvigorated and I found it a most wholesome drink and especially nourishing" (in Jackson and Morgan 1990: 141).

Much that Carpini and Rubruck observed and experienced transgressed the rules of European cooking and eating. Because the central steppe was bare of trees, everyone from the elite downwards warmed themselves and cooked their meat with fires made of ox and horse dung, for they were "very rich in cattle, such as camels, oxen, sheep and goats … they have more horses and mares than all the rest of the world" (Carpini in Komroff 1929: 29). The friars soon came to appreciate this form of fuel. While crossing open country, Rubruck noted they were sometimes obliged to eat meat that was only half-cooked because they had been unable to collect dung for the fire. At first, Carpini had noted with disdain that the Mongols were prepared to eat anything—dogs, wolves, foxes and horses, even mice, and Rubruck mentioned marmots and dormice. But as they suffered hunger and extreme conditions, the friars came to appreciate the importance of these supplementary resources, which had kept the young Chingghiz's family alive, and could be resorted to when conditions turned difficult. There were strict injunctions against wasting food, said to have originated with Chingghiz but probably much older. Every part of the animal was eaten or used in some way, bones were not given to dogs before the marrow had been extracted, and dishes were only washed by rinsing them in the meat broth, after which the liquid used for washing was put back into the pot, both because not a scrap must be wasted, and because water was a precious resource on the steppe. Meat that was not immediately cooked and eaten was chopped into thin strips and wind-dried in the sun for future use. Light in weight, dried meat was easy to transport and to boil up in cauldrons to make broth. Butter was also preserved, and the women boiled the milk from which butter had been extracted into curds, which they then dried in the sun until they were hard. When winter came they put the dried curd into a skin, poured on hot water, and stirred or agitated it until the curd dissolved to make a reconstituted sour milk.

The common people did not use table-cloths or napkins; greasy hands were wiped on their leggings or on the grass. They had "neither bread nor herbs nor vegetables nor anything else, nothing but meat, of which, however, they eat so little that other people would scarcely be able to exist on it" (Carpini in Dawson 1955: 16). The method of serving was very basic, although care was still taken to show preference and status: "One of them cuts the morsels and another takes them on the point of a knife and offers them to each, to some more, to some less, according to whether they wish to show them greater or less honour" (Carpini in Dawson 1955: 17). Rubruck gave a nearly identical account. "With the meat of a single sheep they feed fifty or a hundred men", he asserted. "They cut it up into tiny pieces on a dish along with salt and water, since they make no other sauce … and offer each of the bystanders one or two mouthfuls, depending on the numbers at the meal … the master himself first takes what he pleases" (Rubruck in Jackson and Morgan 1990: 75).

As among the Scythians, there was a marked preference for liquid rather than solid foods, not only the ubiquitous meat broths but several kinds of milk. In Carpini's words:

> They drink mare's milk in very great quantities if they have it; they also drink the milk of ewes, cows, goats and even camels. They do not have wine, ale or mead, unless it is given to them by other nations. In the winter, moreover, unless they are wealthy, they do not have mare's milk. They boil millet in water and make it so thin that they cannot eat it but have to drink it. Each one of them drinks one or two cups in the morning and they eat nothing more during the day; in the evening, however, they are all given a little meat, and they drink the meat broth. But in the summer, seeing they have plenty

of mare's milk, they seldom eat meat, unless it happens to be given to them or they catch some animal or bird when hunting.

(Carpini in Dawson 1955: 17)

Kumiss was prepared in the following way. In the season, the mares were milked in the morning, and the fresh milk churned until it bubbled and fermented, and butter formed. Once the butter was extracted, the newly fermented milk, cloudy and slightly sour to the taste, could be drunk. "After one has finished drinking, it leaves on the tongue a taste of milk of almonds and produces a very agreeable sensation inside," wrote Rubruck (in Jackson and Morgan 1990: 81). Another kind, *karakumiss* or black *kumiss*, was made for the elite. Mares' milk was churned to the point where all the solids sank to the bottom of the churn, leaving a clear, sweet liquid which was highly prized, being described by Rubruck as "a really delightful drink" (in Jackson and Morgan 1990: 82). The quantities of *kumiss* consumed daily were immense. Prince Batu had thirty small camps a day's journey from his own, each of which provided the milk of three thousand mares for ordinary *kumiss*, the milk for *karakumiss* being in addition. In the winter, when fresh milk was not available, the Mongols made drinks from rice, millet, wheat and honey, and wine was brought from distant regions, but "in the summer, as long as they have *kumiss* they do not care about any other food" (Rubruck in Dawson 1955: 97), and were particularly careful not to drink plain water (in Jackson and Morgan 1990: 83). Chinese sources of the 1220s also remark on the Mongols' reliance on milk: "Their way of life is only a matter of drinking mare's milk to assuage hunger and thirst" (Chao Hung, *meng-ta pei-lu* in Buell, Anderson and Perry 2000: 45).

Like the Scythians, the Mongols did not consider inebriation to be offensive: "Drunkenness is considered an honourable thing by them, and when anyone drinks too much, he is sick there and then, nor does this prevent him from drinking again (Carpini in Dawson 1955: 16). As observed by the friars, drinking rather than food was the primary focus of commensality: Mongol feasts were drunk, not eaten. As Carpini put it: "They honour one another greatly, and bestow banquets very liberally, notwithstanding that good victuals are dainty and scarce among them" (Komoroff 1929: 30). Nor did they take offence if foreign guests became drunk, as it showed that they were at ease among them (Chao Hung in Jackson and Morgan 1990: 77 n. 3).

Even in the humblest tents, there always stood a bench at the entrance with a skin full of milk or other drink, and some cups (Rubruck in Jackson and Morgan 1999: 76), and drinking was bound up with religious beliefs and social distinctions. The original religion of the Mongols was shamanism, a form of worship in which ancestors, transmuted into a pantheon of protective spirits, were asked to "provide food, property, game, livestock, long life, happiness, children, peace and friendship and domestic happiness … (and to protect against) grief, illness, wounds

... evil spirits, demons, enemies, passions and misfortunes" (Hessig 1970: 11). By the time *The Secret History* was written and the visits of the friars were underway, the Mongols through their conquests and trade were already coming into contact with Nestorianism, Manichaeism, Roman Christianity, Taoism, Confucianism, Chinese Buddhism and Tibetan Lamaism, followed by Islam. Elements of all would ultimately find their way into the syncretic practice of the greater Mongol Empire, but during the rise of the Mongols, shamanism—though little understood today in its pure form – remained dominant.

Rubruck observed that drinking gatherings in the tent of the master or leading figure of the group was always preceded by ritual offerings. First, the steward sprinkled some of the drink on the household effigies, which included, "by the entrance on the women's side, an idol with a cow's udder for the women who milk the cows, for this is a woman's job. On the other side of the door towards the men is another image with a mare's udder, for the men who milk the mares" (in Dawson 1955: 96). Then the steward stepped outside the tent holding a goblet of drink and sprinkled three times toward the south, genuflecting each time, in honor of fire, then toward the east in honor of the air, toward the west in honor of water, then toward the north for the sake of the dead (Jackson and Morgan 1990: 76). Returning to the tent, the steward and two attendants offered drink to the master and his wife. Before the master drank, he poured a libation of wine onto the ground "as its share." Should the master be mounted, the offering would be poured on the horse's neck or mane before drinking began.

Only after the offerings were made could drinking start, initiated by the master. A musician stood near the *kumiss* pitchers at the door, and when the master began to drink, the steward called "Ha!" and the musician struck up. When the master had drunk, the steward shouted again, the musician stopped, then "they all drink round in turn, men and women alike, and at times compete with one another in quaffing in a thoroughly distasteful and greedy fashion" (Rubruck in Jackson and Morgan 1990: 77). According to Carpini (in Dawson 1955: 57), no Mongol prince ever drank, especially in public, without there being singing and guitar playing for them. At a feast, the guests clapped their hands and danced to the sound of the music while the master was drinking, the men in front of the master and the women in front of the mistress. Drinking games were a feature of these gatherings. Anyone reluctant to take up a drinking challenge would be seized, and his ears pulled vigorously until his mouth opened and the drink could be poured in, while the others clapped and danced. Similarly,

> Likewise, when they want to make a great feast and entertainment for anyone, one man takes a full cup and two others stand, one on his right and one on his left, and in this manner the three, singing and dancing, advance right up to him to whom they are to offer the cup, and they sing and dance before him; when he stretches out his hand

to take the cup they suddenly leap back, and then they advance again as before, and in this way they make fun of him, drawing back the cup three or four times until he is in a really lively mood and wants it: then they give him the cup and sing and clap their hands and stamp with their feet while he drinks.

(Rubruck in Dawson 1955: 97)

In the heart of the steppe, among the common people seen by the friars on their journeys, life was still much as described in *The Secret History*, a pastoral existence in tents of felt, subsisting on a diet that, though sparse and simple, was suited to the climate and terrain and the Mongols' traditional way of life. It was in princely establishments that material change was apparent. In Batu's camp near the Volga, Carpini had seen European goods and plunder on display. When he arrived at the encampment of Guyuk, grandson of Chingghiz soon to be elected Great Qan as successor to his father Ogodei, the friar saw the full wealth of the Mongol Empire. Carpini described a large pavilion of white velvet, large enough to accommodate two thousand men, surrounded by a wooden palisade. The *kuriltai*, the election to Qan-ship, was in process, a decision that was taken by the tribal elite, and for four days the nobles involved and their retinues paraded on horseback on the surrounding plains, dressed in fine silks from China, now under Mongol control. On the first day they wore white, the second scarlet, the third blue and the fourth rich brocade. The saddles, bridles and horse trappings of the nobles were embellished with gold. Deliberations were carried on in the great tent, and when the decision had been made, *kumiss* drinking began at noon and carried on into the evening, "in so great a quantity that it was a rare sight" (in Komroff 1929: 63). Waiting outside to bring tribute and pay honor were Russians, ambassadors from the Kingdom of Georgia and the Caliphate of Baghdad, Saracen sultans, many dukes from China, some four thousand envoys in all. When Guyuk was installed as Qan, the ceremony took place in a grand tent held up by pillars covered in plates of gold. After the new Qan mounted the throne and received obeisances from his subjects, "they started drinking and, as is their custom, they drank without stopping until the evening." Only after the drinking did food make an appearance. Cooked meat was brought in carts without any salt, one joint between four or five men for the people not inside the tent. For those of higher status inside the tent, "they gave meat with salted broth as sauce and they did this on all the days that they held a feast" (Carpini in Dawson 1955: 63).

By the time of Rubruck's visit just a few years later, Guyuk Qan was dead. A preliminary audience with his successor, Mongke Qan, was conducted on the plains, in a tent covered inside in cloth of gold, although the place was heated by a central fire in which burned wormwood, briars and dung. As always a bench stood by the entrance with *kumiss* on it, and although this first meeting was brief, the friar was offered a choice of drinks—*karakumiss*, wine, rice wine or honey mead (in Jackson

اكاه برعقب آن به بيرون بارگاه امندوسه نوبت آفتاب رازانوزدند

5.3 The Enthronement of Kuyuk (Guyuk) the Great Qan, grandson of Chingghiz Qan, which was observed by Friar John of Pian de Carpini. In the foreground, two pitchers of kumiss. Persian School, Timurid Dynasty, c. AD 1485. © The Trustees of the British Museum. Museum number 1948.1211,0.5. Image number AN 90399 and Morgan 1990: 178)—in recognition of the fact that he was an envoy from the West. However, no lavish culinary hospitality was provided. Rubruck recorded "they also brought us some fuel and gave us the meat of one thin little ram for the three of us to be our food for six days. Every day they gave us a dishful of millet and a quart of millet ale and they lent us a cauldron and tripod for us to cook our meat; when it was cooked, we cooked the millet in the broth." The friars may not have fully appreciated that the millet, though humble in their eyes, was something of a luxury on the steppe in those days, obtained through trade or tribute and not part of the daily fare of the common people. The friars received it, as they did the rest of their food, because they were envoys to the Great Qan.

By now, the Mongols were beginning to establish semi-permanent palaces, one being at Karakorum where Mongke held what Rubruck described as "great drinking parties" twice a year, once when the Qan passed through on his way to the summer pastures and once when he returned. The latter was the occasion when the nobles from two months' journey away would gather to pay homage and receive patronage, in the form of treasure and food supplies which the Qan would dispense. Here Rubruck saw the astonishing creation described in the passage at the beginning of this chapter, made for the Qan by a European goldsmith in his service called Master William of Paris. Because it was now thought unfitting that skins of milk and simple pitchers containing other drinks should stand at the entrance of the Qan's grand establishment, Master William was commanded to make a great silver tree which dispensed *kumiss* and other drinks. On the top of the tree was the figure of an angel with a trumpet that was made to blow as a signal for replenishing the supplies of drink. Beyond the silver tree, at the north end of the hall facing the entrance, the Qan sat in great state on an elevated platform so all could see him, at the base of which stood his cupbearer in constant attendance. As before, the men sat on his right, or west, side, the women on the left, and despite the increasing splendor of the appointments and the Mongols' growing wealth derived from conquest and tribute the food remained simple, eating was still incidental, and drinking continued to be the main commensal activity.

The observations of Friar John and Friar William date from the period when the Mongol Empire was still unified. By the second generation, the heirs of Chingghiz were unable to agree a unanimous succession, and control of different territories passed to different Chinggisid lineages. Descendants of the eldest son formed the Khanate of the Golden Horde which survived in Russia until AD 1502; descendants of the second son formed the Khanate of Chagadai which remained in Transoxiana until AD 1687; and the descendants of the fourth son founded the Il-khanate in Persia (Mote 1999: 414–5). These did not remain stable, but split still further. Mongke was succeeded as Great Qan in AD 1260 by his younger brother Kublai. Although the title no longer referred to control of the original vast territory ruled by Chingghiz, Kublai completed the conquest of China, establishing the Yuan Dynasty and becoming the first Mongol and non-Chinese Emperor of China. Kublai was the Great Qan whose court was visited in the 1270s by Marco Polo, whose description of the palace and gardens at Chang-du (Xanadu), re-told by Samuel Purchas, ultimately inspired Coleridge's poem *Kubla Khan*, which begins: "In Xanadu did Kubla Khan a stately pleasure dome decree ..."

According to Polo, Kublai's palace had marble staircases; halls and rooms covered with gold, silver and paintings of birds, beasts and dragons; ceilings embellished with gold and decorations; a roof varnished in vermilion, green, blue and yellow that glittered like crystal; and a great hall so vast that six thousand men could banquet there. Behind the palace were outbuildings where the treasure of the Qan was kept— gold, silver, gems, pearls and much more (in Ricci 1939), and a vast hunting park with rare trees, and an exotic menagerie with leopards and lynxes trained for the chase. But while this magnificence eclipsed that of Mongke, the royal feasts described by Polo were nearly identical.

Although now in a hall rather than in a tent, the Qan sat in an elevated position on the north side, looking toward the south. Attending him were barons—the equivalent of those first appointed by Chingghiz—in charge of the Great Qan's food and drink. Polo reported, "their mouths and noses are muffled up with beautiful silk and gold cloths, in order that no breath or odor of their bodies may come near the Great Qan's food and drink" (in Ricci 1939: 132). On the Qan's left sat his principal wife. On his right, but lower so their heads were level with the Great Qan's feet, were his sons, grandsons and imperial kinfolk, with the heir presumptive higher than the others. Below them, in descending order, were the nobles and barons on the right, and their ladies on the left. Those who were seated were served on small tables, but not all were accorded this honor. The lower-ranked knights and barons who took part in the feast sat on the carpets, and did not have tables. The seating and tables were arranged so that the Great Qan could see everyone: "And everyone knows the place that belongs to him, for the Great Qan has fixed it" (in Ricci 1939: 130), and this was strictly enforced:

> ... there are certain barons whose duty it is to assign their proper places to the strangers who arrive without knowing the customs of the great court. These barons constantly go hither and thither about the hall, seeing whether those sitting at the tables lack anything, and if thereby anyone wants wine or milk or meat or anything else, they at once have it brought by the servants.
>
> (Polo in Ricci 1939: 131)

To be inside the tent at all was an honor; food was distributed to an additional forty thousand gathered outside who had come to pay respects, bring gifts and tribute and seek favors and appointments. In the middle of the hall, according to Polo, stood an elaborate dispenser, similar to the one made for Mongke, from which could be drawn wine, mares' milk, camels' milk and other drinks. The chosen beverage was drawn from the dispenser into large golden vessels, each large enough to hold what Polo reckoned was sufficient wine for eight or ten European men, but were distributed on the basis of one vessel for every two guests, male or female, each of whom dipped what they wanted into golden cups. According to custom, when the Great Qan was ready, instruments struck up, a page offered the ruler a cup and all those present fell on their knees in obeisance, the process being repeated every time the Qan wished to drink. After the guests had eaten, the tables were carried away, and drinking and entertainment by "jugglers, tumblers and such persons who know how to do all kinds of wondrous things" continued into the night.

The birthday feasts of the Great Qan were even more magnificent, with the ruler dressing in robes of golden cloth and his barons, twelve thousand in number, also in silk and gold cloth adorned with precious stones and pearls, encircled with golden belts according to their rank, all given to them by the Qan. The feast of New Year's Day was held to be particularly significant because all that happened on that day was an omen of the year to come. Everyone wore white to ensure that they would be happy and lucky, wished each other luck and good fortune, and exchanged presents of white things, and the Great Qan was presented with a hundred thousand white horses, from which the imperial *karakumiss* would be made. The royal kin, nobles and subjects then gathered for the Qan's blessing, after which all were seated as previously described and the drinking and eating began. Feasts were a regular fixture of the court; in addition to the Qan's birthday and the New Year celebrations, there were other royal birthdays and thirteen annual lunar feasts. For the latter, the Qan provided his guests with thirteen suits of clothing, all of different colors, adorned with pearls and jewels, to be worn only on the days of the appropriate feast, along with special boots of silver thread. Polo noted that since these clothes were worn on one day only, they were not replenished annually, but were expected to last for ten years. The wearing of appropriate clothes—coded by color and decoration—was often a part of formal feasting in antiquity, but the details have usually been lost. In this case, it can be assumed that the colors had symbolic meaning, and in addition to signifying the wealth of the Qan in being able to provide such raiment, the wearing of the same color by a large group would have signified membership of a group—an elite within the elite—while still allowing for distinctions of rank within it.

By now, the material conditions of elite Mongols had been transformed out of recognition, and the condition of the common people had improved substantially. As the Persian historian Ata-Malik Juvayni (1226–83) put it (in Boyle 1958: 22–3):

> Before the appearance of Chingghis Khan they had no chief or ruler. Each tribe or two tribes lived separately; they were not united with one another and there was constant fighting and hostility between them … their clothing was of the skins of dogs and mice and their food was the flesh of those animals and other dead things, their wine was mares' milk … the sign of a great emir among them was that his stirrups were made of

iron, from which one can form a picture of their other luxuries ... [until] the banner
of Chingghiz Khan's fortune was raised ... and they issued forth from a prison into a
garden, from the desert of poverty into a palace of delight ... and it has come to pass
that the present world is the paradise of that people for all the merchandise that is
brought from the west is borne unto them and that which is bound in the farthest east
is untied in their house, wallets and purses are filled from their treasuries and their
everyday garments are studded with jewels and embroidered with gold.

But what about the food at the feasts at which the wealth from the Mongol
conquests were on display? According to Polo, elephants—reportedly five thousand
in number—and an "immense number" of camels, covered with fine cloth, paraded
before those present bearing "the things necessary for this feast"—by tradition skins
of *kumiss* and containers of other drinks. Yet of what was eaten at these grand
events, Polo has only this to say (in Ricci 1939: 132): "Of the food I will not speak,
for anyone can understand that it is in great abundance."

The inference here, borne out by other sources, is that at first Mongol feast foods
changed in quantity, but not in kind. Mongol foodways were initially conservative,
resisting change. Tents at court had gone from felt to linen, silk and cloth of gold;
drinking cups from horn or earthenware to silver and gold, but ceremonies, food
and drink—"meat and milk"—were largely unchanged, except that more people
were involved, provisions were much more plentiful, and the quantity and variety
of alcoholic drinks increased. Over a century later, when their rule over China was
well-established, the Mongol court in China continued to eat steppe food—mutton,
often whole animals boiled up and cut into pieces, served with broth—and to make
offerings to their clan ancestors in the traditional way, sprinkling the ground with
mares' milk and offering *kumiss* and wind-dried meat (Mote 1977: 205). They held
court banquets called "*kumiss* feasts" or "one color" feasts because the guests wore
garments of the same color, changed over the course of three days, and the occasions
"normally seem to have ended in a drunken rout" (Mote 1977: 207).

Yet gradually Mongol feasts and diet began to change, and with them the fortunes
of the Mongol Empire and the peoples' health. In brief, between approximately
AD 1206 and 1279, "the Mongols conquered a good part of the known world ...
from the proceeds of this empire, the Mongol rulers then tried to make more food
available to their nomad subjects and to provide for themselves all they could eat
of their favorite dishes, plus a staggering supply of intoxicating drink" (Masson
Smith 2000: 4). Through trade and tribute, the Mongols gained access to spices—
considered medicinal rather than mere flavorings—and to flour, grains and legumes
of various kinds along with previously unknown foods, also acquiring culinary
techniques and recipes from their new Chinese subjects, and from the Persian part
of their empire. The simple *shülen* broth of the steppes as it had been in the days
of Chingghiz's youth became richer and more complex, thickened with grains and

legumes and embellished with noodles and spices, and instead of small cubes of meat offered on the point of a knife, there were now great quantities of lamb, mutton, goat and other meats, carved and offered on or off the bone. The evolution of Mongol court cuisine can be seen in the *Yin-shan Zhengyao, Proper and Essential Things for the Emperor's Food and Drink,* an imperial dietary manual that was presented to the Mongol Emperor of China (Yuan Dynasty) Tugh Temur, a great-great grandson of Kublai Qan, in AD 1330. While it does not give information on which dishes were considered appropriate for particular occasions, or on how the food was served or consumed, it illustrates the effect on food of the "broader process of political and cultural amalgamation through which the Mongolian world order had taken shape" (Buell, Anderson and Perry 2000: 15), with ingredients, techniques and beliefs regarding health and medicine coming from all parts of the far-flung Mongol Empire (and see Buell 2001).

The Mongols did not have the clear distinction between alcohol and food that the Greeks had. Practical reasons for the nomads' preference for a liquid diet of soup, stews, broths and fresh milk have been given above. However, the centrality of alcoholic drinks has less to do with logistics and nutrition than with the role of alcohol in constructing the Mongols' social and political worlds. Drinking did not only take place during feasts; it was also a part of deliberations or discussions, and happened indoors and outdoors, even on horseback; it was ubiquitous. Remembering the tendencies to fission inherent in Mongol social organization, as well as the consultative process by which decisions were reached, and the ubiquity of *kumiss* pitchers in every tent, however humble, it is easy to see the social role (Douglas 1987) of Mongol drinking—especially with the low alcoholic content of the original *kumiss* at 1.65–3.25 percent (Masson Smith 2000: 3)—as constructive and integrative, actively creating and maintaining a level of community which was entered into by the act of consumption. "Play" rather than "fighting" is the activity associated with drink reported by the friars; drinking showed that one was "relaxed" in the presence of the others. One was expected to drink, even obliged to drink, in the same way that one would be expected to participate in social life more generally. Only later, as the consultative nomadic political processes and tribal organization gave way to other authority structures, and as supplies and potency of drink changed, did the practice become dysfunctional—as did other aspects of the Mongol diet.

The friars had noted the limited use of flour among the Mongol elite, including "dough cooked in water with butter or sour milk and unleavened bread cooked in the dung of oxen or of horses" (Rubruck in Wyngaert: 271–2; in Buell, Anderson and Perry 2000: 48). The *Ying-shan Zhengyao* shows that as soon as flour began to be imported in quantity, a variety of hearth breads, steamed or boiled buns, and noodles became popular, the latter easily incorporated into the favored broths. A liking for lamb, breadstuffs and fried dumplings still distinguishes the cuisine of northwest China, the old center of Mongol domination, as opposed to the rice, fish and pork culture of southeast China. The establishment of the Mongol Empire coincided with the first broad use of distilled brandies and whiskies in East Asia (Buell, Anderson and Perry 2000: 49) so as a result of their conquests the Mongols were able to access a great quantity and variety of alcoholic drinks which were much stronger than those they had previously been used to and which could be stored easily and consumed all year round. These were the liquors glimpsed by the friars and Polo at the court of the Great Qan and which became more widely available with time. *Kumiss* was seasonal, a product of three to five months in summer (Masson Smith 2000: 3) so while the consumption of *kumiss* may have been high in the pre-conquest days on the steppe, it was also limited, and in any case *kumiss* was not as intoxicating as distilled liquor, although it was now in more plentiful supply than it had been in the old days. Increased *kumiss* supplies and the year-round availability of stronger drink led to consistent overconsumption. Here, a parallel can be drawn with the Scythians who, accustomed to mare's milk, developed a taste for stronger drink when they came into contact with it, resulting in the drunkenness criticized by the Greeks. Certainly, many of the Qans from Ogedei onwards, along with their subjects, suffered from what would be called alcoholism today, and the women of the court drank as frequently as the men. Also, due to the increasingly rich meat-based diet, gout and obesity became common afflictions (Masson Smith 2000), exacerbated by the fact that during the Yuan Dynasty the Mongol elite became increasingly sedentary, with seasonal progressions from summer to winter palaces being a pale reflection of the migrations of old.

With this background, it is not surprising that the *Yin-shan Zhengyao* is concerned with matters of health at the royal court, drawing on Chinese, Turkic and Turko-Islamic medical theory and practices, but always within a Mongolian framework, with pan-Eurasian elements adapted to Mongol tastes. Some items in the *Yin-shan Zhengyao* are specifically medicinal, like cinnamon cakes to stop a cough, but all the more general recipes have been devised with a view to health and wellbeing, with many kinds of *shülen* described as being able to "supplement the center and increase *ch'i*." In the vision of world domination set out by Chingghiz, the Mongols sought to take the best from other cultures—everything from military technology and food to administrative techniques and religions—incorporating them into a new Mongol world order while seeking consciously to put a Mongol stamp on them. For this reason, the historian Paul Buell (2001) has called this an attempt by the Mongols to create the first world cuisine. In the *Yin-shan Zhengyao* the categories of court dishes are Mongolian in character but incorporate elements from other cultures. There are recipes for *shülen* (broths, soups and watery stews), the largest category; for dishes in which boiling is the primary form of preparation; for those calling for blood or organ meats; those in which bone plays a conspicuous part; those calling for some Mongolian traditional food especially gathered vegetable foods; and those in which cow's milk, butter, cheese, curds or any other dairy produce plays a role (Buell,

Anderson and Perry 2000: 105). In these, the outlines of the steppe cuisine of old can be discerned, but now spiced, diced and refined to a high degree, enriched with nuts, fruit, ginseng, spices and many other new ingredients. The Mongol preference for liquid foods was new to China, and required new serving vessels. The art historian John Carswell has suggested that the introduction of Mongol court cuisine—which required cups, bowls, servers and pots for the great banquet soups, *kumiss* and many kinds of liquid refreshment—led to the rise in popularity of blue and white porcelain, earlier than previously thought (Buell 2007: 25). The Mongols' enduring legacy to world cuisine is the many soups and broths, *ramen* (Kushner 2012) being a current incarnation, that are popular throughout Eurasia.

But despite the attention paid to health in the *Yin-shan Zhengyao*, the hardiness for which the Mongols had once been noted began to decline as did dynastic longevity. With some justification, the Mongol Empire can be described as having been destroyed by feasting in the sense of overconsumption. The descendants of Chingghiz had ever-shorter reigns, died at earlier ages, and left markedly fewer children, setting off succession disputes and ultimately leading to political fragmentation, for all of which it has been suggested dietary decadence was a primary cause (Masson Smith 2000). The Mongol Yuan dynasty was overthrown in China in AD 1368 and although Mongol influence continued in other regions, the great empire of Chingghiz never rose again. However, when mounted tribes from Mongolia seized power in China and established the Qing Dynasty in AD 1644, they were notably reluctant to give up their traditional steppe foods at court, remembering what had happened to the Yuan Dynasty who they believed had weakened their health and compromised their identity by adopting foreign foods. In sum, the original diet of the steppe nomads and the Scythians before them, although extreme, was in retrospect perfectly suited to a harsh environment and a demanding way of life, while the communal feasts of the early period were a reliable way of sharing scarce resources and of negotiating and perpetuating tribal solidarity. It was the excessive feasts of later times, which took place against a background of trying to maintain the success of the conquest phase in peacetime, in the face of cultural and political complexity as nomadism gave way to a more sedentary lifestyle, that brought the Mongols low. Ironically, the failure of the Mongols seems to lie in the initial success of their imperial project, and their abandoning of the old ways. They should have remembered these words attributed to Chingghiz Qan (in Riasonovsky 1965: 88):

> After us the descendants of our clan will wear gold embroidered garments, eat rich and sweet food, ride fine horses and embrace beautiful women but they will not say that they owe all this to their fathers and elder brothers, and they will forget us and those great times.

CHAPTER SIX

China: The Hidden History of Chinese Feasting

From of old, what have we been doing?
We grow wine-millet and cooking-millet,
Our wine-millet, a heavy crop;
Our cooking-millet, doing well.
Our granaries are all full,
For our stacks were in their millions,
To make wine and food,
To make offering, to make prayer-offering
That we may have peace, that we may have ease,
That every blessing may be vouchsafed.

From *Song 199* (c. 600 BC), in *The Book of Songs*, translated
by Arthur Waley (1937: 209)

At the start of the twentieth century AD, the official popular "history" of China stretched back more than four millennia, to a remote period, about 2852 to 2070 BC, known as the first of the Three Dynasties and the time of the Three Sovereigns and Five Emperors. Seen as a golden age of peace and prosperity in which sages flourished, its rulers were thought to include the wise Yellow Emperor, honored by later generations as the inventor and bestower, among many other things, of centralized government, writing, Chinese medicine and the arts of growing cereals, cooking food and making wine. Here, it was believed, were the roots of a society that seemed to have emerged uncontested from the mists of time with the basic characteristics of Chinese society already fully in place. These were centralized political power, bureaucratic organization carried out by highly literate administrators and an "imperial institution [that], while linked to no church or organized religion, yet claimed that its right to rule was bestowed by heaven's mandate" (Mote 1999: 4), based on just rule. With modifications and occasional interruptions, these institutions were believed to have persisted since time immemorial until the overthrow of the Qing (Manchu) Dynasty and the rise of the Republic of China in AD 1912, but now this conventional view of China's origins is being radically revised through new evidence of early feasting there, as revealed by archaeology.

It is entirely appropriate that feasting should give new insights into Chinese history as a whole because, as K. C. Chang, whose pioneering work applied both anthropological and archaeological methods to the study of China, noted: "few other cultures are as food oriented as the Chinese, and this orientation appears to be as ancient as Chinese culture itself" (Chang 1977: 11). Methodologically, this is both a help and a hindrance. China's vast size, varied geography, diverse foods, different gastronomic traditions, extensive repertoire of culinary techniques and long history stretching over some twenty-four dynasties before the present era have resulted in cuisines that, taken together, are the most elaborate and extensive in the modern world, as they were in different periods of antiquity. Because of this complexity, it will be useful to give some brief and broad outlines before proceeding.

"Chinese" Food

Reflecting the Cultural/Material Turn referred to in Chapter One, contemporary studies of food in and from China treat it as a form of material culture that embodies memory, history and identity heightened by the additional dimension of sensory experience. Presently, several main cuisines are recognized, on the basis of city or region—Cantonese, Hunanese and Szechuan among them—although their number is contested and boundaries constantly shift (Anderson 1988: 194). Despite this, each region is considered distinctive in its ingredients, manner of preparation, organoleptic preferences and signature dishes, and a culinary map of the country would reveal many micro-cuisines dictated by landscape, resources and historical factors. For this reason, China is a favored destination for gastronomic tours in which travelers aim to get to know place and people through eating their food, while foreign language cookbooks on regional Chinese cookery proliferate. Recent academic studies of Chinese food, often in connection with identity, have also had a regional focus, usually concentrating on diaspora communities outside Mainland China, but including Hong Kong.

In addition to Mainland Chinese regional cuisine, there is now an extensive range of "Chinese" foodways created by Chinese migrants who have adapted their cuisine to the ingredients and tastes of the new locales in which they have settled. One notable example is Peranakan/Nonya cuisine. Combining Chinese, Malayan and Indonesian elements, it was developed by Chinese emigrants to the British Straits Settlements in the colonial era. While Nonya cookery began as a domestic cuisine to be eaten at home, another type of migrant food—glossed broadly as "Chinese restaurant cuisine"—was created specifically for public consumption (Ku, Manalansan and Mannur 2013; Coe 2009; Roberts 2002; Wu and Cheung 2004; Wu and Tan 2001), often in special "Chinatown" districts (Tchen 1999). Because commercial success depended on pleasing the palates and preferences of new customers in foreign locales, entirely new dishes were and are invented which subsequently take on an authenticity of their own. A recent example is the dish called "General Tso's Chicken," battered chicken in sweet-sour sauce, supposedly a traditional dish from Hunan province but originally unknown there. The dish was actually invented by a leading chef of the pre-Mao era who, after the fall of the Nationalist government, fled to Taiwan and then to New York, where he opened a restaurant of which his piquant chicken became the signature dish (Dunlop 2007). Such was its popularity abroad that the dish was later taken to China, to be served in Hunan to tourists who expected to find it there.

Restaurants are not alien to Chinese culture, nor is all the food they serve ersatz. Restaurants and eating-houses have been a feature of Chinese life since at least the Tang dynasty, "an inseparable part of being a city-dweller" (Freeman 1977: 158). Unlike Europe, where elite restaurants are of relatively recent establishment, in China eating in good restaurants has long been considered a pleasure and a privilege, for the sake of both the specialist cooking to be enjoyed, and the opportunity to entertain family and friends in a manner often not possible at home, no matter how wealthy, and where there is the additional pleasure of display, eating in a setting where their festivities can be observed by others. Restaurants became the customary site of celebrations to mark key events and the Chinese consider them important cultural establishments, bastions of authenticity and continuity. Although today we are accustomed to thinking of Chinese eateries in terms of take-aways, food to go and *à la carte* menus, the same restaurants that now sell General Tso's Chicken and "regional" dishes to some customers, can also serve another clientele a different kind of cuisine.

A feature of Chinese restaurants in Mainland China before and after the Mao era and without interruption in Hong Kong, Taiwan and diaspora communities— particularly those restaurants patronized by the Chinese community—were and are "banquet meals." These may be on the main menu, on a separate menu, or may be to order in advance only. In Chinese culinary culture, a "banquet" is seen as the proper way to celebrate or mark important family and other events. Why this is the case will become clear in due course, but the following description of a formal restaurant banquet dating from the 1950s will be a useful point of reference. This particular menu is a banquet in the Peking style of cuisine, as served in the diaspora community of Singapore. A Cantonese style banquet would be likely to have fried rice and fried noodles instead of congee. The dishes themselves could change depending on season, but the basic structure is similar across regions and indeed across countries. There are different degrees of elaboration in banquet cuisine. The number of dishes vary, but whether many or fewer, they fall into these categories: Hors d'oeuvres (*Lung Hun*), entrees (*Reh Chao*), main dishes (*Ta Tsai*), roasts (*Kao Hsiao*), "refreshments" (*Tien Hsin*), and hot savory dishes (*Reh Hun*) to go with rice dishes (*Fan Shih*), in established proportions. This is an example of a 32-dish banquet, served in the following order (Chang, 1955: 5):

Lung Hun—Hors d'oeuvres
Four fruits: tangerines, grapes, pears, banana
Four nuts: melon seeds, almonds, walnuts, peanuts
Four cold cuts: smoked fish, sliced ham, sliced chicken, jelly fish

Reh Chao—Entrees
Fried shelled shrimps	Fried fish fillets
Fried spring chicken	Stewed sea slugs

Ta Tsai—Main dishes
Bird's nest soup	Shark fins with brown gravy
White fungus with chicken soup	Braised abalone

Kao Hsiao—Roasts
Roast duck	Roast suckling pig

Tien Hsin—Refreshments
Eight Precious rice	Spring rolls
Pao Tze	Honey cakes

Reh Hun—Hot Savory dishes
Sandy-pot bean curd	Braised pigs shoulder
Simmered chicken	Ham and cabbage soup

Fan Shih—Rice dishes
Rice or congee	Meat dumplings

There was also an established banquet etiquette, as important a part of the event as the food. If everyone entered the room together, there was an elaborate concern for precedence, with people bowing and giving way to each other according to superior/inferior status and age seniority. Precedence also determined the seating. Generally, the higher status seats were at the north or inner side of the room, with the host and hostess sitting opposite the guests of honor, usually at the south or near the serving door. If wines were served, the guests were not supposed to drink until invited to do so by the host (Chang 1955: 2). Recognizably similar banquets were and are found throughout China, and in the Chinese diaspora communities abroad.

The interest in Chinese regional cuisine and in migrant food as an aspect of globalization is recent, reflecting the postmodern persuasion and the interest of the *Annales* School in the mentalities and materialities of specific locales or *terroirs*, and in "everyday eating" or peasant food. One paradigm study in this genre, of communal banquets among poor workers in the New Territories, Hong Kong, in the 1970s, "deals with one hitherto unexplored aspect of China's culinary tradition, namely the use of food as a social levelling device ... [it is] a militant rejection of the hierarchical values that normally find expression at Chinese banquets" (Watson 1987: 389). These *sikh puhn* feasts were an inversion of the usual Chinese banquet—instead of wonderful food elegantly served with due regard for the social rank and seniority of those present, at this meal everything was thrown into a common pot, into which the diners—both rich and poor—had to dig for their meal, fishing among bits of bone and gristle. The surroundings were humble, there were no ceremonies and no toasts, people simply ate and left when they were finished. It was a meal intended to· level the diners, to erase any social differences and eliminate constraining etiquette. In the aggressively egalitarian spirit of the times, it was an event all felt they had to attend, "to show we can all trust each other" (Watson 1987: 392). Looking only at studies like this, it is difficult to appreciate the extent to which the view of China's past social landscape has been flattened, "peasantised" (Cohen 1991: 118) and secularized by the political events of the twentieth century that saw the rise of the People's Republic of China and Maoism, as well as by the current academic preoccupation with workers, the subaltern and the ordinary.

By contrast, other histories of China's food past paint a very different picture, ignoring or diminishing the importance of regionality, drawing broad developmental schema, restoring the importance of the sacred, describing social hierarchies and focusing on elites. These other approaches fall into four categories. First are studies of the domestication and migration of plants and animals that contributed to China's rich larder, including nutrition and material or technological histories (Kiple 2007; Kiple and Conèe Ornelas 2000; Simoons 2001; Crawford 2006; Bellwood 2006; Fuller and Rowlands 2011). Second are the classic social histories of food in Chinese culture (Chang et al 1977; Anderson 1988). Using texts and administrative records, often focusing on specific dynasties, they show how factors such as agricultural innovation, political dissolution and reunification, territorial expansion and a concomitant increase in trade and general wealth, rises and falls in population, and the influx of foreign elements of various kinds including peoples from Inner Asia and new foods from throughout the empire contributed to the development of Chinese cuisine. The Tang Dynasty (AD 618–906) was notable in this regard, when envoys and merchants traveling the sea routes and over land brought exotic delicacies from almost every part of Asia. The best of them were destined for the imperial tables where an official known as the "Provost of Foods" assisted by eight dieticians and sixteen butlers, provided food "in strict accordance with seasonal taboos … and of appropriate character" for royal feasts, state banquets and informal entertainments (Schafer 1963: 141).

Third are the literary histories of food which mine poetry and prose—works of the Tang (AD 618–906) and Song (AD 960–1279) Dynasties, considered literary golden ages, are favorites—to evoke the flavors, pleasures and aromas of past times. These are among the most lyrical descriptions of food in world literature. Foods are enthused over, dishes described in loving detail, drinks relished, as seen in this Han Dynasty (206 BC–AD 220) poem *Summoning the Soul* which attempts to call back the soul of a sick or dying person with enticing food:

> Next to the five grains, six fathoms deep, they place wild rice;
> Cauldrons of well-done stew fill one's gaze, seasoning brings out the aroma;
> Plump cranes, pigeons and swans flavor a badger stew
> Oh soul, return! Taste whatever you will!
> Fresh loggerhead turtle, sweet chicken, blended with Ch'u vinegar;
> Suckling pig in meat sauce, bitter dog, minced Mioga ginger;
> Mugwort and wormwood in a Wu sour, not too juicy or bland:
> Oh soul, return! Choose whatever you like!
> Baked crane, steamed duck, boiled quail all set forth;
> Fried carp, stewed sparrows, broiled kingfisher all presented:
> Oh soul, return! Delicacies are spread before you!
> Four pots of pure wine well-aged, neither harsh nor cloying;
> Clear and fragrant, icy drinks, not served to base men;
> Wu must and white yeast, blended with a Ch'u clear:
> Oh soul, return! Do not be frightened or alarmed!
>
> (in Knechtges 1986: 56)

Again, these studies focus mainly on the aristocracy, the intelligentsia and wealthy commoners whose tastes are described in Schafer's seminal *The Golden Peaches of Samarkand* (1963), delighting in exotic ingredients brought from afar, and in the wine made from highly prized grapes coaxed over arbors and fed with the water in which rice had been soaked:

> As strolling round he chanced to see
> The fruit upon the o'er hanging tree;

We men of Tsin, such grapes so fair
Do cultivate as gems most rare;
Of these delicious wine we make,
For which men ne'er their thirst can slake.

(*The Song of the Grape,* in Schafer 1963: 145)

Paintings and murals provide additional information on the material culture of food. Over many dynasties, men and women, separately and together, are shown at banquets and at other gatherings great and small, sitting companionably at tables set with ceramic and porcelain bowls, cups, tureens, platters, baskets and vessels like those in use today. As depictions of kitchens, street stalls and vendors appear, they too are recognizable. Individual dishes are shown that are identical to those eaten now, like the dumplings celebrated in this ode by the Song poet Shu Xi:

Lovely and pleasing, mouth-watering,
The wrapper is thin but it does not burst.
Rich flavors are blended within,
A plump aspect appears without.
They are as tender as spring wool,
As white as autumn silk.

(in Knechtges 1997: 236)

The impression of culinary continuity is so persuasive that it is generally assumed that "many of the features that we regard today as characteristically Chinese were already in place during the Han Dynasty (206 BC–AD 220) and that Han gastronomy is indeed Chinese cuisine *in statu nascendi*" (Huang 1990: 139). But did Chinese cuisine begin in the Han or is it older, and what meanings and associations are embodied in it?

This bring us to the fourth approach—studies of the relationship between food, politics and religion in ancient China, based on archaeological, palaeographic and textual material that has come to light since the 1970s (see Sterckx 2011, 2005a, 2005b; Cook 1996, 2005; von Falkenhausen 1993, Puett 2004, Boileau (1998–9). These studies begin with the centrality of food in Chinese culture, working from the premise that "Chinese food culture shows material as well as conceptual continuities that stretch over centuries," aiming to show that "... a meticulously stage-managed Chinese banquet today still echoes some of the precepts and rules of etiquette set out in ritual codes traceable to early imperial times" (Sterckx 2005a: 3). Not concerned with food production, food technology or nutrition, these studies are interested instead in how "the culinary arts, food, food sacrifice and eating influenced philosophical and religious perceptions and the ritual setting in which such ideas were expressed" (Sterckx 2005a: 3). They also seek to break down "the enduring preconception" that food culture in China can be fully elucidated as belonging to China's three main religious traditions: "Confucian" ancestor worship and sacrificial religion, religious Daoism and Buddhism (Sterckx 2005a: 3–4).

This approach provides relief from literary studies that often seem to be little more than food lists, and adds another dimension to archaeological studies which have tended to focus on the aesthetic qualities of early food vessels and on typologies, rather than on what they might have been used for, how and why. As will be seen, they also challenge the official view of China's early eras. However, as these studies are impenetrable to non-specialists, it is necessary to begin with a narrative account of past practices in order to visualize them, and to set the new studies and discoveries in context.

"Zhou" Feasting

Until the new discoveries, the Western Zhou Dynasty (1046–256 BC) was the earliest period for which there were written records relating to food rituals and feasting in China. There were several key texts including the Zhou-Li (The Rites of Zhou), the Li-Chi (Book of Rites) and the I-Li (Book of Etiquette and Ceremonial). Although compiled later, they were believed to faithfully reflect society and ritual practice in the Zhou. A warrior society with a hierarchical social organization, Zhou social organization took the form of a pyramidal social structure with the ruler at its apex. Below him was the immediate royal family followed by the hereditary nobility, often distant relatives of the ruler, who provided the upper echelons of court and civic officials, serving as ministers, generals and in other capacities. Below them came the broad mass of the population differentiated in terms of occupations that included artisans, servants, soldiers and even dog attendants. At the bottom of this social pyramid were the chung-jen, "the multitude," lowly peasants who were the mainstay of agricultural and other labor, and then the slaves. Society was patriarchal and patrilineal, producing lineage groups related to a common male ancestor reckoned through the father on the male side. The elite practiced polygamy, having concubines in addition to the principal wife or wives. These women were ranked in order as were their offspring and descendants, adding another element to the hierarchy. As will be seen, all these distinctions were materialized through food.

Kinship-based lineage organizations come with a ready-made structure of inbuilt loyalties, obligations, and rank along the lines of generation, order of birth, gender, consanguinity (blood relationship) and affinity (related by marriage or other form of alliance) (Chang 1980: 166). Kinship determines whom you can marry, whom you must serve, and who must serve you. It is a system in which everyone knows their place and is defined by it, both inside the lineage and outside it, for lineages are seen as ranked relative to each other. Men remain in the lineages into which they are born, while women join the lineages of their husbands but are expected to support the interests of their birth lineages, for one looks to one's kin for advancement and assistance. If the biological kinship network proves insufficient, fictive or honorary kinship can created through adoption, alliance or invented genealogical links which soon become real kinship. And lineages do not only include the living; they can also consist of the dead, including ancestors going back for generations; politics, society, family, the sacred and the secular are inseparable.

This has advantages and disadvantages. On the one hand, lineage organization provides an infrastructure that a leader can mobilize and deploy, and some degree of common interest can be assumed because all lineage members benefit from the success of their line. But lineages are also prone to family tensions and rivalries exacerbated when the leading males of the group in question have multiple female partners, both wives and concubines, who promote the interests of their relatives and children, resulting in fierce rivalries within their generation and those of their descendants. Also, as new generations are born, the size of any lineage group becomes unwieldy, and some form of reorganization has to take place. In some circumstances, this potentially volatile combination of stability and instability, competition and cooperation, can be employed in a gainful manner. Segmentary lineage systems can serve as ready-made organizations of predatory expansion (Sahlins 1961), with junior lines breaking off or segmenting from the main line and moving out to form their own satellite units, taking over territory previously empty or occupied by other groups. As Sahlins described it, the segmentary lineage system consistently channels expansion outward, releasing internal pressure in an explosive blast against other peoples (Sahlins 1961: 337). In early China, these dynamics produced a volatile warrior society continually seeking to expand its territory, its members in constant rivalry, each seeking to advance their status on earth and, as will be seen, in heaven, with food and feasting playing a central role.

According to the *Zhou-Li*, the staff of the Zhou royal household included 152 masters of viands who supervised the planning and preparation of meals for the king, the consort, and the crown prince: 70 butchers, 128 court cooks, 128 outer cooks charged with preparing the sacrificial offerings and food for the military guard and guests; 62 assistant cooks who did the actual cooking on the stoves; 335 masters of the royal domain who provided all of the grain, vegetables and fruits for the royal table; 62 game hunters; 342 fishermen; 24 turtle catchers who provided all of the shellfish; 28 meat-driers; two food doctors who supervised the proper preparation of food and drink; 110 regulators of the wines who supervised the officials who made wines and other drinks; 340 winemakers; 170 beverage makers; 94 ice-house attendants; 31 bamboo basket attendants charged with serving food in the food baskets; 61 meat pickle makers; 62 picklers; and 62 salt makers (Knechtges 1986: 49). The *Li-Ji* gives the following recipe for a dish prepared in elite kitchens. Here we see an elaborate meat-rich cuisine with culinary techniques already well developed,

casting doubt on the claim that the later Han period (206 BC–AD 220) is the fount
of Chinese cuisine.

> For the bake, they took a sucking-pig or a (young) ram, and having cut it open and
> removed the entrails, filled the belly with dates. They then wrapped it round with straw
> and reeds, which they plastered with clay, and baked it. When the clay was all dry,
> they broke it off. Having washed their hands for the manipulation, they removed the
> crackling and macerated it along with rice-flour, so as to form a kind of gruel which
> they added to the pig. They then fried the whole in such a quantity of melted fat as
> to cover it. Having prepared a large pan of hot water, they placed in it a small tripod,
> and the slices of the creature which was being prepared which was filled with fragrant
> herbs. They took care that the hot water did not cover this tripod, but kept up the fire
> without intermission for three days and nights. After this, the whole was served up
> with the addition of pickled meat and vinegar.
>
> (Li-Ji, Nei Zei: 51)

The *I-Li* reveals the extent to which formal feasts and less elaborate dinners were
essential to the conduct of official missions, embassies, visits, district meetings and
military councils, at all levels. The ruler gave feasts to feudal lords, to various
ministers he wished to honor, and to members of his extended family; officials gave
feasts to each other, and in an official context feasts were deemed so essential to
the proper way of doing things that, if a Prince was unable to attend the dinner in
person, the materials including food and gifts were sent to the person who would
have been the guest of honor, and if a feast had been offered to an envoy and the
envoy of a superior state turned up, the original feast would not take place, but
again all the food and gifts that would have been presented were sent to the original
invitee. There was a hierarchy of formal feasts. On a large scale, and given in the
temple, were the Dinner Without Pledging (Toasting), and the Feast With Wine. On a
smaller scale, and given in the private apartments, were The Banquet, the Luncheon
of Game and the Refection, when the delicacies of the season were eaten (Steele
1917: 269). There were variations of each type, depending on the status of hosts and
guests. A Great Officer of superior rank might be honored with a feast of nine meat
stands, while an inferior Great Officer was entitled to only seven stands.

This is an account of a banquet given by a reigning Zhou Duke taken from the *I-Li*,
presented here in narrative form:

After an audience, the Duke sent a retainer to notify those who were invited to the
banquet, while the court steward directed the preparation of the hall and the food.
Not all who attended the audience were asked, and nor would the guests be treated
in the same way. There were different grades of wine both new (must) and aged,
and also Dark Wine, the term for water, which was set out in a different place to the
wines. Great care was taken with the placement of the drinking vessels, containers

and other objects. Whether the wine carriers had round or square mouths; if the ladles were inverted or not; whether the covering cloths were coarse or fine according to the season and if the cup baskets faced west or east were considered matters of great significance. The positioning of those present was equally important; all had their assigned places in the great hall; they had to face in certain directions, and elaborate obeisances were made throughout the proceedings. Elements of religious symbolism and distinctions of social status are apparent, but the nuances of meaning can only be guessed at. Similarly, the architecture and decoration of the setting are unclear, but there were several doors oriented to the cardinal directions, some deemed more important than others. There was also at least one raised dais and sets of stairs the ascent and descent of which were central to the ceremonies and facilitated displays of rank and status.

At the ducal banquet, when all was ready, the Duke ascended the steps and went to his place on the mat, sitting with his face westward. The ministers and great officers then entered and stood inside the door, with their faces north, and graded from the east. The ordinary officers stood in the western part of the hall, facing east and graded from the north. The Duke selected the person who was to have the honor of being the Principal Guest. Protocol demanded that the person so honored refuse out of modesty when the offer was first made, accept when the Duke insisted, and then leave the hall in order to make a ceremonial re-entry.

When the Principal Guest returned, the Master of Ceremonies presented him with wine, dried flesh, relishes (called the "admirable condiments"), hash and a meat stand bearing dismembered joints of cooked meat. Etiquette demanded that the Guest open the proceedings by making an offering and tasting all the foods—if the food taster be not present, the commentary notes—but he might not properly eat until the Prince commands him to do so. Accordingly, the Guest cut a piece of the lung for sacrificing, offered it, tasted it, and returned it to the stand. He poured a libation of wine, sipped it, acknowledged the quality of the wine, then descended in the company of the Master of Ceremonies to perform a ceremonial hand washing and washing of the cup. Returning to his place, the Principal Guest then offered toasts to his host the Duke and to the Master of Ceremonies. The baskets for used cups and the large number of cups found in archaeological excavations attest to their role in ceremonial drinking.

Then the Duke was presented with relishes and a stand bearing joints of meat in order to make offerings as the Principal Guest had done. Goblets of wine were then raised in honor of the Duke by two officials chosen for the role. They kowtowed to the Duke, and he responded with two bows of acknowledgement. The kowtow, which involved kneeling and then touching the forehead to the floor in an act of obeisance and submission to someone of higher status, was a distinctive Chinese form of what Marcel Mauss called "techniques of the body," in which various postures and performative actions embody cultural beliefs and values. "Kowtow" embraced a range of obeisances from full prostration to nods of varying depth and numbers. The kowtow remained a keystone act in a highly hierarchical and ritualized society for millennia, only being formally set aside in the early twentieth century.

The Duke now opened the general pledging on behalf of the assembled guests. Wine was offered to ducal and ordinary ministers along with meats and relishes to make sacrifice, and to the great officers, who were also presented with sacrificial dried flesh and hash, but no joints. When this was over the musicians entered, four in number with two lutes, and sang "The call of the deer," "The four steeds" and "How glorious are the flowers." Bells and a set of 16 striking stones (Steele 1917: 151) suspended from frames were sometimes employed; music was stopped at various points in the proceedings, when obeisances or offerings were being made. When the singing had finished, organ players entered, and performed "The Southern Steps," "White Blossoms" and "The Millet Is in Flower." The ministers and great officers were then told, "The Duke commands you to put yourselves at your ease in his presence." They removed their shoes, and ascended to their sitting mats where they sat and were served the "ordinary dainties," while the food stands previously brought in were removed. The Duke commanded, "Let there be none who does not drink to the full." Then the Principal Guest, ministers and great officers all rose and replied, "Certainly. Dare we not do so?" Wine was offered to the ordinary officers, the cadets and those below them, and then drinking and music followed without restriction, torches being lit when it grew dark. When the Principal Guest had drunk his fill he departed, followed by the ministers and grand officers. The Duke remained behind, and now invited delegates from various states to feast with him. Again, etiquette demanded that the invitation be refused the first time out of deference to the host. The feast was held in the private apartments, and guests dined on dog, although only the Duke and his principal guests had meat stands set for them.

In the *I-Li* further details of etiquette and cuisine are given in the description of the palace dinner that was given by a Prince to a Great Officer (Commissioner) in charge of a smaller mission (Steele 1917: 243–59). At this entertainment, the Princess was also present, but after her entrance nothing more is said of her, and nor are other women mentioned, which is not to say that they were not there, at least as entertainers and as members of the Princess's suite.

Arrayed in his dress clothes, the Commissioner presented himself at the great door of the Palace, made obeisances and was received by the Prince. Goblets of wine and other drinks were set out. The officials and the members of the Princess's household took their assigned places, facing in the correct cardinal direction. More obeisances were made and throughout the hall a series of syncopated movements following strict rules of precedence and propriety began. A stew had been prepared and was brought into the hall in seven tripod vessels (*ding*) born by men who removed the carrying poles and covers and then withdrew, followed by the cooks who had brought in meat stands and the pantry-men who had put ladles into the vessels. In order of precedence, the Great Officers washed their hands in turn, then went forward one by one to ladle out the meat and, when the fish and dried game were cooked, to set the joints on their stands, in a precise manner specified by the *Li-Chi*: "The fish are seven in number, laid lengthwise on the stand, and resting on their right sides. The set of entrails and stomachs are even in number and occupy the same stand. There are seven sides of pork on one stand. The entrails, stomachs and sides of pork are all laid across the stands, and hang down at either side" (Steele 1917: 246–7). When the Great Officers had finished ladling, they returned to their places in the reverse order of their coming.

The Prince descended the stairs to perform a ceremonial hand washing, then returned to his place. The principal viands were then laid out, beginning with a container of wet hash and sauce which was set before the Prince. The Prince now stood on the inside of the inner wall, looking west, while the Commissioner stood to the west of the steps, where he was required to assume an expectant attitude (Steele 1917: 247). The under-steward now brought out six additional holders, placed to the east of the sauce and graded in importance from the west. "There were pickled vegetables, and on their east the pickled hashes. Then came pickled rush-roots with, to their south, elk flesh hash with the bones in, and on the west of this, pickled leek flowers with deer flesh hash following" (Steele 1917: 247). The officers then placed meat stands to the south of the holders, graded from the west, first the beef, then the mutton and then the pork. The fish was placed to the south of the beef, followed by the dried game and the entrails and stomachs, the sides of pork being placed by themselves on the east side.

The under-steward then set out glutinous and panicled millet grains (called "the great harmony") in six round tortoise-shaped covered holders in pairs, with the glutinous millet set opposite the stand of beef, and the panicled millet to the west of it. The "Grand Soup" of beef juice was brought in; this special soup was not seasoned and had no vegetables in it, and was served from an earthenware tureen. The steward brought this in by the temple-door and offered it to the Prince, who placed it to the west of the sauce. Then four tureens of ordinary broth with vegetables were brought in, and placed to the west of the holders, graded from the east—first beef broth with bean vine, then mutton with bitter gourd runners, then pork with vetch vine and beef broth with bean vine again, all with seed pods attached. The Prince now invited the Commissioner to eat. The Commissioner made an offering of the grains, the lungs of the three animals, vegetables from the tureens and wine. Additional courses were then set out—millet porridge (called "the fragrant mass"), rice porridge and the "general delicacies," followed by broiled beef with dry pickled hash, sliced beef, minced beef, broiled mutton, sliced mutton, broiled pork, sliced pork and mustard sauce, and minced fish, all set out in a particular order—and the Commissioner made a second offering from these additional dishes. When the time for the Commissioner to eat finally came, he had to ask to be excused the presence of the Prince, who then withdrew. The Commissioner finished his dinner, ending with the boiled millet. He drank three times, but did not partake of the sauce or the Grand Soup. Taking the spiked millet porridge and sauce, he descended, sat and placed the bowls to the west of the steps, then kowtowed twice to the Prince, who had returned. The Commissioner then took his leave, and assistants picked up the stands with the flesh of domestic animals on them, and carried them to the Commissioner's quarters, but they did not take the fish and dried game.

This degree of ceremonial elaboration is so extraordinary that John Steele, translator of the *I-Li*, deplored the "repetition and unnecessary detail ... that will make the reading of the book almost as wearisome a task as the translation of it" (Steele 1917: xvii–xviii). He also wondered why anyone would have submitted to such meticulous regulation, which will now be considered in light of the discoveries that made possible the new studies of Chinese feasting.

The Dragon Bones

The feasts of the royal Zhou household described above bring to mind the anthropologist Jack Goody's neo-Marxist model (1982) of the emergence of *haute cuisine* in Eurasia. This he related to the development of systems of production with differential access to power, authority and resources, leading to the emergence of social hierarchies based on relations of inequality. These hierarchies are marked by visible and material social distinctions, prime among them the allocation of certain foods to different social classes, with the best kinds of foods—the *haute cuisine* of the elite—characterized by a great variety and quantity of dishes, and by specialist culinary techniques and rare and exotic ingredients. This is fine as far as it goes, but the picture becomes more complex when the ritual and symbolic elements that Goody excludes are added.

Amid the treasures of the British Museum's China galleries lies the broken shoulder blade of an ox, marked with what seem to be random scratches. Easily overlooked among the jade scepters, golden embroideries, flamboyant Tang pieces in the tricolor *sancai* glaze that traveled the Silk Road to influence Western ceramics and elegant imperial porcelain from the Forbidden City in Peking, this apparently humble object is among the Museum's most important pieces. Dating from the Bronze Age Shang Dynasty (c. 1600–1046 BC), this bone and others like it carry the earliest form of writing yet found in China, making the Shang Dynasty the first known period for which both archaeological and textual remains are available. Taken together, they signal a transition from prehistory to history and give insight into a formative period of Chinese culture when cities or urban centers, early states and hierarchical society developed, along with beliefs and practices to which food and feasting were key.

The discovery of the bones was a paradigm of archaeological detective work. "Dragon bones"—the fossilized remains of dinosaurs and other creatures—have long been a prized ingredient in traditional Chinese medicine, excavated in secret and ground up by apothecaries, or sold whole for patients to prepare themselves. When ancient ox bones came to light, they were used in this way, and at the very end of the nineteenth century the markings on the bones came to academic attention. Anecdotally, the discovery was made by a scholar in the process of examining his own medicines purchased from a Beijing pharmacy after falling ill (Allan 1991; Debaine-Francfort 1998). When it became apparent that these markings were an early form of writing, attempts were made to track down their source, which dealers in medicinal supplies and looted antiquities strove to conceal. Finally the bones were traced to the environs of the modern city of Anyang in Henan Province, North China. Starting in 1927, excavations at Anyang and elsewhere—the beginning of systematic modern archaeology in China—have produced not only caches of inscribed bones, but also splendid artifacts that have established the historical authenticity of the Shang as a rich and complex civilization which, in the absence of evidence, had previously been regarded as legendary. It was once thought that the Shang was the only advanced Bronze Age culture in China. Excavations since the 1970s have revealed the existence of other early cultures in Henan, and parallel cultures in different regions, but, as no written records by them have yet been discovered, the northern region and literate Shang culture remain the focus of much of Chinese archaeological and historical interest as a prototype of later Chinese civilization.

The traditional Chinese view of China's past began with what were called the Three Dynasties, the first two regarded as semi-mythical, the last literate and documented. First was the Xia Dynasty, when Huang-di, the sage king or Yellow Emperor, was supposed to have lived, then came the Shang and finally the Western Zhou. Once the existence of the Shang was substantiated by the Anyang discoveries, the search for the Xia began as part of an attempt to trace Chinese culture to its very roots, and give substance to the claim that China is the most enduring civilization in the world. In the process, two other early cultures were found, also in Henan Province. It was once thought that one was the sought-for Xia, but this remains unproven. The following chronology has been suggested: Xia Dynasty (c. 2700–1600 BC), Early Shang/Erligang (1600–1300 BC), Late Shang (1300–1046 BC) and Western Zhou (1046–771 BC). Chronology and categories remain contested, but there are certainly features of material culture found at places other than Anyang including distinctive vessels for food and drink, large-scale architecture including palaces and temples, bronze casting, and elaborate ceremonial paraphernalia that suggest that the Shang culture did not suddenly arise fully formed, as once seemed the case, but instead drew on earlier as yet unsubstantiated foundations.

The ideographic Shang oracle bone inscriptions are not a literary narrative, and the scholarly project of unravelling the meaning of these primary sources is ongoing. At present, some "5,000 individual graphs are known about, of which half have been deciphered with certainty" (Keightley 2006: 183). However, enough is known to give some direct understanding of the way the Shang themselves perceived their world. Like the simple Mesopotamian notations that later gave rise to fully developed cuneiform writing, the bone markings are inventories that link the all-important trinity of the gods, humankind and food. But while the Mesopotamian records are a kind of sacred accountancy, tracking the inward and outward movements of comestibles and other goods in the overall service of the gods, the markings on the Shang bones have another dimension, for they were used in divination and sacrifice, and for that reason are usually now known as "oracle bones."

Divination is "the act of seeking mantic or prophetic information so that good fortune might be welcomed and misfortune avoided" (Field 2008: 3). The Shang practiced pyromantic divination—prophesy by fire—in which ox shoulder blades

6.1 Oracle bone, ox scapula, showing writing. Shang Dynasty. © The Trustees of the British Museum. Museum number 1911.1111.14. Image Number AN 360153

or the plastrons, the bottom or flat under-belly shells, of turtles were subjected to fire or heat until they cracked, in patterns that could be interpreted as "yes/no," "favorable/unfavorable" or "auspicious/inauspicious" answers. Divination with shoulder bones is known as "scapulimancy," and with shells "plastromancy." Records of the rituals were kept on the bones or shells, which were archived in the caches later found by archaeologists. It is these that give insights into Shang society, ritual and feasting, albeit through what is still a dark lens due to the enigmatic nature of the inscriptions. It may be that the bones are all that survive from a lost literature written on perishable silk or wood, although some bamboo with writing has been discovered. Taken together with other artifacts recovered from sites and tombs, the oracle bones reveal a society whose "rulers were not the benevolent sage kings imagined by later philosophers" (Allan 1991: 3) and depicted by artists as posed in idyllic landscapes of misty mountains and limpid streams, lost in contemplation. There was no stable centralized political organization, no administration carried out by highly literate bureaucrats under the aegis of the mythic Yellow Emperor, as long believed. This was a turbulent warrior society with violence at its center, both natural and sanctioned (Lewis 1990), coming from without and from within. Like the Zhou, they were hierarchical and organized into segmentary lineages. With their heartland in the fertile Yellow River Valley, the Shang were a classic "river civilization," benefiting from rich alluvial soil that supported agriculture. But they were also at the mercy of a river and climate that were often unpredictable, and were constantly seeking to maintain and expand their hold on a productive, vast and highly covetable territory that drew the unwelcome attention of rival groups. This required a large and subservient labor force to support agriculture and other activities, clear and easily mobilized forms of social and military organization and ample resources to devote to sacred technology including human sacrifice, and the oracle bones confirm the existence of all of these.

The huge numbers of ox bones and turtle shells that have come to light attest to the centrality and frequency of divination in Shang life. Gnomic and often incomplete though these inscriptions are, "few significant aspects of Shang life were undivined" (Keightley 1992: 33; Keightley 2000), with the oracle bones revealing the major concerns of elite Shang divination. These included military campaigns; hunting expeditions; the founding of new settlements and territorial expansion generally; excursions and travels of the ruler; the prospects for the coming week—which for the Shang was ten days long—and for the coming day or night; the weather; agriculture; sickness; childbirth; distress or troubles of the ruler or members of the royal family and their allies; whether or not orders should be issued; what tribute payments should be demanded and the meaning of dreams (Keightley 1992: 34–5). Should the ruler open a new field for cultivation? Should he send an expedition against enemies? Would there be rain? The divine answer could be yes or no. The Shang ruler acted as diviner on behalf of his people, entering into the divine bargain that is at the heart of sacrifice.

In return for guidance, approval and assistance from the gods, offerings needed to be made, a timeless exchange made explicit in the later *Shih Jing* or *Book of Songs*:

> The divine protectors have arrived,
> May they bestow on us increased felicity,
> May we be rewarded with longevity of ten thousand years ...
>
> Fragrant is the pious sacrifice,
> The spirits enjoy the wine and food,
> The oracle predicts for you a hundred blessings.
>   (from *Shih Jing* Ode 209 in von Falkenhausen 1993: 28; see also Rawson 1991)

In addition to the divinations which were performed when and as needed, there was a cycle of rituals that took a year to complete, and that required five different kinds of sacrifice: the *jung* involving drum music, the *hsi* featuring the feather dance, the *chi* entailing meat sacrifice, the *ts'ai* which used millet and the *hsieh* or great harmony, which involved all (Chang 1994: 30).

A distinctive feature of Shang sacrifice was its interactive nature, mediated through the divination. Instead of simply beseeching and then presenting goods at the altar, Shang divination allowed for the active involvement of the gods in the process, notably in being able to give positive or negative responses through the cracks on bones and plastrons, and in specifying the sacrifices they required. There was a constant give-and-take, and the responses of the gods were not always positive (Puett 2002: 41). Animals, both domestic and wild, along with wine and millet, the grain and drink celebrated in the passage with which this chapter begins, were the usual Shang offerings. The most esteemed sacrifices were human, usually war captives. Sometimes the diviner's question is recorded on the bones, sometimes not. In this example, the diviner asks the gods for approval of the sacrifice:

> *Preface:* divined on the *hsin-zu* day, K'o divined
> *Charge:* Should we offer wine? Should we offer ancestor Ta-chia and Tsu-I ten beheaded men and ten pairs of sheep to thank them?
>
>   (Plutschow 1995)

If a response or approval were not forthcoming, the number and kinds of offerings would be adjusted, and the divination performed again. More animals, of different colors and kinds, might be offered, and more humans. The Chiang peoples, a nomadic non-Shang group, were a frequent source of human sacrifices. This oracle bone asks about the number of human offerings to be made:

> Perform the *yu* ritual to Tsu Yi and sacrifice ten Chiang? Twenty Chiang? Thirty Chiang?
>
>   (Chang 1980: 228–9)

This bone inscription gives an idea of the numbers that could be involved:

> Shall we sacrifice one hundred Qiang people and one hundred sets of sheep and pigs to (High King) Tang, Great Ancestors Jan and Ding, and Grandfather Yu?
>
> (Eno 1996: 43)

Human sacrifices were despatched in different ways depending on the requirements of the ritual and those being honored, with the methods including beheading, burial alive, exposure, drowning or burning at the stake. Drowning was the favored method for offerings to the River God, and the oracle bones record sacrifices of three hundred captives at a single rite (Chang 1980: 194–5). Humans were also sacrificed when important buildings were being constructed, and for interment in tombs, to accompany the dead in the afterlife.

In the British Museum, some distance away from the case that holds the oracle bone, are displayed the bronze vessels and bells for which the Shang period is renowned. Bronze, an alloy of copper usually with tin, had a dramatic effect on the development of human society in antiquity, giving its name to a formative era in which the metal facilitated advances in technology and warfare leading, among other things, to the emergence of urbanism, more complex forms of social organization, and writing. While Bronze Age cultures of the ancient Near East or Western Asia have left behind a substantial legacy of bronze weapons and tools, in early China bronze was mainly

6.2 *Shang Dynasty ritual bronze vessels.* © *The Trustees of the British Museum. Museum number 1954.1019.1. Image Number AN308034*

used for magnificent food and drink receptacles employed in rituals and sacrifices. Unlike the oracle bones which are a recent discovery, these bronze vessels were highly valued and collected in antiquity by Chinese rulers and other members of the elite. Of distinctive form they are richly embellished with curvilinear decoration, including a stylized mask—often compared to a demon—called the *taotie*. The vessels sometimes carry inscriptions like those on the oracle bones, although these were not at first recognized as writing.

The distinctive bronze vessels came in sets of different kinds of vessels of which the *ding* (three-legged cauldron), the *gui* (open vessel with handles) and the *jue* (three-legged wine container) are the best-known individual pieces (see Nelson 2003). Roasted meats would be presented on stands, the different kinds of wine in *jue*, and substantial stews in the *ding*. The number of bronzes that survive in collections around the world attests to the importance of these objects in antiquity, but for a long time they were seen primarily as works of art, rather than as symbolic objects and as functional vessels central to China's never-ending feast. Their original use was dismissed as "ritual" without further attempts at elucidation, understandable enough in view of the lack of contextual material, and some went so far as to argue that the designs on these vessels were purely decorative, without any iconographic, symbolic meaning (Kesner 1991: 29), but this has changed with the discovery of the Dragon Bones and the new material that continues to be unearthed (see Rawson 1993). All give depth, dynamism and meaning to the text which Steele found so burdensome, and which—although respected for its antiquity—was long regarded as little more than an archaic curiosity when first translated into foreign languages at the end of the nineteenth century.

Feasting the Ancestors and Making Gods

After sacrifice came the feast, after the rituals came banquets, but there is a disconnect between the butchered bones in refuse heaps—indicating they were eaten—and the bronze vessels. As there are no narrative Shang descriptions of feasting or cookery as in the *Zhou-Li* and *I-Li*—Shang ideograms simply refer to "feast"—attention has focused on the bronzes, and on their ritual use. Initially, the right to possess these bronze vessels was in the gift of the king, and determined by social rank. The ruler was entitled to nine *ding* and eight *gui*. A duke might only have seven *ding* and six *gui*, a baron five *ding* and three *gui* and a nobleman three *ding* and two *gui* (Rawson 1999, 2007). Their possession went far beyond mere social prestige. Food cooked in other containers might nourish the physical body but it was the bronzes that, through some kind of sacred alchemy, consecrated the contents, transmuting them into viands suitable for offering to and consumption by the gods and ancestors, as is clear in this inscription on a bronze vessel:

Elder Grand Master Initiate (Bo Dashi Xiaozi) and Elder Sire Father (Bo Gung Fu) made a grain vessel selected from the metals of Hao and Lu. Its metal is "Grandly auspicious: Black and Yellow." Fill it with grain cakes, non-glutinous and glutinous rice, and millet. We use it to summon, feast and serve the Ruler King. [We will] use it to summon the Many Deceased Fathers and Many Older Brothers and use it to pray for endless long life and good fortune. May their sons' sons and grandsons' grandsons eternally treasure it and use it to present mortuary offerings.

(May Chengyuan vol. 4: 219 in Cook 2005: 17).

More than this, it appears that the offering of food and wine in bronze vessels was an essential part of a process by which ancestors were changed into spirits who might intercede with the gods on behalf of their descendants, and finally—over time and through continued sacrifices, rituals and offerings involving the bronze vessels—some ancestor spirits were transformed into gods themselves. The *taotie* has been interpreted as a figure in the process of transformation with the decoration adding power to the process (Allen 1993; and see Childs-Johnson 1995) although this is debated. The discovery of human heads in bronze vessels has raised the question of cannibalism, symbolic or actual, but this too is debated. Even the ruler did not address the great gods himself, but asked his ancestors to intercede for him. While the transformation process is not yet fully understood, it could only be accomplished through food and wine offered in bronze vessels. The number of vessels used determined the efficacy and value of the rites, so possession of the bronzes gave their owners sacred and secular power and influence. The greater the number of vessels used, the more powerful the ancestor spirits could become, and the more likely they would ultimately be changed into gods. Seen through an anthropological lens, use of the bronzes allowed the elite to replicate the earthly social order in heaven, transforming their ancestors into spirits and in some cases gods, who could then look after their descendants on earth, and also intercede on their behalf with the non-ancestor gods who stood at the top of the heavenly hierarchy. Placating the spirits and ancestors was seen as an ongoing process, making the bronzes the most valuable objects elite Shang could possess in life and in death, as indicated by their ubiquity in elite tombs, where their presence could also been seen as the first step in the occupants' becoming spirits and gods themselves. As noted above, the bronzes were also used in secular elite entertaining, the number of bronze vessels owned and used being a marker of prestige.

As for the contents of the vessels, the main staple was millet in several varieties, supplemented by wheat, barley, rice and hemp. There were vegetables, beans including soybeans, and fruits such as plum, chestnut, apricot, persimmon, jujube and peach (Sterckx 2011: 14–5). Great soups and stews were favored methods of preparation. Meats both wild and domesticated were eaten by the elite—wild duck and geese, pheasant, quail, rabbit, deer, ox, sheep, pig, chicken and dog. Fish were also consumed and the cooking methods included roasting, baking, boiling, frying, grilling and stewing, with preservation techniques including pickling, drying and salting. While there are no Shang recipes as such, it is clear that the close relationship of the secular and the sacred through food "was already established, and it is assumed that other patterns were also—the meanings and associations of certain foods—were already formed or in formation, emerging in 'the ritual world where table and altar meet'" (Sterckx 2011: 2) that would later develop into a cosmological cuisine.

The bronze vessels come in sets, and although it is not yet possible to discern exactly how the various pieces were used in combination in different rituals, sacrifices and feasts, one type is of particular interest—wine vessels. Wine was essential to both rituals and feasts. Neither was considered complete without it, and it was thought to be essential to pleasing the spirits. Even in early inscriptions, different colors and grades of drink can be discerned, and by the Zhou period several kinds are mentioned including "fine *jiu*" which was used for toasting at large feasts where there was music, singing and dancing; a red colored liquor or *jiu* called *ti*; a grain mash called *sheng*, and a *jiu* for "those below, who were seated on mats outside the central hall and altar" (Cook 2005: 18–19). The spirits were offered a clarified millet drink called *chi jiu*, apparently much enjoyed by them. As the *Shi Jing* (Ode 209 in von Falkenhausen 1993: 28) put it, in a passage that refers to the close of a ritual:

> There ceremonies are now completed,
> The bells and chimes have given their signal;
> The pious descendant goes to his place,
> The officiating invocator makes his announcement:
> "The spirits are all drunk."

It is also possible that the officiators at divinations and sacrifices drank heavily in order to induce an ecstatic state the better to commune with the spirits, and certainly wine was consumed heartily at secular feasts and banquets. Wine vessels are the kind of bronzes found in the greatest quantity in mid- and late Shang elite burials. The main types of bronze ceremonial vessels have been referred to above, of the forty-four different types in all that have been identified to date, twenty-four are wine vessels (Poo 1999: 127). In the tomb of Fu Hao, one of the wives of King Wu-Din—notable in that she was a military leader and priestess, and that her tomb was undisturbed when discovered in 1976, the first unlooted Shang royal tomb to be found—70 percent of the bronze vessels were wine containers (Poo 1999: 127). The large number of wine vessels, both in bronze and in pottery, indicates that drinking played a central part in Shang life, ultimately bringing the Shang Dynasty to an end according to later texts. Di Xin, the last Shang ruler, was supposed to have been addicted to drink, holding orgies, naked revels in the woods and drunken entertainments including one in which guests floated in small boats on a man-made lake of wine, dipping in when they wished to drink and, when they wanted to eat, reaching for roasted meat hung from branches suspended above them. The cautionary passage *Warning Against Drunkenness* in the Zhou *Su Shing* noted of Di Xin:

Greatly abandoned to extraordinary lewdness and dissipation, for pleasure's sake he sacrificed his majesty. The people were all sorely grieved and wounded in heart, but he gave himself wildly up to drink, not thinking of restraining himself but continuing his excess till his mind was frenzied ... though the extinction of the dynasty was imminent, this gave him no concern, and he wrought not that any sacrifices of fragrant virtue might ascend to Heaven. The rank odour of the people's resentments and the drunkenness of his herd of creatures went loudly up on high so that Heaven sent down ruin on Yin and showed no love for it—because of such excesses.

There was an element of propaganda in the foregoing passage, another example of using food and drink as a moral metaphor. In 1046 BC, Xi Din was overthrown by the Zhou, who justified their actions with reference to what became known as the Mandate of Heaven, which held that if a ruler had lost heavenly approval, it was right and just to replace him. The Zhou Dynasty (1046–256 BC), a warrior culture like the Shang, preserved many aspects of Shang culture—archaeological finds attest to the continuing use of bronze ritual vessels and of human sacrifice. Despite the warnings, drinking continued—the *Shi Jing* describes how, after "the ancestral sacrifice, in which every word and movement was minutely regulated, a feast took place in the temple, an occasion for the assembled male kinfolk to become roaring drunk" (Ode 209 in van Falkenhausen 1993: 29). But with time, the archaeological record attests to a cultural change. During the Western Zhou, the number of bronze wine vessels diminished, while food vessels became more numerous (Cook 2005: 22; and see Rawson 1999) and larger, with many capable of serving a great number of people. This shift, with feasts becoming more secular—or increasing the number of secular feasts and banquets—reflected a more elaborate political system in which it was increasingly necessary to "create and maintain social hierarchy and strengthen the social fabric" (Plutschow 1995), through employing more structured and elaborate rituals and expanding ceremonial consumption.

At the end of the Zhou, contending independent states emerged resulting in the turbulent Spring and Autumn and Warring States periods that ended in 221 BC when China was unified under the First Emperor Qin Shi Huang (260–210 BC), creator of the Terracotta Army. The new empire required administration, standardization, consolidation, new laws and their enforcement. A centralized bureaucracy was created that later developed into the Chinese civil service which, with modifications, administered the country until the last imperial dynasty was overthrown in AD 1912. Order and obedience were paramount under a harsh system called Legalism, in which any transgressions met with severe punishments, including burial alive or being tattooed on the face and sent to work on building the Great Wall. Many historical records and philosophical works that predated the formation of the empire were destroyed, either in the conflicts or by the command of the First Emperor who, according to the historian Sima Qian (in Nienhauser 1994: 147), did not wish his radical reforms and single authority to be obstructed by ancient laws and practices.

Nor did he wish to be challenged by the many new teachings called the Hundred Schools of Thought that had grown up during the wars, including what would later become Confucianism and Taoism.

During the long Han Dynasty (206 BC–AD 220) that followed the short-lived Qin Dynasty, many of the First Emperor's reforms were retained, but a less severe form of government was sought, and a figure from the past was reinvented for the present. The philosopher Confucius (c. 551–479 BC) was a personage around whom many later layers of mythologizing and interpretation have been wrapped (see Eno 2003). As with Karl Marx, much was done and said in his name that he never envisioned. On the level of the individual, Confucianism was a humanistic philosophy in which virtue, propriety and ethical behavior were achieved through the control and cultivation of the self, while familial relations were governed by filial piety—the loyalty, obedience and respect due to parents and elderly family members. Both ritual and etiquette were seen "to be based upon ethics and also to be a means of inculcating ethics, while such ethics were themselves validated as being elements in a total, morally good cosmic order" (Cohen 1991: 117). Ritual and etiquette—li— became an example of Elias's civilizing process (Elias 2000) in which manners are an instrument of state formation, forging a common culture and also serving as an instrument of power and social control for those groups who could best exploit it. During the Han period, the personal morality of Confucianism was transformed into State Confucianism, which replaced the Legalism of the Qin as the ideology of government. The principles of filial piety were applied to the relationship between the individual and the state, to which loyalty and obedience were now owed. Instead of social control enforced from outside as with Legalism, under State Confucianism control was seen as coming from within, driven by Confucian values. Raised from the individual to the collective level, State Confucianism imposed a degree of order so profound that, in its full ramifications, it transcended all things (see Ebrey 1991). Imperial China became a paradigm of Mary Douglas's (1970) model of high-grid, tightly controlled and controlling societies, in which roles, statuses and behavior are precisely defined, reinforced by rigid codes, systematized foodways and highly regimented ritualized behavior based on "Confucian principles." Or rather, on interpretations of what Confucius may have said or thought, for much of the literature attributed to Confucius was the work of his followers, and so gnomic that it required volumes of commentaries and re-interpretations down the centuries. Here is an example of a simple family meal, conducted according to the Confucian way:

> Sons, in serving their parents, on the first crowing of the cock, should all wash their hands and rinse their mouths, comb their hair, draw over it the covering of silk, fix this with the hair-pin, bind the hair at the roots with the fillet, brush the dust from that which is left free, and then put on their caps, leaving the ends of the strings hanging down ... [Sons'] wives should serve their parents-in-law as they served their own ... Thus dressed, they should go to their parents and parents-in-law. On getting to where

they are, with bated breath and gentle voice, they should ask if their clothes are [too] warm or [too] cold, whether they are ill or pained, or uncomfortable in any part; and if they be so, they should proceed reverently to stroke and scratch the place. They should in the same way, going before or following after, help and support their parents in quitting or entering [the apartment]. In bringing in the basin for them to wash, the younger will carry the stand and the elder the water; they will beg to be allowed to pour out the water, and when the washing is concluded, they will hand the towel. They will ask whether they want anything, and then respectfully bring it. All this they will do with an appearance of pleasure to make their parents feel at ease. They should bring gruel, thick or thin, spirits or must, soup with vegetables, beans, wheat, spinach, rice, millet, maize, and glutinous millet—whatever they wish, in fact; with dates, chestnuts, sugar and honey, to sweeten their dishes; with the ordinary or the large-leaved violets, leaves of elm-trees, fresh or dry, and the most soothing rice-water to lubricate them; and with fat and oil to enrich them. The parents will be sure to taste them, and when they have done so, the young people should withdraw.

(*Nei Zei*: 2–4 in Legge 1885)

Instead of abandoning the old ways as under the Qin, in the Han Dynasty "tradition" was used to support the new regime and ideology. Attempts were made to recreate the literature and records lost during the Qin, allegedly from memory and from fragments of Zhou works that no longer exist. The key works in this reconstituted canon, known as the *Four Books* and the *Five Classics*, were long regarded as authoritative accounts of the Zhou and Shang, with the *Li-Chi*, *Zhou-Li* and *I-Li* focusing particularly on ritual. It was once believed that Confucius himself had compiled these books. This is no longer believed—but whoever wrote them, do they give an accurate picture of feasting in antiquity?

Until now there have been two points of view—either that the accounts in the *Li-Chi*, *Zhou-Li* and *I-Li* are accurate, or that they are entirely invented – but from an anthropological perspective, the interesting thing is what has been left out. There are striking lacunae in the account of Zhou feasting given above drawn from these texts. Offerings are made—but to whom? Food is described in detail, but what precisely is the social context? What the new discoveries make clear is what has been carefully excised—the divination, the transforming sacrifices to the gods, societies in which the significant political units are lineages, not the state, and above all the bronze vessels. The books are also inconsistent in style and often contradictory, with many sections incomplete. These have been glossed over, or explained away as being parts of a larger corpus that has not survived, but instead they bespeak heavy-handed editing with a political agenda. Under Confucian influence, feasts were recast in a bureaucratic mode, and instead of the proper conduct of ritual as an essential part of worship of the gods, the performance of ritual became an end in itself, as a form of self-discipline and submission to the state. Instead of worshipping the deified ancestors of the elite, the people now paid filial respect to their own ancestors, giving them offerings in a practice that continues to this day. Hierarchy was emphasized, because in the Confucian scheme of things hierarchy—social order—was seen as consolidating, not divisive. The ritual system became secularized, an aesthetic and ethical practice—with secular rituals becoming the natural laws that held Chinese society together. In answer to Steele's question, this is why people followed them, for as the anthropologist Laura Nader (1997) would put it, ritual had become a controling process, with social control disguised as "the way things are done." Yet for all they removed, Confucianists retained the importance of feasting and the banquet, albeit as celebrations of the state and of the family. And nor did sacred eating entirely disappear. The ruler—now Emperor—remained the ritual head of the state, conducting rituals on its behalf, following the precedents set out in the reclaimed texts. In time, the Emperor, his clan and officials had to perform a hundred rituals that included offering sacrifices to Heaven and the ancestors—not deified—and giving banquets to officials and foreign envoys (McDermott 1999: 2). The Emperor also had to eat ritual meals—according to the "monthly ordinances" he "was to eat millet and mutton in spring, beans and fowl in summer, sorghum and dog in autumn and millet and pork in winter." This diet "symbolized the idea that, by partaking of all ingredients in his realm following a cyclical pattern, a ruler symbolically tasted the cosmos itself and thereby helped ensure the harmonious passage of time and season" (Sterckx 2011: 18).

While much has been excised, what the new discoveries indicate is that the accounts of feasting in the texts are not entirely invented. There are sufficient correspond-ences between the number of dishes presented at feasts in the texts and the number of bronze vessels known to have been used in Shang rituals, along with the ritual placements of offerings to glimpse the broad outlines of practices that should become clearer with the discoveries that are ongoing. For now, it is sufficient to see the shadowy feasts involving sacrifice, divination and transforming ancestors into gods that lurk behind the constrained proceedings portrayed in the *Five Classics*. In addition to the rites, there is the question of the food symbolism in the texts. There are oppositions—seasoned as opposed to non-seasoned dishes; preparations such as millet porridge with significance beyond their apparent simplicity; particular combi-nations and flavors—that suggest symbolic eating. Five is a magic number associated with many aspects of Chinese belief and practice, and it is central to the key concept of *wu wei*, the five flavors—pungent, sweet, sour, salty and bitter—which appear in the ritual texts. As the *Li-Chi* put it: The five sapors (flavors), which are combined in six different ways to form the twelve types of dishes, follow on immediately from each other and each in turn (according to the season) form the basis of the food one takes (in Lo and Barrett 2005: 398).

The five flavors and their associated foods "resonate in the model of the Five Phases, with a corresponding season and generate nutritional and health benefits accord-ingly" (Sterckx 2011: 18), as part of a "correlative cosmology"—a cosmology that establishes elaborate correspondences between nature, the individual human being and society" (Harper 1998: 9). In this scheme of things, the natural world was seen as comprised of Five Elements or Five Agents—earth, wood, fire, metal and water—each associated with a cardinal direction, a color, an emblematic beast, a flavor, a bodily organ and a season. All were conceived of in terms of flows, processes, attributes, qualities and consequences which had to be kept in dynamic harmony through continual effort, lest calamity follow—anything from personal ill health or other misfortune to catastrophic harvests, the end of a dynasty and the fall of the state.

> Fire: south, red, phoenix, bitter, summer, heart
> Water: north, black, tortoise, salty, winter, spleen or kidneys
> Wood: east, green, dragon, sour, spring, liver
> Metal: west, white, tiger, pungent, autumn, lungs
> Earth: centre, yellow, *quilin*, sweet, late summer, stomach.

Here can be seen a system in which health, nutrition and magic combine in the making of a cuisine. In its later forms a fundamental distinction was made between *fan* (grains and other starch) and *ts'ai* (vegetables, meat and fish). Food, like everything in the natural world, was deemed to have energy (*qi*) in a system which classified the *qi* of things as "*yin*" (cool/light/female) or "*yang*" (hot/heavy/male). Beef and garlic, for example, were *yang*, watermelon and green tea *yin*. Within these categories, some things were more *yin* or *yang* than others, and the *qi* could be further modified by the manner of cooking, such as deep frying, steaming or braising, as well as by the quality and provenance of the ingredients. The outlines of these symbolic and culinary systems can be discerned in banquets today, and in the 1950s banquet given above; a cosmological cuisine with ancient magic at its heart. It was once thought that the system originated in the Han period, but the new discoveries suggest much earlier origins, in the Zhou and Shang. The prospect of further details emerging in future is what makes studies of food and feasting in China so interesting.

Guided by these symbolic and nutritional principles, feasting and banquets continued to be central to social and political life in China. Diet and etiquette remained an organizing trope through the Yuan and Ming Dynasties (AD 1271–1368 and AD 1368–1644) by which time "if every rule was followed scrupulously, it would make eating virtually impossible" (Mote 1977: 225). The Qing Dynasty (AD 1644–1911) was not Chinese but Manchu or Mongol (see Chapter Five) so they had two parallel court cuisines: six grades of Manchu banquet with Mongol cuisine, and five grades of Han banquet, with Chinese food. These were distinguished by the number and kinds of dishes included, but the fine points of differentiation were lost on Westerners, who were in any case deeply suspicious of what they were offered. As always, the state banquet had the potential to be a diplomatic minefield in which

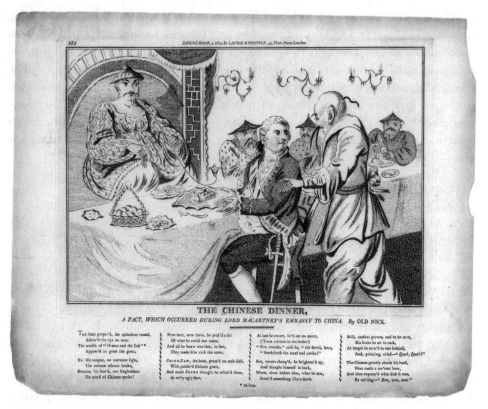

6.3 *"A Chinese Dinner." Lord Macartney is offered dog at a Chinese state banquet. By Old Nick, 1805. © The Trustees of the British Museum. Museum number 2000.0723.18. Image number AN 124692*

the clash of culinary cultures could have profound political consequences. This Lord Macartney discovered during his visit to China in 1792 when he was offered dog, which the Chinese considered a delicacy although he took it as an insult, an incident that was satirized in the British press.

Foreign attendees of grand banquets in the late nineteenth and early twentieth centuries were struck only by their length and the profusion of the dishes. "Forty or fifty courses followed one another," one correspondent to *The Times* of London reported, "til all the guests succumbed, though being assured that many more dishes were in readiness … the banquet rose and fell, as it were, like a gale of wind or a grand epic. The palate was alternately stimulated and recruited; the appetite was forced and left to repose; the dishes came in courses, reached a climax, and after a pause, gave way to a new act in the drama."

In the Qing Dynasty, as for millennia before, food, feasting and etiquette were the very embodiment of "the norms of meaning and value that the civilization lived by" (Mote 1977: 225). So deeply rooted were these old values that, when he became Chairman of the People's Republic of China in 1949, Mao Tze-Dong, in a manner reminiscent of the First Emperor, forbade large banquets and ancestor commemorations and swept aside the Confucian hierarchies in favor of total leveling democratization. But banqueting survived in the diaspora communities, and was resumed with enthusiasm in post-Mao mainland China, where the never-ending feast goes on.

CHAPTER SEVEN

Japan: Banqueting Beyond a Bridge of Dreams

There was food, six trays made of nettle-tree wood with mother-of-pearl inlay. The surface was embossed in places. The cloth too was intricately woven and inset with ivory. The food boxes, chopstick-rests, sake cups and bowls had all been prepared by the Imperial Table Office ... Fifty banquet settings [came] from the Bureau of Palace Storehouses, fifty meals from the Granary and twenty meals for retainers from the Kitchens of the women's quarters at the Palace. Officials from the Imperial Table Office came to the bottom of the steps, here women servants took the food and presented it ... Akimitsu and the other nobles held a banquet in the east wing; they sat in the southern gallery, facing north and ranked west to east.

> An account by a Heian courtier of a banquet at the Palace to celebrate an Imperial birth, written in AD 1008. (In Bowring 1996: 76)

Japan may have the oldest cuisine in the world. In the 1960s, radiocarbon dating established that the ancient hunter-gatherer Jomon culture of Japan had produced pottery some two thousand years before it was made elsewhere, disproving the old assumption that pottery was invented by settled farmers, and since the 1990s the working date for the earliest Jomon pottery has been pushed back to c. 16,500 years ago. Analysis of the residue on Jomon cooking pots along with remains unearthed by archaeologists has revealed a diet rich in nuts (acorns, walnuts and chestnuts), game (especially deer and wild boar), seeds and grains, fruits and a wide range of marine foods including shellfish, fish and seaweed. There are indications that the fish—including yellowtail, flounder, mackerel and shark—were dried, smoked or salt-cured on the coast and sent inland, and evidence that wine was made from fermented fruit. Although this basic diet remained remarkably stable for many centuries, it is not just the ingredients but the highly stylized mode of presentation that distinguishes Japanese cuisine and feasting, raising the question of how and why this visually striking way of eating developed.

"Japanese" Cuisine

Teriyaki steak, *sukiyaki,* pork *tonkatsu, chicken tori-age, tempura* and many other "traditional" Japanese dishes with which the world is now familiar date only from the latter part of the early modern period (AD 1600–1868) and most especially from the following Meiji era (AD 1868–1912) (Ashkenazi and Jacob 2000, Ishige 2001). Between AD 1639 and 1853, Japan closed itself to foreign influences and visitors. During this time and stretching back into antiquity, it is claimed that Japanese food was "austere" and "monotonous" (Cwiertka 2006: 95) even among the well-to-do, especially outside the urban centers. With the opening of Japan in 1854 at the insistence of the West, new foods, culinary techniques and dietary beliefs entered the country. These were introduced to—indeed imposed on—the population, presented as a duty to be undertaken in the service of Japan's reinvention and emergence as a modern nation state. The improvement of the national health was central to this project. Japanese officials were impressed by the physique and vitality of Westerners which they attributed to what the foreigners ate, so the adoption of a Western diet, or at least the incorporation of foreign elements into Japanese-style meals, was mandated. The most dramatic of the changes involved the consumption of meat, spearheaded by an announcement from the palace in 1872 that the Emperor Meiji was now regularly eating beef and mutton. For centuries the eating of most meats had been discouraged or forbidden for religious reasons.

A dish that entered the country at this time is the *katsu*. "*Katsu*" is the Japanese way of saying "cutlet," referring to thin pieces of pork or veal covered in breadcrumbs and fried, also known as *escalope* and *schnitzel,* that were regarded as the height of fine dining in the West in the nineteenth century when the Meiji reforms were being implemented. Frying in oil was not an indigenous Japanese culinary technique, breadcrumbs were previously unknown and the eating of meat was still shocking to many, but the Japanese took up the *katsu* with alacrity. Following the lead of the Japanese royal family, the elite had adopted foreign-style dining, eating their *katsu* while seated on chairs at a Western table set with crystal, china and silver cutlery, as part of a meal presented in courses in the European way. As Western food spread through the general population, the *katsu* became naturalized, served in the Japanese

7.1 Early Japanese encounters with Western food. Dutch men and women around a table at a banquet, Nagasaki School. The animal head on the table denotes what to the Japanese seemed a barbaric way of eating. © The Trustees of the British Museum. Museum number 1951.0714.0.33. Image number AN 512177

fashion on low tables with diners sitting on the floor. Instead of being presented whole to be cut with knife and fork, the Japan-ized *katsu* was served pre-sliced in pieces that could be eaten with chopsticks, artistically arranged on a plate accompanied by the standard Japanese meal elements of rice, soup, side dish and pickles, served all at the same time. The *katsu* was accompanied by a dipping sauce as is customary with Japanese meals although the sauce was not a traditional preparation of soy or vinegar but a mixture of two Western condiments then considered highly fashionable and exotic by the Japanese—tomato catsup and Worcestershire sauce.

Today the *katsu* is seen as "typically Japanese," and so it is in Cwiertka's terms as part of the "multicultural" national cuisine that helped to construct the modern nation state which emerged in the Meiji era, but that is not the whole story. The *katsu* may have entered Japan as a borrowed food, but it did not remain foreign. Instead, it was drawn into a system of aesthetics, practices and customs with roots deep in the Japanese past. These dictate what should be served with the *katsu*, how it should be cut, presented and garnished, on which occasions it was considered suitable fare, and the kinds and colors of dishes that should be used.

The Japanese have a word—*moritsuke*—for the seven ways food should be arranged, depending on the foods and the vessels (Hosking 1995: 98):

1. *sugimori,* strips and slices of food in a slanting pile; 2. *kanemori,* slices placed overlapping each other; 3. *tawaramori,* blocks or rounds placed horizontally in a pyramid; 4. *hiramori,* flat slices of sashimi arranged vertically or a representative selection arranged on a plate; 6. *yosemori,* two or three contrasting ingredients arranged next to each other; 7. *chirashimori,* like *yosemori* but with space between the ingredients.

There is another term, *takamori,* piling food high above the vessel, which "is nowadays restricted to service of the gods and the emperor" (Hosking 1995: 98), and there are additional rules. The plates and vessels much be chosen to suit the food; round pieces of food should be placed on square dishes and square pieces of food on round dishes, and the color and pattern of the dishes must suit the season (Hosking 1995: 211).

The process of appropriation inevitably involves modification by the adopting culture, but not to the extent seen in Japan where the rules of *moritsuke* and a highly stylized and ritualized way of eating persists, on both formal and informal occasions, applied to indigenous food and to adopted dishes like the *katsu.* Japan is usually studied in terms of its political history, its literature and its art, but rarely in terms of the anthropology of its food and feasting rituals, the persistence and distinctiveness of which demand investigation. Where and how did they originate, why do they persist and what do they tell us?

Samurai Feasting

A good place to start is the period that most people think of when "traditional Japan" is mentioned—the heyday of the *samurai.* From the Kamakura era (AD 1192–1333) onwards, Japan was ruled by a militaristic administration or "shogunate," under a military leader called the *shogun,* supported by provincial lords, *daimyo,* and by warriors called *samurai* or *bushi.* Together, they controled military and political power in the country, with the emperor playing a purely ceremonial role, a state of affairs that continued, with some interruptions and modifications, until the start of the Meiji era. The anthropologist and culinary historian Naomichi Ishige has singled out the late Muromachi period (AD 1337–1573) to the beginning of the Edo period (AD 1603–1868) as a key era of social and culinary change in Japan. Initially, the meals of the Kamakura-period warriors who seized power at the end of the Heian era were plain and simple, in contrast to the elaborate elite repasts of the regime they had recently removed from power. The first *shogun,* Minamoto no Yoritomo, punished *samurai* who affected the showy style of the former nobility, and his successors maintained a similar policy through the Kamakura era. But as the new warrior class solidified its economic and social base and feudal control was exerted on every level of society, the military elite began to imitate the cuisine and etiquette of the old aristocracy, while at the same time, new practices were introduced. In AD 815 tea from China had been brought to the Japanese royal court, where it was used as medicine, but not taken up more widely. Reintroduced in the early thirteenth century in the form of powdered leaves (*matcha*), tea became popular at all levels of society, giving rise to the tea ceremony, *chanoyu*, with associated snacks and a new style of formal meal, *kaiseki ryori*, in which all the ingredients were seasonal and fresh. Also developed at this time was a style of eating called *shojin ryori*, vegetarian cooking, created in the monasteries under the influence of Buddhism. Tofu, first recorded in AD 1183, was a staple of *shojin ryori* (Ishige 2001: 76). All of these made lasting contributions to the Japanese cuisine of today, but *honzen ryori* is generally considered the most influential. First "institutionalized as the banqueting fare of the upper-class samurai and the nobility," it then spread "among the general populace, and up through the first half of the twentieth century, *honzen ryori* was always served at formal dinner parties" (Ishige 2001: 98).

Honzen ryori is a style of formal banqueting that "appeared around the thirteenth century and reached its full form as the official banquet style during the Muromachi period" (Ishige 2001: 98). *In honzen ryori* dining, food was served on a number of small, low tables called *zen*. Individual trays or low tables had been used since ancient times; what made *honzen* banqueting notable was the degree of elaboration and formalization achieved. At official *honzen ryori* banquets in the mansions of the military elite, the guests—usually male—would be seated on the floor in positions dictated by their social rank. The host and guest of honor would face the rest of the diners, whose status was made evident by where they were seated in rows in relation to the host, the closer positions being the most coveted. Carefully prepared dishes of food were arranged on small tables which were then brought out to the guests. Order of service, the number of tables presented to each guest and the number and type of dishes on the tables varied according to the social status of the diner, materializing the social hierarchy and demonstrating the ability of the host to stage such a costly and elaborate event. Nothing was left to chance. There were rules that covered all aspects of presentation, preparation, consumption and dining etiquette, recorded in handwritten culinary manuscripts called *ryorisho* that have received new attention as a result of the development of food studies in Japan.

Most of the surviving handwritten *ryorisho* manuscripts date from the sixteenth century, but there are some from the fifteenth century which reference earlier works now lost. Created by and for the master chefs who were responsible for preparing grand banquets (Rath 2008: 44) and also consulted by those responsible for arranging and supervising these events, *ryorisho* provide a remarkable *emic* or inside view of *honzen ryori* banqueting. Tables were presented to guests in sets of three, five or seven. One *zen* served as the main table with the others arranged around it, and each *zen* would have a specified number of dishes on it. This meant that diners had to sit some distance from each other, in order to accommodate the tables. One standard presentation was a three table "5–4–3" meal in which the main table was set with five side dishes in addition to soup and rice, the second table had four side dishes in addition to soup and the last table three side dishes in addition to soup. No drinks were served, but each of the soups was different, as in this 5–4–3 meal described in the *Yamanouchi ryorisho*, compiled in AD 1497 (after Rath 2010: 62–5).

First Table: rice; soup of bamboo shoots; dried sea bream; octopus; pickles; cooked fish salad; *sushi* (fish in vinegar, not the *sushi* of today).

Second Table: heron soup; salted sea bream; sweetfish; salmon roe; sea bass simmered in vinegar.

Third Table: cold soup with separate rice; grilled sweetfish; dried fish; salted abalone.

There are records of seven-*zen* banquets which included service of eight soups and twenty-four side dishes for each person, although this would only have been for the leading guests. The kinds of dishes considered appropriate to various occasions were specified, but the dishes would not be identical every time. For example, a fish soup would be specified, but the chef could be given the latitude to choose the kind of fish to be used, thereby allowing him to demonstrate his expertise within an overall structure.

The 5–4–3 meal described above does not seem particularly appetizing by modern Japanese standards. Banquet meals consisted of four types of food, mainly served cold: *himono* (dried and salted food), *namamono* (fresh food), *kubotsuki* (fermented or vinegar-dressed food) and *kashi* (desserts) (Ishige 2001: 73). Because of the difficulties of transportation and storage, fresh food was limited. The basic cookery techniques, established since at least the ninth century, were grilling, simmering, boiling and steaming. Virtually no cooking was done with fat or oil, and seasoning was restrained, consisting mainly of salt, vinegar and an early form of soy sauce (Ishige 2001: 71–2). Much effort had to be expended on making the basic ingredients palatable—and the appeal of the final dishes was largely visual. In the *ryori*, the emphasis is on preparation and presentation, rather than on flavor.

The foundation of *honzen ryori* banqueting lay in the cutting of the food, which was elevated to a high art. The "cutting was often the most important part of making the dish" (Rath 2010: 58), and many *ryorishi* manuals devoted as much attention to cutting as to cookery, one giving forty-seven different ways of cutting carp. In the militaristic period, the parallels between the samurai and his sword and the elite chef and his kitchen knife (*hocho*) were emphasized, with the knife described as "a sword for the kitchen" (Ishige 2001: 206), and sometimes a demonstration of culinary knife work was part of the banquet spectacle, with the chef brought on to demonstrate his art, a practice that continues in Japanese restaurants today. However, knife work was not regarded as mere entertainment. As described in the manuals, the strokes and movements of the knife-wielding chef were as carefully choreographed as those of a sword-master. "Holding the knife in the right hand, lift it high upward to the right while raising your right knee and straightening your hips" (in Rath 2010: 44), began one instruction. Going beyond technological expertise, the text reveals that cutting was seen to have a spiritual dimension. As another manual put it: "This is the knife that invites the presence of the divine" (Rath 2010: 48).

Close examination of the texts reveals a similar approach to the proper use of the cutting board (Ishige 2001: 207). Merely a piece of wood to the untutored eye, for initiates and connoisseurs the cutting board was a culinary altar. The board was divided into five areas—the four corners and the center—each of which was associated with a color, a direction and an element which had to be kept in dynamic harmony. Items were to be cut and arranged on different areas of the cutting board in different sequences, depending on the food and the occasion, for spiritual reasons. "Protective astral bodies have descended into these places from heaven. One should not think this is untrue. The Five Agents protects all four. These five agents are wood, fire, earth, metal and water. There are further oral instructions about this" (Rath 2010: 49), as one *ryori* put it. Much information about culinary beliefs and practices was never committed to paper, but treated as secret knowledge for initiates only, passed on by word of mouth. For this reason, the *ryori* cannot tell the whole story, but the glimpses they offer are suggestive.

From the cutting board, the food was transferred to dishes, usually lacquer ware, earthenware and, from the thirteenth century, ceramics. The *ryori* dictated that the shape, material and decoration of the vessels had to correspond to the status of the guest, the occasion and the food served. Once selected, the vessels had to be placed in precise positions on the *zen*, and placement diagrams were often included. More than symmetry underlay these arrangements: like the chopping boards, the tables and the dishes were seen as invisible maps, redolent with symbolic meanings which are no longer fully understood. The color of the dishes and of the foods played a role, as did the shape of the food on the plates, with some foods and shapes being considered male and some female—an earlier version of *moritsuke*. As for the food itself, the elite foods were game, choice fish and seafood, and rice—although other grains were also eaten—with some foods particularly prized for their symbolic meanings and associations, the crane being associated with longevity. The most spectacular element of *honzen ryori* cuisine in the Muromachi period was dishes intended primarily for display and admiration, notably grand arrangements of what appeared to be living things such as crabs, lobsters or game birds, prepared with exquisite attention to detail, surrounded by things that suggested their natural habitats. A variation was foods made to look like something else—a fish decorated to look like a boat, or dried squid and abalone transmuted by culinary artistry into butterflies, flowers or other things thought to be auspicious (see Rath 2010: 79); the modern equivalents are still to be seen on contemporary Japanese banquet tables. Then as now, the correct form was for guests to make a great show of admiring these creations and not to eat them on the spot, although, after the banquet, pieces might be taken away.

It is now possible to imagine a Muromachi formal *honzen ryori* banquet, held in the shogun's palace or one of the splendid mansions of the warrior elite, who had by now abandoned the restrained ways of their predecessors. The "beauty in simplicity" or *wabi* that would become the foundation of the tea ceremony in a later period was the very opposite of late Muromachi banqueting at which the profusion of dishes bespoke luxury and ostentation. Yet beneath the splendid surface, tensions ran high. In this warrior society, formal banquets were political events, the arena in which decisions were made public, achievements announced and celebrated, and favor or disapproval displayed for all to see, keenly watched by rivals jostling for position. For all the seething emotions, the participants were required to sit virtually immobile. The banquet took hours, proceeding at a slow pace that was often interrupted for proclamations, announcements of promotions, the giving of awards and the bestowing of ceremonial gifts. For the shogun, hosting the *daimyos* was an opportunity to demonstrate shogunal wealth and authority; for the *daimyos*, hosting the *shogun* was a chance to show loyalty and respect by providing an appropriate feast presented in the correct manner. Any lapse in procedure or provisioning—intentional or not—would be interpreted as an insult to the guest. And then there were the strict rules of dining etiquette which had to be observed.

The correct way to eat was to alternate mouthfuls of rice with the contents of the side dishes; it was considered vulgar to just eat the non-rice dishes (Ishige 2001: 176), and it was thought rude to speak while eating. Diners at a formal banquet also had to observe the correct way to eat particular dishes; the proper use of chopsticks which had to be deployed in different ways depending on what was served; the degrees of appreciation and admiration that had to be expressed; the sequence in which the many dishes offered were to be eaten; and which dishes were not meant to be eaten, only admired. One had to present oneself at banquets dressed in the attire appropriate to one's rank and to the occasion, correct down to the tiniest detail. Procedures and ceremonies were so complicated that it was necessary to have professional specialists and advisers who could be hired—or bribed—to make sure newcomers to the *shogun's* court or the mansions of the *daimyos* conducted themselves in the correct manner. Knowing the proper way of doing things was essential in order to demonstrate one's background, status and suitability for advancement, while a *faux pas* could have disastrous consequences. The great Edo period samurai epic *The Forty-Seven Ronin* or *The Forty-Seven Loyal Samurai* turns on just such a sequence of events. Lord Asano, new to the *shogun's* court and given the responsibility for supervising a banquet, is supposed to receive instruction from Lord Kira, the *shogun's* master of ceremonies. Lord Asano fails to reward Kira to the latter's satisfaction. Offended, Kira gives Lord Asano incorrect advice on ceremonial procedure, causing him to disgrace himself. In the confrontation that followed, a humiliated Lord Asano assaulted Kira in the *shogun's* palace, an offence for which he was obliged to commit *seppuku*, ritual suicide. After biding their time, Lord Asano's loyal samurai retainers avenged their dead master by killing Lord Kira, and then committed *seppuku* themselves.

For all their luxury, late Muromachi *honzen ryori* banquets were an ordeal, relieved only by the drinking party that followed the formal meal. *Sake* or rice wine, which came in several grades, was the drink of the elite. After the rigid constraints of the banquet, the guests were finally allowed to behave in a relatively free and easy manner (Ishige 2001: 74) at an after-banquet *sake* drinking party that might go on for hours, often ending in drunkenness. Official events were often preceded by ceremonial drinking, in which host and guests drank three rounds of *sake*, the order of service again depending on status. A round involved each person drinking three small cups of *sake*, for a total of nine drinks. The guests might then proceed to a formal event such as a banquet or a ceremony, or the drinking could be continued, often with entertainment. In this case, snacks as specified in the *ryorishi*—often dried fish—were supplied. Drinking was at will, often to excess, and the atmosphere was full of the conviviality so missing in formal banquets. Attendance at the after-banquet drinking party was considered obligatory (Ishige 2001). After the isolation and separation of formal banqueting, *sake* drinking recreated community, literally. Then as now, etiquette demanded that people not pour their own *sake* (Ohnuki-Tierney 1995: 229). *Sake* was poured for you, then you returned the favor, and it was returned again, in an endless round of exchanged drinks.

The end of the Muromachi period saw a prolonged and devastating civil conflict between the *daimyos* known as the Onin War (AD 1467–77), followed by the emergence of the Tokugawa shogunate which ruled Japan during what became known as the Edo period (AD 1603–1868), until the Meiji Restoration. The Tokugawa regime imposed strict social controls at all levels of society, including the closing of the country to foreign influence for two centuries, and some of the strictest regulations were applied to food and banqueting. The excesses of late Muromachi feasting were eliminated. Game birds were now reserved for the aristocracy, and even among the elite, rank determined what could be eaten—dried sea cucumber and skewered abalone were now only for *daimyo,* not for lower samurai. Seven-tray presentations were done away with; the *shogun's* leading advisers were allowed three trays with ten side dishes, but *daimyo* were limited to two trays with two soups and seven side dishes, and middle rank *samurai* could only have two trays with two soups and five side dishes (Rath 2010, 2008). Generally, lavish banqueting was discouraged, and the amount of *sake* that could be served was now limited. Commoners were

7.2 Sake *cups with pictures of the Six Immortals of Poetry, a stack of three dishes, a jug, blossoms and poem. Ryuryukyo Shinsai, woodblock print, c. Bunka Era.* © *The Trustees of the British Museum. Museum number 1902.0202,0.374. Image Number AN 758688*

forbidden the use of lacquered *sake* cups and highly ornamented food boxes while the peasants, for whom banqueting of any kind was not an option, had their staples restricted to brown rice and grains like barley and millet instead of white rice.

At the same time, the development of printing made books available to an ever-wider audience, and the old handwritten *ryorisho* manuscripts gave way to a new genre of printed books, *ryoribon*, which described the banquets of past times in detail. Although most of the population would not have attended grand banquets even if they still existed, were not now legally entitled to eat the foods described and, in most cases, could not have afforded them even if entitled, and above all did not mix with their social superiors, these books became extremely popular. The mysteries of elite etiquette for entertaining, the intricacies of fish-cutting and formal food presentation, the correct conduct of ceremonial *sake* drinking and much more were revealed to a wider audience for the first time. In an era of imposed restraints on consumption, "fantasy," "vicarious pleasure" and even "voyeurism" (Higashiyotsuyanagi in Rath 2010: 118) have been suggested, but there is a more convincing anthropological explanation which turns on Elias's (2000) civilizing process. As in Victorian England—like the Tokugawa era, a period of profound social change which saw the emergence of a new middle class—these books acted as a conduit of dreams and aspirations. In the climate of the times, to know how things should be done—even if the opportunity to put knowledge into practice never or rarely arose—was regarded as a worthy accomplishment in itself (O'Connor 2013), a source of social stability through conformity. Self-improvement was part of the civilizing process, and knowledge of elite banquets was a form of education with one or two elements like ceremonial toasting filtering down to the common people for use on special occasions such as weddings (Rath 2011: 114). However, since the ingredients of elite cookery and banquets themselves were closed to the lay readership, and as the advanced technical details of cutting and cooking were of practical use only to the relatively few professional *hochonin* or master cooks, and later to Edo-period restaurant chefs, the emphasis in the books shifted.

Instead of being applied guides, the *ryoribon* gradually became distanced from cookery and preparation, evolving into manuals of style, with practicality giving way to aesthetics. Food was discussed and debated in the abstract—the relative merits of different combinations, the interplay of color and texture, the amusements of juxtapositions, the word play in the names given to some foods, the philosophical meanings of specific dishes or even of whole imagined menus. The discussion of food became a cultural discourse, an activity in which the bourgeoisie could indulge freely and which the samurai and higher elite also took up, a hobby for some and serious dialogue for others. With time, the symbolic meaning and sacred associations explicit in the early *ryorisho* were translated into a canon of appearances and aesthetics. Things were considered good and beautiful because they were done in a particular way, and the mystic element of ceremonial banqueting glimpsed in the Muromachi era retreated. Rarely, if ever, has there been such a clear example of how a culinary aesthetic develops.

Most studies of Japanese food and feasting focus on the Edo period and later, with the Muromachi representing a distant past that requires no further understanding, but this is only part of the story. The persistence of formal feasting can be seen in

7.3 *New Year dinner service, c. 1949. Japanese Cookbook, Japan Travel Bureau, Tokyo, p. 131*

the following description of the proper way to serve a New Year celebration dinner in Japan, published by the Japan Travel Bureau in 1949 (see Fig 7.3).

Three trays are used, and correct placement of the dishes on the tray and the food on the dishes is clearly as important as the food itself (Kagawa 1949: 130):

Tray 1
Plate (1)
A) Broiled lobsters in their shells
B) Small turnips of chrysanthemum shape
C) Sweet boiled chestnuts

Small Bowl (2)
Sweet boiled black soy bean

Covered Bowl (3)
Zoni (rice cake soup)

Tray 2
Toso sweet *sake* mixed with some Medicinal Herb powder (4)

Tray 3
Plate (5)
Crane in its nest (A boiled egg on cuttlefish cut into strips and dried)
Young grass *kinton* (sweetened white kidney bean mixed with powdered green tea)
Broiled *wakasagi* (small fish) on skewers

Plate (6)
Nuku-zushi—vinegared boiled rice mixed with many-colored ingredients

Bowl (7)
Soup

In Japan, the New Year has always been the great festival of celebration, in which food plays an important role, both as part of the hospitality offered to renew family and friendship bonds for the coming year, and because partaking of certain foods at this time is symbolic, bringing luck, fortune, health and wealth in the next annual cycle. Here the past in the present can be detected in the presentation of three separate table trays, and although the number of dishes is much reduced from 5–4–3, they all have a symbolic significance glimpsed in the original *ryorisho*—the crane, represented by egg and cuttlefish, the rice with multicolored ingredients, and *toso-sake*, of which the text notes: "this is *sake* mixed with a small quantity of four kinds of medical herb powder. This has been used since the Heian period (AD 794–1186) in the New Year Season as a means of avoiding evil and prolonging life" (Kagawa 1949: 134). In food studies, there has been too much of tendency to take aestheticism as a given, to accept the concept of "eating with the eyes" without asking how and why this came about. To truly understand the persistence of this culinary symbolism and stylized way of eating—the foundations that lie beneath mere "aestheticism"—one has to find out about the original rules recorded in the handwritten *ryorisho*. Where did they come from, and why did they exist? And for this, it is necessary to cross a bridge of dreams.

Across A Bridge of Dreams

As I Crossed A Bridge of Dreams is the title of a work, also known as the *Sarashina Diary*, written by a lady of the royal court in Heian period (AD 794–1185) Japan. It is part of a remarkable body of literature, the best known of which is *The Tale of Genji* (Waley 1965) by Murasaki Shikibu, often called the world's first novel, which gives insight into aristocratic life in Japan in the ninth century AD, when the imperial court, and not that of the shogun, was still the center of power in the country. A better term for *The Tale of Genji* and others of its genre, called *"monogatari,"* is "ethnographic novel," as they are lightly fictionalized narratives based on historical events and close observation of a seemingly dreamlike society very different to the militaristic Muromachi era which followed it. Set in a place known as the City of Crystal Springs and Purple Hills, now Kyoto, the *monogatari* depict an enclosed imperial world in which life seems to be an endless procession of ceremonies, amusements and celebrations dictated by an elaborate ritual calendar and rules of procedure. Princes and princesses, lords and ladies move between palaces and mansions as though they were pieces on a chessboard, according to protocol that is never fully explicit but which everyone seems to know and obey, and in which supernatural elements, ghosts and spirits play important roles. As in an enchanted fairy tale, refreshments and banquets appear and disappear seemingly by magic, prepared by unseen hands, and goods and tribute flow in to the capital from unknown hinterlands, enriching the city. The capital was the symbolic center of the nation, the palace complex was the symbolic center of the city, within the palace complex were the country's administrative and ceremonial offices, and at the heart of it all dwelt the Emperor (W. McCulloch 1999a). The Emperor's residential compound, a palace within a palace, consisted of many low buildings with deep eaves and wide verandas, overlooking exquisite gardens and connected by walkways and galleries. Clustered around the Emperor's private apartments were those of his Empress and consorts, about six in number, who had their own separate establishments. The aristocrats spent much of their time at court, and their mansions were located near to the palace complex (H. McCulloch 1999). It was in this imperial enclave that *monogatari* were written by court ladies. When these *monogatari* first reached the West in translation, it was easy to think of them as little more than romantic tales, but subsequent study of the diaries kept by leading male officials, and other records of the period, have substantiated their portrayal of the otherworldly Heian court in which banqueting played a central though elusive role.

The Heian Context

The Chinese *Wei Zhi* chronicle of AD 239 recorded the visit of envoys from a queen, Himiko (see Kidder 2007), who was both shaman and ruler of one of the many small tribal states that then flourished in Japan, where society was stratified into a governing class, general citizenry and slaves. The *Wei Zhi* also includes the earliest written account of dietary culture in Japan, noting: "there are people who are specialized in diving into the water for fish and shellfish;" "rice and millet are cultivated;" "as the climate is warm, raw vegetables are eaten in both summer and winter;" "they have ginger, citrus fruits, *sansho* pepper and *myoga* ginger but do not know how to use them in cooking;" "at meals they eat with their fingers from a small dish with attached base;" and "they are fond of drinking wine" (Ishige 2001: 26). After intertribal warfare and a period of unification, a single state emerged under a ruler from whom the present imperial line of Japan descends. As early as the second century AD there were embassies from Japan to China and by the fifth century these had become systematic and lengthy missions charged with bringing material goods and knowledge of Chinese culture back to Japan. There was also inward migration from China and Korea during unsettled times on the continent. The Chinese contribution to nascent Japanese society has been called "incalculable" (Borgen 1982: 1), although the Japanese position has always been that it was not a wholesale importation or imposition of Chinese culture, but rather a selective picking and choosing in which the Japanese were always in control. Among the things that came to Japan during the Nara era and earlier were Chinese writing and literature, elements of Taoist belief and practice, Confucian values and forms of bureaucratic organization, Legalistic law codes, Buddhism, luxury goods, chopsticks and new food plants including the mandarin orange. The Nara period (AD 710–794) and the Heian that followed it are considered the beginning of the historic era in Japan, the first for which dependable written records are available. Then, in AD 894, these missions were discontinued. Diplomatic contact between China and Japan ceased until it was resumed by the Muromachi Shogunate five centuries later and Japan embarked on a period of developing "Japanese-ness," which gave rise to the distinctive culture and feasting of the Heian period.

Initially, Japanese society was organized on the Chinese model of a pyramidal centralized state. At the apex was the emperor, who held the dual role of secular and sacred leader. Beneath him were the imperial family and the aristocracy, supported by a meritocratic administrative bureaucracy. During the Heian period, political power passed into the hands of the aristocratic Fujiwara clan who controlled the government by acting as chancellor or regent for the emperor, thus ruling indirectly. Under the Fujiwaras, the emperor was obliged to play a symbolic role, although all acts of state continued to be done in his name. Domination of the emperor was made easier by the Fujiwara practice of marrying their daughters to the ruler and members of his close family, with leading Fujiwaras becoming the father-in-law and eventually grandfather or other relative of the sovereign. The Fujiwaras also encouraged emperors to retire early, preferably to be succeeded by child emperors with Fujiwara mothers who they could more easily control through acting as regent during their minority. And above all, the Fujiwaras supported the importance and performance of the rituals and ceremonies of which formal banqueting was a central part.

Heian life was not regulated by secular codes so much as by rituals that had the force of law. After progressing beyond the mere imitation of Chinese modes, a distinctive Japanese institution emerged for which there was no Chinese equivalent (Hérail 2006: 33). This was the *Jingi-kan*, the Office of the Gods, responsible for the sacred administration of the country. It was one of the two great departments of government, the other being the *Daigo-kan*, the Office of State, which oversaw the secular administration of the country. As the power of the Fujiwaras increased, the importance and visibility of the *Daigo-kan* decreased while that of the *Jingi-kan* rose, several factors contributing to this overshadowing of the secular by the sacred. First, it was important that the *Daigo-kan* not serve as a political center from which Fujiwara power could be challenged. This was partly accomplished by removing the meritocratic element of office-holding in the *Daigo-kan*, and partly by promoting the importance of sacred ritual as a means of social and political control. From the beginning of the clan's rise, Fujiwaras had been instrumental in codifying and implementing ritual procedures observed at court and many became experts in precedence and protocol, enabling them to dominate and direct proceedings. In the Heian capital, "ceremony and ritual were primary concerns of government and private citizens alike. During the period of the Fujiwara regency ... ceremony and ritual were conceived to be at the very center of life and government, more time and wealth being expended on them than on perhaps any other single category of public or social activity at court and among the nobility" (W. McCulloch 1999b: 123). Second, it was vital for both the Fujiwaras and the imperial family that the importance of the throne be constantly and visibly reinforced (Bock 1970: 17), but in a way that did not threaten Fujiwara hegemony. Instead of playing a political role, the emperor, who was considered a living link between heaven and earth due to his descent from Amaterasu no Okami the Sun Goddess, "presided over the chief court rituals and ceremonies which were widely considered the most significant contribution a ruler could make to his own and the general welfare, lying as they did at the very foundation of a healthy state" (W. McCulloch 1999b: 123). Third, it was necessary to use ritual to regularize the nation's tangled background of religious beliefs, a potential source of socio-political instability.

Religious belief in Japan during the Heian period was complex, contested and syncretic. The shamanism referred to in early Chinese accounts of Japan was an animistic worship of *kami*—numerous indigenous nature spirits, elemental forces, local deities and the gods and goddesses of sun, moon and storm, ranked in hierarchical order. A figure of 3,132 (Bock 1970: 59) *kami* has been given, but they were countless. Out of this grew what became the state cult, called *Shinto* today, the veneration of a particular set of indigenous deities connected to the imperial family, who claimed divine descent from them. Interwoven with these were imported beliefs including a version of the two-principle (*yin yang*) and five-element system brought from China—the dynamic interplay of cosmic forces that had to be kept in constant harmony and balance, known as *Ommyodo* in Japan (Tubielewicz 1980). To these

7.4 Ebisu, one of Japan's many indigenous deities or kami, *feasting on fish. Painting, ink on paper, school of Katsushika Hokusai. © The Trustees of the British Museum. Museum number 1913.0501.0.325. Image number AN758688*

were added Buddhist elements from the mystic *Tendai* and *Shingon* sects then in fashion among the aristocracy, which posed a threat to the authority of the *kami* and the state cult. The importance of ritual generally was intensified by Confucianism which, while not a religion itself, held that ritual and its proper observation was a moral duty and cardinal virtue. These elements came together in a convoluted web of beliefs and practices that included geomancy, astrology, divination, prediction, malevolent spirits and hauntings, the belief in unlucky directions (Frank 1998) and unlucky days, and the interpretation of dreams and omens. A special office called the *Ommyodo* Bureau drew up a calendar of ceremonies for the year which, while acknowledging the introduced elements, promoted and strengthened traditional *kami* worship, the basis of the imperial state. The annual calendar—an endless procession of festivals, offerings and ceremonies meant to ensure the well-being of the nation and the fertility of the land—was followed scrupulously by the court led by the emperor, according to detailed manuals of procedure such as the *Engi-shiki* and others which have not come down to us (Philippi 1959: 1), which set out exactly how ceremonies were to be conducted, including where to stand at different stages of the rite, what to wear and when to perform ritual claps. Every ceremony was accompanied by food offerings and the vessels in which they were to be cooked and presented to the gods, provided by the *Jingi-kan* and listed in minute detail in the *Engi-shiki* of which the following is representative. If the ceremonies were taking place outside the palace, the food was usually presented in raw form, along with cooking pots and implements for preparing the food for offering, sent by the *Jingi-kan*.

> ... 5 *to* of white rice, 2 *to* of glutinous rice, 1 *to* each of soybeans and red beans, 2 *to* of sake, 4 *soku* of rice-in-ear, 2 *kin* each of abalone, bonito and assorted dried meat, 5 salmon, 2 *to* assorted *sushi* (fish in vinegar), 2 *kin* of *wakame*, 2 *kin* assorted seaweeds, 2 *to* of salt, money for purchase of fruit (amount according to season), 2 white-wood boxes, 4 cypress-wood boxes, one high table, 2 earthenware jugs, 4 cooking pots, 20 uncovered dishes, 4 gourds ... .
>
> (Bock 1970: 64–5)

Presentation was accompanied by the recitation of *norito*, ritual verses, in a special sonorous sing-song style, the original purpose of which "was to perform magic by way of words" (Philippi 1959: 2) through hypnotic cadence, repetition and the ritual formulae themselves. Addressed to the *kami*, *norito* begin respectfully—*hear me, all of you Sovereign Deities; I humbly speak before you*—before going on to ask for blessings in an elliptical and allegorical manner. There are *norito* for different shrines and ceremonies, but food offerings and food imagery are involved in all, as is this passage that recurs in a number of the surviving rituals:

> The first fruits of the tribute presented by the lands of the four quarters have been lined up:
> The wine, raising high the soaring necks
> Of the countless wine vessels filled to the brim;
> The fruits of the mountain fields
> The sweet herbs and the bitter herbs
> As well as the fruits of the blue ocean
> The wide-finned and the narrow-finned fishes
> The sea-weeds of the deep and the sea-weeds of the shore,
> All these various offerings do I place, raising them high
> Like a mountain range, and present.
>
> (Philippi 1959: 32)

Here can be seen the origins of the *takamori* style of food presentation—the high piles represent the sacred mountains where the *kami* were believed to live. Like their worshipers, the *kami* were ranked hierarchically. All were honored, but those of superior rank received offerings placed on top of offering tables, while lesser *kami* had their offerings placed below the tables, upon mats (Bock 1970: 60 n. 149). The meticulous performance of ceremonies and rites great and small was believed to keep chaos and misfortune at bay and to ensure the fertility of the land and people, with offerings a form of sacred food technology, intended to please the gods. "So far as the cosmic harmony was preserved by correct ritual behavior or at least was not disturbed by errors of conduct, then the duty of the sovereign and his great ministers was fulfilled" (Sansom 1958: 167). Although the Fujiwaras exploited the system to their advantage, as their diaries show they were also subject to its rules and beliefs.

The strange clock-like movements of people in the *monogatari*, operating according to unseen rules, is partly explained by this ritual schedule, and partly by the complex social hierarchy that further dictated behavior. Court ranks, set out in the Yoro Code of AD 757 were so central to elite Japanese culture that they remained in place until the Meiji era. There were nine court ranks divided into senior and junior, with senior first rank at the top, and junior ninth rank at the bottom, and each of the lower six ranks were further subdivided into upper and lower. "Court ranks entitled the holder to present himself at the Imperial Palace, to occupy a specific seat at public and private functions, and to participate in ceremonies and other official events" (McCulloch and McCulloch 1980 II: 790). Family connections usually determined which rank a man was given when he began at court at the age of about twenty. Thereafter his progress up the court hierarchy depended on family influence, the favor of patrons and his own abilities. Providing valuable service to the throne also led to elevation in court rank—in AD 725, two minor functionaries were awarded Fifth Rank for having introduced the mandarin orange to Japan (von Verschuer 2003: 222). Ladies-in-waiting and imperial consorts and concubines also held court rank, with awards and advancement conferred by the emperor. Alongside these court ranks there were official ranks associated with office (Sansom 1958: 170–1). In addition, "There was a separate system of four un-subdivided ranks for formally designated Imperial Princes and Imperial Princesses. Other Princes and Princesses received ranks ranging from First to Fifth" (McCulloch and McCulloch 1980 II: 790 n. 2). Within the imperial and aristocratic families, there were internal hierarchies based on seniority between lineages, on the differences arising from polygamy and on birth order within nuclear lines, resulting in minute gradations of status. Social distinctions were mirrored in etiquette and in material culture, ranks and sub-ranks being entitled to wear different clothing in particular colors and fabrics, to ride in specified palanquins, to be served before or after others, to carry certain sorts of fans, to receive prescribed gifts at official presentations and much more. Because food varied according to rank, every meal and mouthful reinforced the social order.

Maintaining these distinctions was an important part of maintaining social and cosmic order and the display of hierarchy began at birth. The *Okagami monogatari* tells of an aristocratic infant who, having lost his mother in childbirth, was raised by his aunt, the Empress Anshi, like one of her own children—except that the orphan's meal table was one inch shorter than those of his imperial cousins (H. McCulloch 1980: 160).

Fujiwara power rested on politics not arms. There were no *samurai* and, as this was a time of peace, culture rather than military prowess became the arena in which courtiers sought to distinguish themselves. Poetry, the arts, specialized knowledge, sartorial style and material display flourished, turning the period into a golden age of taste and refinement. This was true of women as well as men. At court, the Fujiwara consorts kept bevies of well-born ladies-in-waiting chosen for their elegance and learning, making their households into literary salons for their amusement and that of the emperor and courtiers, and leading aristocrats also held artistic entertainments in their mansions. It was in this glittering, competitive and anxious setting that ethnographic narratives like *The Tale of Genji* and *As I Crossed a Bridge of Dreams* were written by court ladies, and Heian banquets were held.

Invisible Food and Elusive Banquets

It is a common assumption among culinary historians and anthropologists of food that if more early histories and ethnographies were written by women instead of by men, there would be more detailed accounts of food, but this is disproved by the Heian case. Of course, aristocratic Heian women did not cook, so there would be no culinary details such as those found in later *ryori* manuals. Yet in terms of material culture, the detail in Heian *monogatari* written by women is unsurpassed. Every sense is appealed to. The seductive scents of incense, the sheen on lacquer work, the rustle of the silken robes worn by men and women, the beauty of hand-painted fans are all described—but food is absent from the scene. In her *Diary*, Murasaki Shikibu, author of *The Tale of Genji*, writes of a grand event: "Everything was of silver—the food boxes, the plates and the *sake* cups" (Bowring 1996: 88), but does not mention the food itself. In *The Tale of Genji*, in a chapter called "The Flower Feast," the emperor gives a banquet under a great cherry-tree in the southern court of the palace. There was a poetry competition, then music and dance performances, the beauty of which brought tears of admiration to the eyes of the guests. Prizes were awarded—and then the banquet was over, without food and drink being mentioned (Waley 1965). Readers of *monogatari* are told that banquets are held, but the proceedings and food are not described. While the *sake* parties that follow the formal banquets are mentioned—a practice that the *monogatari* show was well established by the Heian period—it is only the entertainments, the witty things said, the flirtations and the loveliness of the cups and vessels that are commented upon.

This is also the case in the description of the banquet to mark an Imperial birth with which this chapter began. There is no Heian poetry that celebrates the delights of food, such as was being written in contemporary Song Dynasty China.

Only once is the curtain lifted on private entertainments in the palace—the episode of the imperial cat banquet. Cats were first brought to Japan from China in the reign of the Emperor Ichijo (reigned AD 986–1011). At first cats were rare and expensive, pets for the elite alone, and the Emperor and the Empress Teishi became very fond of them. In the year 999, one of the Emperor's cats gave birth, an event attended by leading ministers, who were required to be present at the birth of royal children. The Emperor's favorite kitten was given court rank as a Lady of the Fourth Rank with her own lady-in-waiting, and a banquet was held to celebrate the birth at which special rice cakes were ceremonially presented to the infant cat (Morris 1967:

7.5 *Small, portable food tray-table made of lacquered wood, an essential of formal Japanese banqueting for over a thousand years.* © *The Trustees of the British Museum. Museum number As1972.Q.1427. Image number AN694870001*

272–3; Hérail 1987 I: 240), as they would to any royal newborn. Here merriment can be detected but generally the attitude to eating was humorless. Food was thought "vulgar" (Morris 1979: 159), and for both men and women, if one had to eat in public, the thing to do was to pick daintily, not consume heartily. One diarist, Sei Shonagaon, author of *The Pillow Book*, went so far as to write, "I cannot bear men to eat when they come to visit ladies-in-waiting at the palace" (Morris 1967: 254).

Yet although food is culturally invisible in the *monogatari*, administrative records show that food was flowing into the capital, and through the palace kitchens. At the palace, food for the courtiers, administrators, people in the ministries and all those working in the complex was prepared by the Office of the Palace Table using tribute food conveyed from the provinces. The Office also sent food and supplies out to shrines, temples, mansions and other sites when official rites and celebrations required. Among the foods made here were salted and pickled meats, vegetables in vinegar, sauces made of fermented beans and bean soups like *miso*, and the ingredients consisted primarily of fish, shellfish, seaweed, beans, vegetables and fruits. There were specialists in condiments and a hundred and sixty cooks working in rotation, supported by assistants. The Office had to turn out everything from snacks to full banquets, and portions and the foods to be served were carefully itemized and differentiated according to court rank (Hérail 2006: 346). It was also responsible for all the plates, bowls and dishes, different according to rank and occasion.

The Office of the Imperial Table was responsible for the food prepared for the emperor, and also for the royal serving vessels, draperies and napkins. Here, chefs worked in rotation, preparing food not only for the royal table but also food that was offered to the gods. Because of this, the purity of the kitchens, the utensils, the persons of the cooks and the provisions was paramount. There were periodic purifications of the royal cooking fires and a special god who presided over the imperial kitchens. If ever the royal household had to relocate due to a house fire or for ritual reasons, the kitchen god was taken to the new residence in ceremonial procession, with a large escort of attendants (Hérail 2006: 372). Provisions for the emperor came from areas in the countryside set aside to produce food specifically for the imperial table, and from chosen suppliers who sent in different kinds of fish, fowl, nuts and regional specialities such as nashi pears and figs. Provisions were also grown in the imperial gardens, where gardeners looked after pear, peach, mandarin, persimmon, plum and red date trees (von Verschuer 2003: 28), medlars and sweet chestnuts. Blackberries, barley, soy, azuki beans, cowpeas, turnip, several kinds of chives, ginger, melon, eggplant/aubergine, radish, lettuce, cruciferous vegetables, taro and other things were also cultivated there. Finally, there was the Office of *Sake*, responsible for brewing the drink that figured in all ceremonies, banquets and collations, in many qualities and flavors, from dry to sweet (Hosking 1995: 215). There was *sake* with herbs steeped in it, *sake* flavored with flower petals, and a special black *sake* colored with ash for use in rituals, and the Office of *Sake* was considered so important that it had four gods enshrined in it, who were honored with their own festival twice annually (Bock 1970: 70). There was also an Office of Water which furnished the palace and the court with pure water for drinking and cooking, and also with ice. The Office of Water had its own protective *kami*. One of the duties of the Office of Water was the preparation of a dish of several boiled grains—described as "prophylactic"—which had to be consumed by the emperor and court on the fifteenth day of the first month (Hérail 2006: 376). The *Engi-shiki* is precise about how much acreage and how much fertilizer was necessary for every crop in the palace gardens (von Verschuer 2003); supply records show exactly what was coming in from the different provinces and administrative accounts throw light on other details, including storage—special rooms had to be set aside for the storage of the many portable tables required for banquets. But details of the banquets remain elusive, partly because Heian culinary texts similar to the Muromachi *ryorisho* have not come to light—although it is reasonable to assume that these later texts are based on Heian practice—and partly because in the Heian period as in the Muromachi and later, ritual procedures were often not committed to paper, remaining secret knowledge that was transmitted orally. In terms of the visual appearance of banquets, the best sources are visual—rare surviving scroll paintings (Hosking 2001)—but they beg the question of what was going on from the participants' point of view.

A Heian source that has only relatively recently begun to be studied is the diaries kept by high ranking male courtiers (Yienprugksawan 1994). Not intended as literary works for circulation like the *monogatari*, they are private records of events in their authors' professional lives. These diaries also show a disregard for food, except in the context of ceremony, etiquette and presentation, with which they appear to be obsessed. A paradigm example is the diary kept between AD 998 and 1021 by Fujiwara no Michinaga (AD 966–1028), the greatest of the Fujiwara regents (Hérail 1987, 1988, 1991). In his prime, Michinaga bestrode the court like a colossus. Three of his daughters became empresses, two of his sons regents, and two of his grandsons emperors, and he was father-in-law to a retired emperor and a crown prince, so his diaries give a unique *emic* account of life at the center of power at the Heian court, and here finally banquets can be glimpsed.

Michinaga's diaries describe rounds of meetings on court business that alternate with artistic events such as poetry competitions and musical performances. Entries show that there were rituals and ceremonies of different kinds nearly every day and night, although these are so well known and taken for granted that Michinaga usually does not describe them, unless he has arranged or sponsored them, and they do him credit in some way. The mention of banquets is also usually perfunctory, along the lines of "Banquet to inaugurate the new residence, the Emperor attended" (Hérail 1991: 225, my translation) or "The Dowager Empress offered a banquet on the ninth night. The protocol observed followed the precedent set by similar banquets [customarily held on the ninth night after a birth]" (Hérail 1991: 12, my translation). In the following passages, Michinaga gives rare detail. The first occasion was a highly select banquet for grandees of the court, given by Michinaga as head of the house of Fujiwara:

> 5 March 1008. I organize a grand banquet ... The guests begin to arrive around four o'clock ... and take their places in the customary order [according to rank] ... With the second service of *sake*, small cakes of pounded rice were served. With the third service of *sake*, I have rice and soup brought out. During this time, the falconer passed among the guests, displaying his birds. At the fourth service, wild vegetables still on their branches are served. At the fifth service, there were meats stuffed with forcemeat. At the sixth service, I myself presented the cup of s*ake* to the guests seated in the inner place of honour. The cup then circulated to the rear, finally arriving where the junior courtiers sat. I gave the order for gratuities to be presented to the scribes, secretaries and minor officials. During this time, the *sake* cups continued to circulate. I invited the guests of honour to put themselves at their ease. Dried fish and *sake* were served. After the musicians were summoned, many rounds of *sake* were offered. Then began the distribution of presents to the guests, beginning with those of lesser rank ...
>
> (Hérail 1988: 224, my translation)

The second occasion to receive special mention was a joint celebration of the fiftieth day after the birth of an imperial prince, Michinaga's grandson, and the Boiling of the Seven Herbs, one of the annual ceremonies observed at court, attended by the emperor, grandees and courtiers, the splendor of which was marred for Michinaga by a *faux pas* at the end.

> February 1, 1010. The Emperor took his place ... and the grandees were given special seats in the south gallery. Tables of food were placed before the grandees, and then the Emperor was served ... There was a fine white cloth embroidered with motifs of pine, paulownia and oak branches. On each sort of branch an ornamental dish was placed. On the paulownia was placed a pair of phoenixes, on which rested the emperor's chopsticks. On the pine was placed a dish in the shape of a hollow crane. For the rest, the large oak leaves served as dishes ... Then the tray with *sake* for the Emperor was brought in. It was a tray of bamboo on which had been placed a cup in the shape of a parrot and, in a pot of lapis lazuli, a Chinese spoon adorned with vegetable motifs ... *Sake* was served to the Emperor and then to the grandees. After the cups had circulated several times, I called for the music ... During this time the grand master of the Empress's household sang of the delights of the *sake* of Shinpo, and everyone joined in ... After the event was over and the Emperor had retired, the Minister of the Right, looking at the service that had been set before the Emperor, tried to take something from the hollow crane dish and in doing so upset the tray. The astonishment of all who witnessed this scene was without measure: the crane was not to be touched. Shouldn't it have been covered? What a lack of attention, truly what a lack of attention! This tray service had been promised to the Emperor to use for his breakfast.
>
> (Hérail 1988: 368–9, my translation)

On another occasion, just after he had attained a high office, Michinaga was exultant because he had received the red lacquer serving ware that was the mark of his new status. That Michinaga, the most powerful man in the land, could have been so keenly interested in such details was not unique. The diaries of other grandees reveal similar preoccupations, although not always with Michinaga's attention to detail, or resources to stage such grand entertainments. Again, the food is usually not mentioned although at the housewarming banquet given by Fujiwara no Yorinaga in AD 1136, honored guests were served with *ayu* river fish prepared in several ways, bass, sea bream, trout, octopus, carp, pheasant, spiny lobster, various dried fish, steamed abalone, grilled octopus, plovers, turbot, crab, sea squirt and jelly fish (Hosking 2001: 105). In the main, diarists simply state that banquets and other events were carried out "as prescribed," "in the correct manner, "according to precedent," although when there were lapses, these were noted. The imperial cat banquet only came to light because Fujiwara no Sanesuke, an expert in court protocol, thought it so improper that he was moved to record his disapproval. Another diary records an incident where the kitchen had made a mistake, and one of the main guests of honor had not been given the pheasant drumstick his status demanded. Quickly, a drumstick was taken from the tray of a courtier of slightly lower rank and slipped onto that of the honored guest, while the lower ranked courtier extinguished the lamp in front of his tray so others could not see that he was now missing a plate.

The diaries of male courtiers and surviving manuals of procedure show that, far from being superficial, these details were regarded as of fundamental importance. Seating was another preoccupation—who was sitting where, who was seated first, who was facing in what direction—because seating materialized the ranking system referred to above. The same level of concern for precedence and position seen at grand banquets was also applied to the smaller communal meals held within the palace, where all eating was highly formalized. In the diaries, enough is said to make clear that the formal banquets seen in the Muromachi era were already well estab-lished in the Heian period. There were minor differences in service. The multi-table style had not yet been adopted in the early Heian. The guest of honor had his own table about a meter square, and the guests sat facing him clustered in groups around tables some two meters square, and the tables of high status guests were higher than those of low status. An alternative was the presentation of several table trays in sequence, as in Michinaga's banquet. However, the food was largely the same as in the Muromachi era both in substance and presentation, as shown in the scroll paintings, and there were different grades of banquet cuisine, depending on the status of host and guests (Hosking 2001). The banquets were as protracted as those of the Muromachi period, featuring awards, proclamations, performances and ceremonial gifting, with the post-banquet *sake* drinking coming as a welcome relief at the end.

Two questions now arise—what accounts for the cultural invisibility of food in the *monogatari* and diaries, and what does the Heian banqueting reveal about the origins of Japan's ritualized eating? The indigenous religion of Japan is the worship of the *kami*, and the Japanese origin myths give insight into the Japanese cultural attitude to food. According to the ancient chronicles the *Kojiki*, the *Nihonshoki* and other sources, the brother of the Sun Goddess went to visit the deity of food, variously named as Ogetsuhime or Ukemochi, sometimes described as male and sometimes as female. Wishing to honor the guest with a banquet, Ukemochi/Ogetsuhime expelled rice, fish and "smooth-haired and rough haired" animals—usually glossed as "game"—from her nose, mouth and rectum, spreading the food upon a hundred tables. The divine guest was so disgusted—"How filthy! How vile!"—that he drew his sword and killed Ukemochi/Ogetsuhime. Hearing of the outrage, the Sun Goddess sent a messenger to the scene, where, according to the *Kojiki*, he found that the body of the dead *kami* was continuing to produce food and useful things:

> From the crown of the god's head came horses and oxen. From his forehead sprang millet, and from his eyebrows silkworms. From inside his eyes came millet, and from inside his stomach rice. From his genitals came wheat and large and small beans. The messenger collected all these things and went, giving them in offering [to Amaterasu]. Then, Amaterasu no Okami said, "These things can be eaten as food by the people." So millet, wheat and beans became the seed crops of the dry field, and rice the seed crop of the paddy.
>
> (for variants see Philippi 1987: 404–5 n. 11)

Two things are apparent here. First, that the Japanese relationship with food began with disgust, which helps to explain the deep ambivalence about food and eating that pervades Japanese culture even today, reflected in the invisibility of food in the *monogatari*, and the displacement into aestheticism—the preoccupation with vessels, with elaborate preparation in which the food is distanced from its origins, and the interest in the look of things rather than with taste, in both the Heian and later periods. It also explains the Japanese concern with food-related purity and pollution seen in ritual and everyday life. Purity "was the condition for spirits to be present and for the state to function" (Ooms 2009: 257). In the Heian period, purity and pollution became "central cultural concerns in the capital. Contemporaries linked it even with what one could call Japanese identity" (Ooms 2009: 267), with Fujiwara no Sanesuke reflecting in his diary that the concern with pollution was distinctly Japanese because pollution taboos did not exist in China. Ceremonies great and small required that participants be in states of ritual purity achieved through observing food taboos including fasting. Purification rites were frequent, food presented for offering had to be purified and, as seen above, it was vital that the emperor's food and water be pure. This in turn throws light on the restricted nature of indigenous Japanese cookery techniques, seemingly inexplicable when compared to the wide borrowings from China and the Asian mainland in antiquity in other fields, and never before explained. Visually exquisite, Heian food was not nutritious, due to the lack of fat and the high proportion of salted and pickled foods. Even among the aristocracy, the poverty of the diet led to chronic ill health (H. McCulloch 1980), often referenced in the diaries and *monogatari*—and yet the Japanese clung to their restricted techniques. Why only boiling, simmering and grilling? Why was frying and cooking with oil not adopted? Water and fire were the two purifying and cleansing elements in the worship of the *kami*, their purity constantly reinforced through rituals. I argue that Japan's fire-and-water cookery is essentially a cleansing ritual, passing the food through fire and water to purify it. In this context, oil and frying are polluting, and the Japanese continued to reject them until a much later era, under very different circumstances.

This leads to the second thing that emerges in the myth—that the first food event was a sacred feast followed by an offering, thus fusing feast, ritual and the sacred, and placing them at the center of Japan's cosmology and origin narrative. The offerings enumerated in minute detail in the *Engi-shiki* were at the center of the endless round of ceremonies and rituals that were re-enactments of the first feast, as were the banquets in which food full of symbolic meaning was prepared and arranged as if on small altars, and also piled up in the *takamori* style. Even the vexed problem of seating—later explained entirely in terms of rank—originally corresponded to the sacred and auspicious directions so important in ritual. The Heian annual ritual calendar set out a series of ceremonies that often included the consumption by the emperor of symbolic foods, drinks and meals that were meant to ensure his health and that of the nation—the Boiling of the Seven Herbs that figures in Michinaga's celebrations is one example, as is the grain gruel prepared by the Office of Water. Often described as "medicinal," these were originally seen as magical, transformative and protective foods. Beginning with the emperor, their use would have spread to the imperial family, then the court, and finally over the centuries to the general population, as seen in the imitation crane served at the 1949 New Year banquet, and in *toso-sake* included in the same meal—seven centuries after the end of the Heian period.

Sake is one of the oldest drinks in the world still in everyday usage. Considered the national drink of Japan—*nihonshu*—it is still a part of religious rites, formal banqueting, social and business entertaining and family events. As seen above, it appeared as an offering to the gods in the earliest chronicles, and its other name— *sei shu*, pure liquor—is a reminder of its ritual role, and of the fact that it too is considered purifying. Yet despite its remarkable persistence at the heart of Japanese culture for nearly two millennia, in the study of Japanese foodways *sake* has been overshadowed by tea, a much later introduction. During the late Muromachi, opulent tea-drinking parties became fashionable, similar in format to the Heian *sake* drinking parties, but with tea added to the menu. In the following Edo period under the Tokugawa shogunate, an austere style of tea drinking, *wabicha*, associated with Zen Buddhism was taken up widely. Its practice involved a light meal, then the ceremonial preparation of the tea and its consumption, with *sake* usually removed from the menu. *Wabicha* ultimately gave rise to its own specialized cuisine, *kaiseki ryori*, in which there were fewer dishes, the food presented in small servings and arranged on the plates in a different way, with each person's meal generally served on a single tray without legs. The reduction was relative; there were still different grades of tea-food, and over time these meals became less austere. *Kaiseki ryori* is usually described as "simpler" and "fresher" than the old banquet food, but on inspection it is something rather more. Tea ceremony is a ritual, involving etiquette every bit as demanding as that of formal banquets in the old style. In the tea ceremony, much is made of the purity of the water, and the drink produced at the end of the intricate tea-making process takes on a semi-mystical aspect, while the contemplation and concentration essential to proper tea making and consuming is equivalent to religious meditation. It is possible to see this shift from *sake* to tea drinking as a reflection of the attempt by Zen Buddhism to displace the indigenous Shinto religion from its central position, as happened periodically until the Meiji Restoration, when Buddhism was actually banned. Substituting tea for *sake* broke the links to the *kami*. The eclipse of *sake*, the appropriation of the *sake* drinking parties, the use of tea etiquette to exert social control in the way banquet etiquette was formerly used, the invention of *kaiseki ryori* and the change in presentation—placing food on plates in arrangements that rejected the elaboration, symmetry and symbolism of the old style placement based on Shinto practice—was more than a change in fashion. It was a war fought though feasting.

Feasting as social narrative requires as long an historical perspective as possible. The Japanese case has demonstrated that to see food only in the context of the early modern period onwards gives a partial view. The complexities of Heian society and religion are often overlooked, but they explain the prime importance placed on maintaining order, and on food as the means by which this was to be achieved. There was always a tension between the cultural disdain for food rooted in the origin myth, and the clear importance of food in ritual and as a means of maintaining social and political control. The references in the *ryorishi* to knife work that "invites the divine," to moving food in specified and auspicious directions, to combinations of symbolic colors and shapes, to seasonality having less to do with fresh food than with harmonizing with the annual cycle—no longer fully understood even in the Muromachi era—repeat procedures and principles employed in the ritual offerings at shrines and temples in the Heian period as seen in the *Engi-shiki* and probably in the Nara period and even before, although reliable written records are lacking. Just as the repetition of rituals and ceremonies reinforced both cosmic and social order, the consumption of ritualized food at formal banquets allowed this order to be internalized. One of the striking features of formal Japanese feasting was its extreme rigidity, reversed at the end by the excesses of the obligatory after-banquet drinking party. That banquets lent themselves so well to materializing and maintaining the hierarchical social order under the Fujiwaras and possibly earlier regimes of which knowledge is scarce may have been fortuitous, but over time the sacred and secular fused, and although the knowledge of the sacred faded, ritual practice is embedded in the formal banquet, which remains at the core of official life, and in the everyday culinary conventions that make indigenous and appropriated dishes so visually distinctive, in Japan's version of the never-ending feast.

CHAPTER EIGHT

Epilogue: After the Feast

Men of the "second house" will stand holding torches between the individual tables of the king's sons and the emirs; and when the meal has been generously served, incense in good quantity will be burnt around the tables of the king's sons and of the emirs, the large drinking-cups will be set down, and the *sa pan ekalli* will take his stand saying, "give to drink, O cup-bearer".

(Kinnier Wilson 1972: 43)

This description of the start of post-feast drinking from the *Nimrud Wine Lists* is a fitting opening to this brief Epilogue—equivalent to a bibulous after-party—for what has emerged strongly from this historical anthropology of feasting in antiquity is the importance of alcohol. Although the default definition of feast as "a communal food consumption event that differs in some way from everyday practice" (Bray 2003: 1) suggests that in antiquity the main focus at feasts and in associated rituals and ceremonies was on food, the preceding chapters show otherwise. As reflected in this volume, in ancient texts liquid offerings to the gods are referred to more frequently than offerings of food; in museum collections, the wares and implements for drinking far outnumber those for eating and, although artistic representations of drinking are common, those of eating are relatively rare. As Bottéro (1994: 10) says of Mesopotamia, so generally in the ancient world, drink was celebrated and esteemed more than food. In ancient Sumerian, the word for feast translates literally as "the pouring of beer" (Michalowski 1994: 29). What accounts for the pre-eminence of drink?

As a field of academic study, alcohol initially suffered even more opprobrium and moralizing than food but, following the Turn, it has emerged in archaeology and ancient history as a form of material culture which, viewed through "the lens of practice, politics and gender" (Dietler 2006: 229), throws light on the broad political economy in which it is embedded, on strategies of manipulation and domination, and on social differentiation, colonization and trade. These broad outlines are discernible in all the preceding chapters, but as the anthropology of history shows, they are not the whole story. In Mesopotamia, for example, the archaeological record evidences a shift from small-scale female brewers to large-scale male brewers, also described as the loss of access to productive facilities, through the appearance of references to men in production records and a concomitant decline in references to women, as well as the increase in large workshop-made storage jars not suited to domestic use. But to the anthropologist, the eclipse of the brewing goddess Ninkasi speaks more eloquently of a change in the status of women. The economic effect at the domestic level can easily be imagined, but what can the psychic shock of Ninkasi's demotion have been, and how might it have influenced engendered belief and behaviour? Ancient historians focus on agricultural production and the labor roles and social relationships entailed in the making of beer, but an anthropological dimension is added by knowing that it was driven by "fear in a handful of dust," and perceived by the people as the need to provide drink for the gods, who were themselves often portrayed as drinking and being drunk. In Mesopotamia, as elsewhere in the ancient world, drink always came back to the gods.

Belief and religion are aspects of the past that archaeologists and many historians find challenging. They tend to acknowledge that "alcohol has frequently played a prominent role in rituals of both a religious and secular nature ... [and] the association between alcohol and religion is one with deep antiquity" (Dietler 2006: 241), and then move quickly on to focus on secular ceremonies, production, politics, ceramic objects, culinary remains and residues. By contrast, the key questions in the anthropological manual *Notes and Queries*—Are any ceremonies connected with drinking? Are there any myths or traditions connected with drinks or drinking customs?—lead to the heart of the relationship between people, drink, belief and the gods.

In origin myths, alcohol was not invented by man, it was always a gift from the gods, a gift that is returned through offerings and libations. The quality that distinguishes drink from food, apart from hallucinogens, is its psychoactive properties—its ability to alter perception. The consumption of alcohol produces a kind of embodied magic in which the experience of reality is transformed. Senses are heightened, time and space are transcended, the mind can leave the body or experience it in a different way, boundaries dissolve and the divine becomes accessible. In this context, drunkenness is not necessarily a bad thing, in antiquity it could be seen as a form of divine possession. The experience is intensified and manipulated through music, dance, ceremonies, rituals and the dynamics of group participation. Through drinking, one directly experiences the power of the gods, and to an extent becomes one with them. Thus drinking was an act of worship that constantly reaffirmed the power of the gods and the temples that served them.

Similar processes can be seen in secular rituals in a context in which the divide between the sacred and the secular is not as clear as it is today. When palaces took over from temples as the centres of authority and kings and princes claimed to rule because of divine approval, alcohol was still central to worship in the temples and in religious festivals, but the state now provided the drink to the population on a regular basis through rations, and through great public feasts and celebrations. This appropriation of the former temple monopoly reaffirmed the power of the state and consolidated the identification of the new divine kings with the gods. The state provision of drink—involving a huge mobilization of resources—has always puzzled ancient historians and archaeologists. As one put it "It is not clear to me why an emergent leader would want to foster a stupefied labour force" (Peregrine 1998: 314), although it is not possible to say just how debilitating the state drinks were. Social control through dependence, a reward to build loyalty and a means of minimizing the stress that accompanied social change, conflict and enforced labor have all been put forward as explanations. Elements of all were no doubt involved but, from an anthropological perspective, paralleling the role of alcohol in religion, the fundamental importance of alcohol can be seen to lie in the active properties of the substance itself, which was able to literally impress the power of the state onto and into the body through drinking.

As an animate, active substance, alcohol is dualistic in nature, having two faces, one constructive, the other destructive. As the Greek poet Panyasis (fifth century BC) put it: "Wine drives all sorrows from men's hearts when drunk in due measure, but when taken immoderately it is a bane" (in Athenaeus II: 163). Both faces were on display at feasts. Wine could constructively facilitate sociality and enhance performance—singing, dancing, the playing of music, the recitation of poetry and the verbal artistry of debate. The offering of drink to a visitor or stranger in hospitality forms an immediate bond. But just as often, the destructive face was seen in copious drinking followed by disorderly behaviour, sexual license and general abandon in which the normal order was challenged, and things were said and done that would not have been permitted under normal circumstances. This was true on occasion even of the ancient Greeks, who normally disapproved of excess, moderated their own consumption through the practice of mixing wine with water and only drinking a limited number of cups, who believed that wine had been given to them by a foreign demigod Dionysius, and whose own gods did not drink wine, but nectar. Elsewhere, not everyone went to extremes, but very often a considerable degree of intoxication was expected and even obligatory—for example the enforced drinking in the encampments of the Mongol Qans and at the royal court in Heian Japan.

As this study shows, in the feasts of antiquity, the consumption of food and of drink was not integrated from start to finish, as it tends to be today when there might be an aperitif or cocktail to begin a banquet, and a liqueur, port or brandy at the end, with wine or other alcohol served throughout the meal. Instead, in the ancient world, wine was often part of a feasting sequence that went drink-food-drink or food-drink. One got through the food, in order to get to the drinking. The informality—even abandon—induced by drink stands in sharp contrast to the rigors of formal feasting centered around food, materializations of larger social formations and values that were also often onerous. Drink parties and the drinking parts of feasts were a particular kind of "focused, bordered world" with their own etiquette and "specific discourse strategies including 'gaming' and 'drink talk'" (Michalowski 1994: 33). The drinking provided an opportunity for social negotiation, "a structured setting within which one's social relationships beyond his everyday associations can be extended, defined and manipulated" (Frake 1964: 131). Here drunkenness was integrative, hence the obligation to drink. It acted as a form of release and consolidation, dispersing the tensions that had built up in an earlier phase of the feast, or outside the feast itself, and drawing people together who may previously have been separated by the etiquette of the food part of the feast or by external social events, although neither release nor consolidation necessarily involved full equality. After the drinking, order and sobriety returned, but that order could have been modified by what had taken place during the drinking, making drink and the drinking parties agents of change, in a way that did not constitute a direct challenge. However, a bigger question lies beyond these functional explanations.

The primacy of drink at the feast, in religion and in state ritual forces us to ask—Why do people drink? The active chemical substance ethanol or ethyl alcohol—C_2H_5OH—is the same for all drinks, whether wine, cider, mead, beer, ale or spirits (Heath 1987). Archaeologists are finding evidence of drinks earlier and earlier in prehistory, and academic controversy is ongoing as to which came first, cooked food or alcohol. The great staples of antiquity—millet, barley, wheat and rice—were all valued as much for the drink they produced as for their use as cooked food. In all societies and periods of history, people have used the basic techniques of solution (dissolving), suspension, infusion, decoction (boiling), distillation and fermentation and an array of ingredients to produce an alcoholic repertoire that is dizzying in its variety and ingenuity. Wine can occur naturally without human agency when fruits become over-ripe and ferment, but the other drinks require the intervention of brewers, distillers and other preparers. Why go to so much trouble? Food sustains life, but to value drink over food suggests that it is considered more important than life. The "life" at issue here is not biological, not mere survival, but *social* life. The unproblematic assumption of the social sciences is that socialization is a desirable thing, a step forward in human development, something that everyone wants to be a part of. But is that always true? In phenomenological terms, alcoholic drink allows the drinker to break through the embodied, socialized and temporal structure of human existence. If only briefly, it frees people from social restrictions and identities, lifts them above the everyday and allows them to touch the divine. This is what gives drink its power. The antiquity and primacy of alcoholic drink suggests that this is the deepest and most fundamental of human impulses; one that can be manipulated and appropriated by religion and the state, but which remains at the core of our being. It has been asserted that cooking makes us human (Wrangham 2009). *The Never-Ending Feast* suggests that drinking makes us more than human. And to us, it seems, that matters more.

Indeed, for all the material remains of vanished feasts that archaeologists uncover on an ongoing basis, the ancient literature that has so far come to light—with the exception of Chinese and Greek and Roman texts—is not littered with detailed gastronomic and culinary descriptions. Athenaeus (IV: 128–30) writes of two friends, Hipplochus the Macedonian and Lynceus the Samian, who made a pact to describe to each other any sumptuous banquets at which they were present, when they were apart. The result was "banquet letters," the full corpus of which is now lost, but from which Athenaeus quotes this letter from Hipplochus:

> Caranus celebrated his marriage with a banquet at which the number of men invited to gather was twenty … no sooner had they taken their places on the couches, than they were presented with silver cups, one for each, to keep as their own. Each guest, also, had been crowned before he entered with a gold tiara … after they had emptied their cups, they were each given a bronze platter of Corinthian manufacture, containing a loaf as wide as the platter; also chickens and ducks, ringdoves, too, and a goose, and an abundance of suchlike viands piled high; and each guest took his portion, platter and all, and distributed it among the slaves who stood behind him. Many other things to eat were handed round in great variety, after which came a second platter of silver, on which again lay a huge loaf and geese, hares, young goats and curiously moulded cakes besides, pigeons, turtle-doves, partridges and other fowl in plenty. "This also," he says "we presented to the slaves in addition …" When he had at last pleasantly taken leave of all sobriety, there entered flute-girls and singers and some Rhodian sambuca-players. To me these girls looked quite naked, but some said they had on tunics. And after a prelude they withdrew … After that was brought in a fortune rather than a dinner, namely a silver platter … large enough to hold the whole of a roast pig—a big one too—which lay on its back upon it; the belly, seen from above, disclosed that it was full of many bounties. For roasted inside it, were thrushes, ducks and warblers in unlimited number, pease puree poured over eggs, oysters and scallops, all of which, towering high, was presented to each guest, platters and all. After this, we drank, and then received a kid, piping hot, again upon another platter as large as the last, with spoons of gold … our attention was next engrossed in a warm and almost neat drink … [then] we were all presented with a crystal platter being about two cubits

in diameter, lying in a silver receptacle, and full of a collection of all kinds of baked fish; also a silver bread-rack containing Cappadocian loaves, of which we ate some and gave the rest to the slaves.

Eventually, after the performance of a wedding hymn by a hundred-strong male chorus, entertainment by dancing-girls attired as nereids and nymphs and the serving of pieces of Erymanthian boar on silver skewers, the banquet came to an end. The signal to conclude was sounded on the trumpet, a Macedonian practice at dinners attended by many guests, according to Athenaeus. After which the guests went on their way with boxes and baskets packed full of delicacies from the feast, a final gift from the host.

Whether this is an accurate description or food-as-metaphor, today's scholars and food enthusiasts would welcome the full correspondence between these two feast-loving friends, and more fulsome accounts of this kind from many other cultures, but, at least at present, they are not to be found, and perhaps never will be. For one of the great lessons of anthropological fieldwork—here in the form of "going among the texts" as Sahlins called it—is that you do not always find what you expect or want to find. Instead, even if it seems counterintuitive, you must learn to see things as the people themselves see them, *emic*-ally.

When dealing with the past, it is necessary to guard against "presentism"—to keep present-day values and perspectives from creeping into one's work, which is what *The Never-Ending Feast* shows has happened with prevailing assumptions that the feasts of the past were wholly pleasurable events, characterized by equable and convivial commensality. Instead, as seen in the preceding chapters, at the banquets of antiquity—total social facts *par excellence*—it was difference rather than community that was on display. Far from being the enjoyable experiences imagined *etic*-ally from the outside and portrayed in the art and literature of later periods, seen *emic*-ally from the inside in the foregoing chapters, the formal feasts and banquets of antiquity were often excruciating, intensely competitive events that challenge the consolidating, community-forming aspect of commensality emphasized in many current studies of feasting. It is telling that almost as soon as detailed accounts of drink emerge, we find that they were socially differentiated. In early Mesopotamia there were many types of beer, including dark, sweet dark, reddish brown and golden, and many different grades of it, starting with "best" and "first class," and this was the case for all kinds of drink throughout the ancient world. "Display" and "luxury" have been shown to be simplistic terms in view of the nuances conveyed through the differentiation of seating at feasts, of the number of dishes offered, the type of vessels used and quantity and quality of food and drink offered, the gifts given and the robes worn. The fixed tables of the modern period were not customary in antiquity. The bringing out of pre-set small tables and parading with them through the feasting room or rooms in front of the guests gave everyone the opportunity to see who was served what, who was who in the social hierarchy, and who was in or out of favor on that particular occasion. How galling it must have been to be served with fewer dishes than one's rival, to be offered an inferior grade of drink in a relatively plain cup, to be seated well away from the prestige areas, and how much worse if one had been recently demoted after giving offence or had simply been supplanted. Sneaking into a better position was not an option. Major-domos and staff who patrolled the eating part of the feast, making sure that people were in their assigned places and that etiquette was strictly observed, seem to have been universal. And even if one was not in the first rank within the main hall, how much better to be there than in the outer rooms where people of lesser status ate, or even outside the feasting structure, in the courtyard or on the fields beyond, where the common people ate. Inclusion and exclusion were relative. Being present but in a lowly position for all to see was far worse than being absent from the feast altogether. Production-based functional studies emphasize the cooperative aspect and consumption-based cultural studies the competitive; both are necessary, but this work on feasting suggests that concepts of sociality/commensality need to be refined, both in the context of the feast and more generally.

While presentism is to be avoided, comparisons between past and present are to be encouraged, for the feast has had different incarnations over time, and the differences are instructive. In the longitudinal view, the early modern period has seen the greatest changes to feasting, under the influences of democratization, migration and globalization, as a survey of current food writing shows. Great calendrical feasts such as Christmas and Easter are still observed, but at least in the West they tend to take place on a household level with 'extended family' and friendship groups smaller than formerly. Regions, social and religious groups and nations may be united in eating the same festival foods at the same time of year, but they do so in private collectivities. Where then do the differences and competition, formerly materialized through feasting, find expression? It is possible that much of this has been displaced onto the conspicuous consumption of goods of all kinds that characterizes late modernity. But at the same time, hierarchy remains—in the many kinds of food snobberies; in the rivalry to get the best table in smart restaurants and the continuing importance in these establishments of the *maitre d'*, the modern version of the precedence and seating experts of old; or the reverse one-upmanship of knowing all about the latest kinds of street food. Formal dining at the highest level, and diplomatic and state banquets and private clubs, preserve many of the old hierarchical forms in a modern idiom. There are changes and continuities, but the feast is never-ending.

And yet for all the gastronomic flourishes, variety and comfort of feasting today, something significant is missing compared to most of the banquets of antiquity—the sheer gusto with which large quantities of drink and food were once consumed, as Athenaeus (IV: 144) anticipated long ago, when he wrote:

For it is anything that transcends the usual that gives pleasure, which is the reason why all men except tyrants look forward with joy to holiday feasts. For since the tables set before tyrants are always heavily laden, they have nothing special to offer on feast-days, so that here is the first particular in which they are at a disadvantage compared with men in private station, namely in the delight of anticipation. Then secondly, he said, I am sure that you have learned that the more abundantly one is supplied with things which go beyond his needs, the more quickly he suffers from satiety as regards eating.

It may have been noticed that I did not give my own succinct definition of "feast" in the Introduction. This was intentional, a methodological means of letting the feast speak for itself. The technique is called an "operational definition." Instead of starting with a formal definition, which risks over-determining and limiting the analytic perspective, a working definition emerges from the material itself. The method is not new. As *Notes and Queries* (1929: 174) put it—"It is the primary aim of the fieldworker to record what exists among a given community, there is no immediate need for him to occupy himself with the exact definition of the terms employed by students at home. If the fieldworker employs a standard term in order to describe the character of the people with whom he is dealing, there is a danger that he will overlook those local distinctions which may render his particular application of that term somewhat misleading." This was an ideal method for 'going among the texts' with the aim of producing an holistic and synthetic study of feasting in societies separated in time and space, drawing on anthropology, history, archaeology, art and literature. Operational definitions are *emic*; by not imposing typologies, templates or theoretical limitations, they allow nuanced similarities and differences to emerge from a culture-rich narrative. The strength of the method can be seen here in the importance of alcohol, which would not have emerged in the same way if the standard default emphasis on food had been followed.

As noted in the Introduction, the primary academic objective of this work has been to use the "anthropology of history" developed by Marshall Sahlins in order to stimulate future collaborative work, and to provide a starting point for new synthesizing theories, rather than to develop such theories here. Another aim has been to revive narrative. Also as noted, there are wider objectives. And so we find ourselves back in the British Museum, among once-strange objects that have become familiar. The display cases of Greek drinking vessels are no longer silent—some bespeak the shared pleasures of cup and couch, others were witness to contests of oratory, even sometimes awarded as prizes, and the use of the large vessels for mixing wine and water can now be appreciated. The majestic panels carved in pale stone that now grace the Assyrian galleries were the backdrop for Ashurnasirpal II's feast, the greatest yet known in history, that lasted ten days and involved 69,574 guests. What had seemed like purely decorative patterns on the vessels in the vast collection of later Chinese ceramics are now revealed to be symbolic motifs and colors that link cuisine and cosmology and, over the ceremonial Shang and Zhou bronzes, the spirits they once transformed from ancestors into gods seem to hover. The ewer that once held Mongol *kumiss* asks us how a single drink/food could have sustained the feasting and fighting that built the greatest empire of its time, and in the Japan gallery we encounter the accoutrements of highly formal feasts that served up symbols that were meant to be eaten with the eyes. Meaningless in isolation, all have been presented here in a holistic manner that answers the questions: what were these feasts of antiquity like, and why were they so important? We understand now why the Museum is full of bygone feasts, but only after having taken the approach presented here. Curators at the British Museum were customarily called "Keepers," and while it is entirely right that museums should preserve cultural heritage, they should not keep knowledge to themselves. There are fashions in museum studies and displays as with all things, but the current penchant for displays that look like modernist art galleries, with minimalist labels bearing not much more than find and accession details, gives little impression of the living past, and almost never in its own words as taken from ancient texts. Through them we can hear peoples no longer mute and see now-vanished landscapes; we can appreciate the consequences of changes in diet, and the *longue durée* of environmental manipulation. Above all, as far as possible, we can achieve the anthropological aim of 'being there'. Objects need *cultural* context, theory and research need to be reinvigorated through synthesis, and museum displays should follow the precedent set here. We must learn to ask new questions of the past and of the present. This is an open invitation to undertake more synthesizing studies of the never-ending feast.

References and Bibliography

Ainian, Alexander Mazarakis (2006), "The Archaeology of *Basileis,*" in Sigrid Deger-Jalkotzy and Irene S. Lemos (eds), *Ancient Greece: From the Mycenaean Palaces to the Age of Homer.* Edinburgh: Edinburgh University Press, pp. 181–211.

Allen, Sarah (1991), *The Shape of the Turtle: Myth, Art and Cosmos in Early China.* Albany: State University of New York Press.

—(1993), Art and Meaning, in Roderick Whitfield (ed.), *The Problem of Meaning in Early Chinese Ritual Bronzes.* London: Percival David Foundation of Chinese Art/School of Oriental and African Studies.

Allsen, Thomas T. (2001), *Culture and Conquest in Mongol Eurasia.* Cambridge: Cambridge University Press.

Alster, Bendt (2005), *Wisdom of Ancient Sumer.* Bethesda, MD: CDL Press.

Ammianus Marcellinus (1986), *The Roman History of Ammianus Marcellinus,* C. D. Yonge (trans). London: Penguin Books. Also from 2009, Project Gutenberg.

Anderson, E. N. (1988), *The Food of China.* New Haven and London: Yale University Press.

Antonini, Chiara Silvi (1994), "On Nomadism in Central Asia between the Saka and Xiongnu: The Archaeological Evidence," in Bruno Genito (ed.), *The Archaeology of the Steppes: Methods and Strategies,* pp. 287–330. Naples: Istituto Universitario Orientale.

Appadurai, Arjun (1981), "Gastropolitics in Hindu South Asia." *American Ethnologist,* 8: 494–511.

—(1988), "How to make a national cuisine: cookbooks in contemporary India." *Comparative Studies in Society and History,* 30(1) 3–24.

Ashkenazi, Michael and Jacob, Jeanne (2000), *The Essence of Japanese Cuisine.* Philadelphia: University of Pennsylvania Press.

Athenaeus (1927–41), *The Deipnosophists,* Charles Burton Gulick (trans.) in seven volumes (1927–41), and S. Douglas Olson (trans.) in eight volumes (2007–12). Cambridge, MA and London: Loeb Classical Library, Harvard University Press.

Beidelman, T. O. (1989), "Agonistic exchange: Homeric reciprocity and the heritage of Simmel and Mauss." *Cultural Anthropology* 4(3), (August): 227–59.

Bellwood, Peter (2006), "Asian Farming Diasporas: Agriculture, Languages and Genes in China," in Miriam T. Stark (ed.), *Archaeology in Asia*. Malden and Oxford: Blackwells, pp. 96–118.

Bendall, Lisa (2004), "Fit for a King? Exclusion, Hierarchy, Aspiration and Desire in the Social Structure of Mycenaean Banqueting," in P. Halstead and J. Barrett (eds), *Food, Cuisine and Society in Prehistoric Greece*. Sheffield: University of Sheffield Press.

—(2008), "How Much Makes a Feast? Amounts of Banqueting Foodstuffs in the Linear B Records of Pylos," in A. Sacconi, L. Godart and M. Negri (eds), *Proceedings of the XIIth International Colloquium of Mycenology* (February). Rome: Biblioteca di Pasiphae.

Bentley, Amy (2012), "Sustenance, Abundance and the Place of Food in U.S. Histories," in Kyrie W. Clafin and Peter Scholliers (eds), *Writing Food History, a Global Perspective*. London and New York: Berg.

Bentley, Jerry H. (2006), "Beyond Modernocentrism: Toward Fresh Visions of the Global Past," in Victor H. Mair (ed.), *Contact and Exchange in the Ancient World*. Honolulu: University of Hawaii Press, pp. 17–29.

Binford, Louis (1962), "Archaeology as anthropology." *American Antiquity* 28(2): 217–25.

Black, Jeremy (2002), "The Sumerians in Their Landscape," in Tzvi Abusch (ed.), *Riches Hidden in Secret Places*. Winona Lake, IN: Eisenbrauns, pp. 41–62.

Black, Jeremy and Green, Anthony (1992), *Gods, Demons and Symbols of Ancient Mesopotamia*. London: The British Museum Press.

Boas, Franz (1928), *Anthropology in Modern Life*. London: George Allen and Unwin.

Bock, Felicia Gressitt (1970), *Engi-Shiki: Procedures of the Engi Era*. Tokyo: Sophia University Press.

Boileau, Gilles (1998–9), "Some ritual elaborations on cooking and sacrifice in late Zhou and Western Han texts." *Early China*, 23–4, 89–124.

Bonatz, Dominik (2004), "Ashirnasirpal's headhunt: an anthropological perspective." *Iraq* 667(1): 93–101.

Bonfante, Larissa (2011), *The Barbarians of Ancient Europe: Realities and Interactions*. Cambridge: Cambridge University Press.

Borecky, Borijov (1965), *Survivals of Some Tribal Ideas in Classical Greek*. Prague: Universita Acta Universitatis Carolinae, Philosophica et Historica Monographia 10.

Borgen, Robert (1982), "The Japanese mission to China, 801–806." *Monumenta Nipponica* 37(1): 1–38.

Bottéro, Jean (1985), "The cuisine of ancient Mesopotamia." *The Biblical Archaeologist,* Vol. 48(1) (March), 36–47.

—(1987), "The culinary tablets at Yale." *Journal of the American Oriental Society,* 107(1) (January–March): 11–19.

—(1995a), *Textes Culinaires Mesopotamiens*. Winona Lake, Indiana: Eisenbrauns.

—(1995b), *Mesopotamia: Writing, Reasoning and the Gods*. Chicago: University of Chicago Press.

—(1999), "The Most Ancient Recipes of All," in John Wilkins, *Food in Antiquity*. David Harvey and Mike Dobson (eds). Exeter: University of Exeter Press, pp. 248–55.

—(2001), *Religion in Ancient Mesopotamia*. Chicago and London: University of Chicago Press.

—(2004), *The Oldest Cuisine in the World: Cooking in Mesopotamia*. Chicago and London: University of Chicago Press.

Bowie, A. M. (1997), "Thinking with drinking: wine and the symposium in Aristophanes." *Journal of Hellenic Studies* 117: 1–21.

Bowman, Raymond A. (1970), *Aramaic Ritual Texts from Persepolis*. Chicago: University of Chicago Press.

Bowring, Richard (1996), *The Diary of Lady Murasaki*. London: Penguin.

Boyle, John Andrew (1958), *Ala-a-Din Ata-Malik Juvaini's History of the World Conqueror*. Cambridge, MA: Harvard University Press.

Braun, David (ed.) (2005), *Scythians and Greeks: Cultural Interactions in Scythia, Athens and the Early Roman Empire*. Exeter: University of Exeter Press.

Bray, Tamara (2003a), "The Commensal Politics of Early States and Empires," in Tamara Bray (ed.), *The Archaeology and Politics of Food and Feasting in Early States and Empires*. New York, Boston and London: Kluwer Academic/Plenum, pp. 1–13.

—(2003b), "To Dine Splendidly: Imperial Pottery, Commensal Politics and the Inca State," in Tamara L. Bray (ed.), *The Archaeology and Politics of Food and Feasting in Early States and Empires*. New York, Boston and London: Kluwer Academic /Plenum, pp. 93–142.

—(ed.) (2003c), *The Archaeology and Politics of Food and Feasting in Early States and Empires*. New York, Boston and London: Kluwer Academic/Plenum.

Bremmer, Jan (1994), "Adolescents, Symposion and Pederasty," in Oswyn Murray (ed.), *Sympotica*. Oxford: Clarendon Press, pp. 135–48.

Briant, Pierre (2002), *From Cyrus to Alexander: A History of the Persian Empire*. Winona Lake, IN: Eisenbrauns.

Brosius, Maria (2007), "New Out of Old? Court and court ceremonies in Achaemenid Persia," in A. J. S. Spawnforth (ed.), *The Court and Court Society in Ancient Monarchies*. Cambridge: Cambridge University Press, pp. 17–57.

Buccellati, Giorgio (1964), "The Enthronement of the King and the Capital City," in Robert M. Adams (ed.), *Studies Presented to A. Leo Oppenheim (From the Workshop of the Chicago Assyrian Dictionary)*. Chicago: The Oriental Institute of Chicago, pp. 54–61.

Buell, Paul (2001), "Mongol Empire and Turkicization: The Evidence of Food and Foodways," in Reuven Amitai-Preiss and David O. Morgan (eds), *The Mongol Empire and its Legacy*. Leiden, Boston and Koln: Brill, pp. 200–23.

—(2007), "Food, medicine and the silk roads: the Mongol-era exchanges." *Silk Road Foundation Newsletter* 5(1): 22–35.

Buell, Paul D., undated, *How Genghis Khan Changed the World*. http://www.mongolianculture.com/How%20Genghis%20Khan%20Has.pdf

Buell, Paul D., Anderson, Eugene and Perry, Charles (2000), *A Soup for the Qan*. London and New York: Kegan Paul.

Burkert, Walter (1985), *Greek Religion*. Oxford: Basil Blackwell.

—(2004), *Babylon, Memphis, Persepolis: Eastern Contexts of Greek Culture*. Cambridge, MA and London: Harvard University Press.

Burton, Joan (1998), "Women's Commensality in the Ancient Greek World," *Greece and Rome* 45(2): 143–65.

Bylkova, Valeria (2005), "The Lower Dnieper Region as an Area of Greek/Barbarian Interaction," in David Brown (ed.), *Scythians and Greeks. Culture Interactions in Scythia, Athens and The Early Roman Empire*. Exeter: University of Exeter Press, pp. 131–47.

Chang, Esther (1955), *Chinese Banquets*. Singapore: Tan Liang Khoo Printing.

Chang, K. C. (1977), "Introduction" in Chang, K. C. (ed.), *Food in Chinese Culture: Anthropological and Historical Perspectives*. New Haven: Yale University Press, pp. 3–21.

—(1980), *Shang Civilization*. New Haven: Yale University Press.

—(1994), "Shang Shamans," in Willard J. Peterson, Andrew H. Plaks and Ying-shih Yu (eds), *The Power of Culture*. Hong Kong: The Chinese University Press, pp. 10–36.

Childs-Johnson, Elizabeth (1995), "The ghost head mask and metamorphic Shang imagery." *Early China* 20: 79–92.

Cifarelli, Megan (1998), "Gesture and alterity in the art of Ashurnasirpal II of Assyria." *The Art Bulletin* 80(2) (June): 210–28.

Civil, Miguel (1964), "A Hymn to the Beer Goddess and a Drinking Song," in Robert M. Adams (ed.), *Studies Presented to A. Leo Oppenheim (From the Workshop of the Chicago Assyrian Dictionary)*. Chicago: The Oriental Institute of Chicago, pp. 67–89.

—(1994), *The Farmer's Instructions: A Sumerian Agricultural Manual*. Barcelona: Editorial Ausa.

Coe, Andrew (2009), *Chop Suey: A Cultural History of Chinese Food in the United States*. Oxford and New Haven: Oxford University Press.

Cohen, Andrew C. (2005), *Death Rituals, Ideology and the Development of Early Mesopotamian Kingship*. Leiden and Boston: Brill/Styx.

—(2007), "Barley as a Key Symbol in Early Mesopotamia," in Jack Cheng and Marian H. Feldman, *Ancient Near Eastern Art in Context: Studies in Honour of Irene J. Winter*. Leiden: Brill, pp. 411–22.

Cohen, Mark E. (1993), *The Cultic Calendars of the Ancient Near East*. Bethesda, MD: CDL Press.

Cohen, Myron (1991), "Being Chinese: the peripheralization of traditional Chinese identity," *Daedalus* 120(3) (Spring): 113–34.

Collon, Dominique (1992), "Banquets in the Art of the Ancient Near East," in R. Gyselen (ed.), Banquets d'Orient. *Res Orientales* IV: 23–30.

Comaroff, John and Comaroff, Jean (1992), *Ethnography and the Historical Imagination*. Boulder, CO: Westview Press.

Cook, Constance A. (1996), "Scribes, cooks and artisans: breaking Zhou tradition." *Early China*, 20: 241–77.

—(2005), "Moonshine and Millet: Feasting and Purification Rituals in Ancient China," in Roel Sterckx (ed.), *Of Tripod and Palate: Food, Politics and Religion in Traditional China*. London and New York: Palgrave Macmillan, pp. 9–33.

Cooper, Jerrold S. (1983), *Reconstructing History From Ancient Inscriptions: The Lagash-Umma Border Conflict*. Malibu: Undena Publications.

Crawford, Gary W. (2006), "Early Asian Plant Domestication," in Miriam T. Stark (ed.), *Archaeology in Asia*. Oxford and Malden: Blackwells.

Crawford, Michael and Whitehead, David (1983), *Archaic and Classical Greece: A Selection of Ancient Sources in Translation*. Cambridge and New York: Cambridge University Press.

Curtis, John and Razmjou, Sharokh (2005), "The Palace," in John Curtis and Nigel Tallis (eds), *Forgotten Empire: The World of Ancient Persia*. London: British Museum Press, pp. 50–103.

Curtis, John and Tallis, Nigel (2005), "Introduction," in John Curtis and Nigel Tallis (eds), *Forgotten Empire*. Berkeley and London: University of California Press, pp. 9–11.

Cwiertka, Katarzyna J. (2006), *Modern Japanese Cuisine: Food, Power and National Identity*. London: Reaktion.

Dalley, Stephanie (1998), "Introduction," in Stephanie Dalley (ed.), *The Legacy of Mesopotamia*. Oxford and New York: Oxford University Press, pp. 1–8.

Dalley, Stephanie and Oleson, John Peter (2003), "Sennacherib, Archimedes and the water screw: the context of invention in the ancient world," *Technology and Culture* 44(1): 1–26.

David Braun (ed.), *Scythians and Greeks. Cultural Interations in Scythia, Athens and The Early Roman Empire*. Exeter: University of Exeter Press.

Davidson, James (1998), *Fishcakes and Courtesans*. London: Fontana Press.

—(1999), "Opsophagia: Revolutionary Eating at Athens," in John Wilkins, David Harvey and Mike Dobson (eds), *Food in Antiquity*. Exeter: University of Exeter Press, pp. 204–13.

Dawson, Christopher (1955), *The Mongol Mission*. London and New York: Sheed and Ward.

Day, Ivan (2014), www.historicfood.com, http://foodhistorjottings.blogspot.co.uk (accessed September 2014).

Debaine-Francfort, Corinne (1998), *The Search for Ancient China*. London: Thames & Hudson.

Deger-Jalkotzy, Sigrid (2006), "Late Mycenaean Warrior Tombs," in Sigrid Deger-Jalkotzy and Irene S. Lemos (eds), *Ancient Greece from The Mycenaean Palaces to the Age of Homer*. Edinburgh Leventis Studies 3. Edinburgh: University of Edinburgh Press, pp. 151–79.

Dentzer, Jean-Marie (1971), "L'Iconographie Irannienne du Souverain Couché et le Motif du Banquet." *Annales Archéologiques Arabes Syriennes-Revue d'Archéologie et d'Histoire*, XXI: pp. 43–9.

—(1982), *Le motif du banquet couché dans le Proche-Orient et le monde grec du VII siècle avant J.-C.* Rome: Ecole Francaise de Rome.

Detienne, Marcel (1989), "Culinary Practices and the Spirit of Sacrifice," in Marcel Detienne and Pierre Vernant (eds), *The Cuisine of Sacrifice Among the Ancient Greeks*. Chicago: University of Chicago Press.

Dickenson, Oliver (2006), "The Mycenaean Heritage of Early Iron Age Greece," in Sigrid Deger-Jalkotzy and Irene S. Lemos (eds), *Ancient Greece from The Mycenaean Palaces to the Age of Homer*. Edinburgh Leventis Studies 3. Edinburgh: University of Edinburgh Press, pp. 115–22.

Dietler, Michael (2006), "Alcohol: anthropological/archaeological perspectives." *Annual Review of Anthropology*, 35: 229–49.

Dietler, Michael and Hayden, Brian (eds) (2001a), *Feasts: Archaeological and Ethnographic Perspectives on Food, Politics and Power*. Washington and London: Smithsonian Institution Press.

—(2001b), "Introduction: Digesting the Feast," in Michael Dietler and Brian Hayden (eds), *Feasts: Archaeological and Ethnographic Perspectives on Food, Politics and Power*. Washington and London: Smithsonian Institution Press, pp. 1–20.

Donbaz, Veysel (1988), "Complementary data on some Assyrian terms." *Journal of Cuneiform Studies* 40(1) (Spring): 69–80.

Donlan, Walter (1989), "The social groups of dark age Greece." *Classical Philology* 80(4) (October): 293–308.

Douglas, Mary (1970), *Natural Symbols: Explorations in Cosmology*. London and New York: Routledge.

—(1977), "Introduction," in Jessica Kuper (ed.), *The Anthropologists' Cookbook*. London and Boston: Routledge and Kegan Paul.

—(1987a), "A Distinctive Anthropological Perspective," in Mary Douglas (ed.), *Constructive Drinking: Perspectives on Drink from Anthropology*. Cambridge and New York: Cambridge University Press, pp. 3–15.

—(ed.) (1987b), *Constructive Drinking: Perspectives on Drink from Anthropology*. Cambridge and New York: Cambridge University Press.

Douglas, Mary and Isherwood, Baron (1979), *The World of Goods: Towards an Anthropology of Consumption*. London and New York: Routledge.

Dunlop, Fuschia (2007), "Human Resources." *New York Times* Magazine, February 4 2007, http://www.nytimes.com/2007/02/04/magazine/04food.t.html (accessed September 13, 2012).

Dusinberre, Elspeth R. M. (1999), "Satrapal sarids: Achaemenid bowls in an Achaemenid capital." *American Journal of Archaeology* 103(1) (January): 73–102.

Ebrey, Patricia Buckley (1991), *Confucianism and Family Rituals in Imperial China*. Princeton: Princeton University Press.

Edens, Christopher (1992), "Dynamics of trade in the ancient Mesopotamian 'world system.'" *American Anthropologist* New Series, 94(1) pp. 118–39.

Elias, Norbert (1983), *The Court Society*. New York: Pantheon Books.

—(2000), *The Civilizing Process*. Oxford and Malden, Blackwells.

Ellison, Rosemary (1981), "Diet in Mesopotamia: the evidence of the barley ration texts (c. 2000–1400 BC)." *Iraq* 43(1) (Spring): 35–45.

—(1983), "Some thoughts on the diet of Mesopotamia from c. 3000–600 B.C." *Iraq*, 45(1) (Spring): 146–50.

—(1984), "Methods of food preparation in Mesopotamia (c. 3000–600 BC)." *Journal of the Economic and Social History of the Orient* 27(1) (1984): 89–98.

Ellison, Rosemary; Renfrew, Jane; Brothwell, Don and Seeley, Nigel (1978), "Some food offerings from Ur, excavated by Sir Leonard Woolley and previously unpublished." *Journal of Archaeological Science* 167–77.

Endicott-West, Elizabeth (1986), "Imperial governance in Yuan Times." *Harvard Journal of Asiatic Studies* 46(2) (December): 523–49.

Eno, Robert (1996), "Deities and Ancestors in Early Oracle Inscriptions," in D. S. Lopez Jr. (ed.), *Religions of China in Practice*. New Haven: Princeton University Press, pp. 41–52.

—(2003), "The background of the Kong Family of Lu and the Origins of Ruism." *Early China* 28: 1–41.

Ferguson, Priscilla Parkhurst (2004), *Accounting for Taste: The Triumph of French Cuisine*. Chicago: University of Chicago Press.

Field, Stephen L. (2008), *Ancient Chinese Divination*. Honolulu: University of Hawaii Press.

Finet, Andre (1992), "Le Banquet de Kalah Offert Par le Roi d'Assyrie Asurnasirpal II (883–59)," in R. Gyselin (ed.), *Banquets d'Orient. Res Orientales* IV: 31–44.

Firth, Raymond (1967), *The Work of the Gods in Tikopia, 2nd Edition*. London and New York: University of London/The Athlone Press.

Fisher, Nick and van Wees, Hans (eds) (1998), *Archaic Greece: New Approaches and Evidence*. London and Swansea: Duckworth and The Classical Press of Wales.

Flannery, Kent and Marcus, Joyce (2012), *The Creation of Inequality: How our Prehistoric Ancestors set the Stage for Monarchy, Slavery and Empire*. Cambridge, MA and London: Harvard University Press.

Fletcher, Joseph (1986), "The Mongols: ecological and social perspectives." *Harvard Journal of Asiatic Studies* 46(1) (June): 11–50.

Frake, Charles O. (1964), "How to ask for a drink in Subanum." *American Anthropologist* NS 66; 6 pt 2: 127–32.

Frank, Bernard (1998), *Kata-imi et Kata-tagae: étude sur les interdits de direction à L'époque Heian*. Paris: College de France, Institut des Hautes Etudes Japonaises.

Freeman, Michael (1977), "Sung Dynasty," in K. C. Chang (ed.), *Food in Chinese Culture: Anthropological and Historical Perspectives*. New Haven and London: Yale University Press.

Fuller, Dorian Q. and Rowlands, Mike (2011), "Ingestion and Food Technology: Maintaining Difference Over the Long Term in West, South and East Asia," in T. C. Wilkinson, S. Sherratt, and S. Bennet (eds), *Interweaving Worlds—Systematic Interactions in Eurasia 7th to 1st Millennia BC*. Essays from a conference in memory of Professor Andrew Sherratt. Oxford: Oxbow Books, pp. 37–60.

Garnsey, Peter (1999), *Food and Society in Classical Antiquity*. Cambridge: Cambridge University Press.

Geertz, Clifford (1973), *The Interpretation of Cultures*. New York: Basic Books.

Gelb, I. J. (1965), "The ancient Mesopotamian ration system." *Journal of Near Eastern Studies* 24(3) (July): 230–43.

—(1982), "Measures of dry and liquid capacity." *Journal of the American Oriental Society* 102(4) (October–December): 585–90.

Genito, Bruno (1994), "Foreword," in Bruno Genito (ed.), *The Archaeology of the Steppes: Methods And Strategies*. Naples: Istituto Universitario Orientale, pp. xv–xx.

—(ed) (1994), *The Archaeology of the Steppes*, Naples: Istituto Universitario Orientale.

Gibson, McGuire (1974), "Violation of Fallow and Engineered Disaster in Mesopotamian Civilization," in T. E. Downing and Gibson McGuide (eds), *Irrigation's Impact on Society*. Tucson: University of Arizona Press, pp. 7–10.

Gold, Barbara K. and Donahue, John F. (eds) (2005), "Roman dining." *American Journal of Philology*, special issue.

Goody, Jack (1982), *Cooking Cuisine and Class*. Cambridge: Cambridge University Press.

Gordon. E. I. (1959), *Sumerian Proverbs*. Philadelphia: University of Pennsylvania Museum.

Gorman, Robert J. and Gorman, Vanessa B. (2007), "The *Tryphê* of the Sybarites: a historiographical problem in Athenaeus." *The Journal of Hellenic Studies* 127: 38–60.

Goulder, Jill (2010), "Administrators' bread: an experiment-based re-assessment of the functional and cultural role of the Uruk Bevel-Rim Bowl." *Antiquity* 84: 351–62.

Grayson, A. Kirk (1991), *Assyrian Rulers of the Early First Millennium I (1114–859 BC)*. Toronto: University of Toronto Press.

Grayson, A. Kirk; Frame, Grant; Frayne, Douglas and Maidman, Maynard (1987), *Assyrian Rulers of the Third and Second Millennia BC (to 1115 BC)*. Toronto: University of Toronto Press.

Guralnick, Eleanor (2004), "Neo-Assyrian textiles." *Iraq* 66: 221–32.

Hall, Jonathan M. (2007), *A History of the Archaic Greek World c 1200–479 BCE*. Oxford: Blackwell Publishing.

Halstead, P. and Barrett J. (eds) (2004), *Food, Cuisine and Society in Prehistoric Greece*. Sheffield: University of Sheffield Press.

Hamilakis, Yannis and Konsolaki, Eleni (2004), "Pigs for the Gods." *Oxford Journal of Archaeology*, 23(2): 135–51.

Harper, Donald J. (1998), *Early Chinese Medical Literature: The Mwangdui Medical Manuscripts*. London and New York: Kegan Paul International.

Hartog, François (1988), *The Mirror of Herodotus*. Berkeley, Los Angeles and London: University of California Press.

Hayden, Brian (2001), "Fabulous Feasts: A Prolegomenon to the Importance of Feasting," in Michael Dietler and Brian Hayden (eds), *Feasts: Archaeological and Ethnographic Perspectives on Food, Politics and Power*. Washington and London: Smithsonian Institution Press, pp. 23–64.

—(2014), *The Power of Feasts from Prehistory to the Present*. Cambridge: Cambridge University Press.

Hayden, Bryan and Villeneuve, Susanne (2011), "A century of feasting studies." *Annual Review of Anthropology* 40: 433–49.

Heath, Dwight B. (1987), "Anthropology and alcohol studies: current issues." *Annual Review of Anthropology* 16: 99–120.

Hegmon, Michelle (2003), "Setting theoretic egos aside: issues and theory in North American archaeology." *American Antiquity* 68(2): 458–69.

Henkelman, Wouter F. M. (2010), "Consumed Before the King: The Table of Darius, that of Irdabama and Irastuna and that of his Satrap Karkis," in Bruno Jacobs and Robert Rollinger (eds), *The Achaemenid Court*. Wiesbaden: Harrassowitz, pp. 667–776.

Hérail, Francine (1987), *Notes Journalières de Fujiwara no Michinaga. Vol. I*. Geneva: Librarie Droz.

—(1988), *Notes Journalières de Fujiwara no Michinaga. Vol. II*. Geneva: Librairie Droz

—(1991), *Notes Journalières de Fujiwara no Michinaga. Vol. III*. Geneva: Librairie Droz.

—(2006), *La Cour et l'Administration du Japon a l'époque de Heian*. Geneva: Librairie Droz.

Herodotus (1998), *The Histories*, R. Waterfield (trans.). Oxford: Oxford University Press.

Herrenschmidt, Clarisse and Lincoln, Bruce (2004), "Healing and salt waters: the bifurcated cosmos of Mazdean religion." *History of Religions* 42: 629–83.

Hessig, Walther (1970), *The Religions of Mongolia*. London: Routledge and Kegan Paul.

Hicks, Dan (2010), "The Material-Cultural Turn: Event and Effect," in Dan Hicks and Mary E. Baudry (eds), *The Oxford Handbook of Material Culture Studies*. Oxford: Oxford University Press, pp. 25–98.

Hobsbawm, Eric and Ranger, Terence O. (eds) (1984), *The Invention of Tradition*. Cambridge: Cambridge University Press.

Hocart, A. M. (1970), *The Life-Giving Myth, with an Introduction by Rodney Needham*. London: Methuen & Co.

Holzman, John D. (2006), "Food and memory." *Annual Review of Anthropology* Vol. 35: 361–78.

Homan, Michael M. (2004), "Beer and its drinkers: an ancient Near Eastern love story." *Near Eastern Archaeology* 67(2) (June): 84–95.

Homer (1961), *The Iliad of Homer*, Richard Lattimore (trans.). Chicago and London: University of Chicago Press.

—(1991), *The Odyssey*, E. V. Rieu (trans.), rev. edn. London: Penguin Books.

Hornsey, Ian Spencer (2003), *A History of Beer and Brewing*. London: Royal Society of Chemistry.

Hosking Richard (1995), *A Dictionary of Japanese Food: Ingredients and Culture*. Rutland, Vermont and Tokyo: Tuttle.

—(2001), "A Thousand Years of Japanese Banquets," in Harlan Walker (ed.), *The Meal: Proceedings of the Oxford Symposium on Food and Cookery*, pp. 104–12.

Huang, H. T. (1990), "Han Gastronomy: Chinese Cuisine in *Statu Nascendi*." *Interdisciplinary Science Reviews* 15(2) (June): 139–52.

Ingold, Tim (2012), "Toward an ecology of materials." *Annual Review of Anthropology* 41: 427–42.

Ishige, Naomichi (2001), *The History and Culture of Japanese Food*. London and New York: Kegan Paul.

Jack, Albert (2010), *What Caesar Did To My Salad*. London: Particular Books/Penguin.

Jackson, Peter and David Morgan (eds) (1990), *The Mission of Friar William of Rubruck*. London: Hakluyt Society.

Jacobsen, Thorkild (1970), *Toward the Image of Tammuz and Other Essays on Mesopotamian History and Culture*, William L. Moran (ed.). Eugene, OR: WIPF & Stock.

—(1987) *The Harps That Once ... Sumerian Poetry in Translation*. New Haven and London: Yale University Press.

Jacobsen, Thorkild and Adams, Robert M. (1958), "Salt and silt in ancient Mesopotamian agriculture." *Science*, New Series, 128(3334) (November): 1251–8.

Jennings, Justin; Antrobus, Kathleen L.; Atencio, Sam J. et al. (2005), "Drinking beer in a blissful mood': alcohol production, operational chains and feasting in the ancient world." *Current Anthropology* 46(2) (April): 275–303.

Joffe, Alexander H. (1998), "Alcohol and social complexity in ancient western Asia." *Current Anthropology* 39(3) (June): 297–322.

Jones, Martin (2008), *Feast: Why Humans Share Food*. Oxford: Oxford University Press.

Jong, Albert de (2010), "Religion at the Achaemenid Court," in Bruno Jacobs and Robert Rollinger (eds), *The Achaemenid Court*. Wiesbaden: Harrassowitz, pp. 533–58.

Josephus, Flavius (2006), *Jewish Antiquities*. London: Wordsworth Editions.

Joyce, Rosemary A. (2012), "Life with Things: Archaeology and Materiality," in David Shankland (ed.), *Archaeology and Anthropology: Past, Present and Future*. London and New York: Berg, pp. 119–32.

Kagawa, Aya (1949), *Japanese Cookbook: 100 Favourite Recipes for Western Cooks*. Tokyo, Japanese Travel Bureau.

Keightley, David N. (1992), *Sources of Shang History: The Oracle Bone Inscriptions of Bronze Age China*. Berkeley and London: University of California Press.

—(2000), *The Ancestral Landscape: Time, Space, and Community in Late Shang China, Ca. 1200–1045 B.C.* Berkeley: Institute of East Asian Studies/University of California Press.

—(2006), "Early Writing in Neolithic and Shang China," in Miriam T. Stark (ed.), *Archaeology of Asia*. Malden and Oxford: Blackwells, pp. 177–201.

Kertzer, David I. (1988), *Ritual, Politics and Power*. New Haven and London: Yale University Press.

Kesner, Ladislav (1991), "The *Taotie* reconsidered: meanings and functions of Shang theriomorphic imagery." *Artibus Asiae* 51(1/2), pp. 29–53.

Kidder, J. Edward Jr. (2007), *Himiko and the Elusive Chiefdom of Yamatai*. Honolulu: University of Hawaii Press.

Kilian, Klaus (1988), "The emergence of the Wanax ideology in the Mycenaean palaces." *Oxford Journal of Archaeology*, 7(3): 291–302.

Killen, John T. (2006), "The Subjects of the Wanax: aspects of Mycenaean Social Structure," in Sigrid Deger-Jalkotzy and Irene S. Lemos (eds), *Ancient Greece: From the Mycenaean Palaces to the Age of Homer*. Edinburgh Leventis Studies 3. Edinburgh: Edinburgh University Press, pp. 87–109.

Kinnier Wilson, J. V. (1972), *The Nimrud Wine Lists. (Cuneiform Texts from Nimrud)*. London: British School of Archaeology in Iraq.

Kiple, Kenneth F. (2007), *A Moveable Feast: Ten Millennia of Food Globalization*. Cambridge: Cambridge University Press.

Kiple, Kenneth F. and Conèe Ornelas, Kriemhild (eds) (2000), *The Cambridge World History of Food*. Cambridge: Cambridge University Press.

Kirch, Patrick V. and Sahlins, Marshall (1992), *Anahulu: The Anthropology of History in the Kingdom of Hawaii*. Vol. 1 (Historical Ethnography by Marshall Sahlins) and Vol. 2 (The Archaeology of History by Patrick V. Kirch). Chicago and London: University of Chicago Press.

Kitto, H. D. F. (1957), *The Greeks*. London: Penguin.

Klein, Jakob A., Pottier, Johan and West, Harry G. (2012), "New Directions in the Anthropology of Food," in Richard Farndon, Olivia Harris, Trevor H. Marchand et al. (eds), *The SAGE Handbook of Social Anthropology*. London: Sage Publications, pp. 293–302.

Klotz, Frieda and Oikonomopoulou, Katerina (eds) (2011), *The Philosopher's Banquet*. Oxford: Oxford University Press.

Knechtges, David R. (1986), "A literary feast: food in early chinese literature." *Journal of the American Oriental Society* 106(1) (January to March): 49–63.

—(1997), "Gradually entering the realm of delight: food and drink in early medieval China." *Journal of the American Oriental Society* 117(2) (April to June): 229–39.

Komroff, Manuel (1929), *Contemporaries of Marco Polo*. London: Jonathan Cape.

Kotaridi, Angeliki (2011), *The Legend of Macedon: A Hellenic Kingdom in the Age of Democracy in Heracles to Alexander the Great*. Oxford: Ashmolean Museum of Art and Archaeology, pp. 1–24.

Kramer, Samuel Noah (1963), "Cuneiform studies and the history of literature: the Sumerian sacred marriage texts." *Proceedings of the American Philosophical Society* 107(6) (December 20): 485–527.

Ku, Robert Ji-Song; Manalansan IV, Martin F.; and Mannur, Anita (eds) (2013), *Eating Asian America*. New York and London: New York University Press.

Kuhrt, Amelie (2002), *'Greeks' and 'Greece' in Mesopotamian and Persian Perspectives* (21st Meyers Memorial Lecture). Oxford, Leopard's Head Press.

—(2010), "*Der Hof der Achaemeniden*: Concluding Remarks," in Bruno Jacobs and Robert Rollinger (eds), *The Achaemenid Court*. Wiesbaden: Harrassowitz, pp. 901–12.

Kuper, Jessica (ed.) (1977), *The Anthropologists' Cookbook*. London and Boston: Routledge and Kegan Paul.

Kushner, Barak (2012), *Slurp: A Social and Culinary History of Ramen*. London: Global Oriental/Brill.

Ladurie, Emmanuel Le Roy (1978), *Montaillou*. London and New York: Penguin Books.

Lambert, W. G. (1993), "Donations of Food and Drink to the Gods," in J. Quaegebeur (ed.), *Ritual and Sacrifice in the Ancient Near East*. Leuven: Uitgeverij Peeters in association with the Departement Orientalistiek, pp. 191–201.

Langness, L. L. (1977), "Ritual, Power and Male Dominance in the New Guinea Highlands," in Raymond D. Fogelson and Richard N. Adams (eds), *The Anthropology of Power*. New York, San Francisco and London: Academic Press, pp. 3–22.

Leach, Edmund (1989), *Claude Levi-Strauss*. Chicago: University of Chicago Press.

Legge, James (trans.) (1885), *The Book of Rites*. Oxford: Clarendon Press.

Levi, Mario A. (1994), "The Scythians of Herodotus and the Archaeological Evidence," in Bruno Genito (ed.), *The Archaeology of the Steppes: Methods and Strategies*. Naples: Instituto Universitario Orientale, pp. 634–9.

Levi-Strauss, Claude (1967), *Structural Anthropology*. New York: Anchor Books.

Lewis, David M. (1997), "The King's Dinner," in P. J. Rhodes (ed.), *Selected Papers in Greek and Near Eastern History*. Cambridge: Cambridge University Press, pp. 332–41.

Lewis, Mark Edward (1990), *Sanctioned Violence in Early China*. Albany: State University of New York Press.

Limet, Henri (1987), "The cuisine of ancient Sumer." *The Biblical Archaeologist* 50(3) (September): 132–47.

Lincoln, Bruce (2007), *Religion, Empire and Torture*. Chicago and London: University of Chicago Press.

Lion, Brigitte; Michel, Cecile and Noel, Pierre (2000), "Les Crevettes dans la documentation du Proche-Orient Ancien." *Journal of Cuneiform Studies* 52: 55–60.

Lissarrague, François (1990), *The Aesthetics of the Greek Banquet: Images of Wine and Ritual*. Princeton: Princeton University Press.

Lo, Vivienne and Barrett, Penelope (2005), "Cooking up fine remedies: on the culinary aesthetic in a sixteenth-century Chinese materia medica." *Medical History* 49(4): 395–422.

Luke, Joanna (1994), "The Krater, 'Kratos,' and the 'Polis.'" *Greece & Rome*, second series, 41(1) (April): 23–32.

Luukko, M. and van Buylaere, G. (2002), *The Political Correspondence of Esarhadon*. Helsinki: SAA. 16.

Macfarlane, Alan (1988), "Anthropology and History," in John Cannon et al., *The Blackwell Dictionary of Historians*. Oxford: Blackwells.

Machida, Margo (2013), "Devouring Hawai," in Robert Ji-Song Ku, Martin F. Manalansan IV and Anita Mannur (eds), *Eating Asian America*. New York and London: New York University Press, pp. 323–53.

Mair, Victor H. (2006), "Introduction: Kinesis versus Stasis, Interaction versus Independent Invention," in Victor H. Mair (ed.), *Contact and Exchange in the Ancient World*. Honolulu: University of Hawaii Press, pp. 1–16.

Malinowski, Bronislaw (1922), *Argonauts of the Western Pacific*. London: Routledge and Kegan Paul.

Mallowan, Max (1972), "Cyrus the Great (558–529 BC)." *Iran* 10: 1–17.

Maran, Joseph (2006), "Coming to Terms with the Past: Ideology and Power in Late Helladic IIIC," in Sigrid Deger-Jalkotzy and Irene S. Lemos (eds), *Ancient Greece from The Mycenaean Palaces to the Age of Homer*. Edinburgh Leventis Studies 3. Edinburgh: University of Edinburgh Press, pp. 123–50.

Masson Smith, John Jr. (2000), "Dietary Decadence and Dynastic Decline in the Mongol Empire." *Journal of Asian History* 34; 1: pp. 35–52.

—(2003), "The Mongols and the Silk Road." *Silk Road Foundation Newsletter*, 1: 1. http://silkroadfoundation.org/newsletter/volumeonenumberone/mongols.html (accessed September 2014).

Mauss, Marcel (1966), *The Gift: Forms and Functions of Exchange in Archaic Societies.* London: Cohen & West.

McBride, W. Blan (1977), "Import-Export Business Operation in Early Mesopotamia." *Business and Economic History* 6, Mesopotamia. http://www.h-net.org/~business/bhcweb/publications/BEHprint/toc61977.html (accessed September 2014).

McCulloch, Helen Craig (1980), *Okagami—the Great Mirror: Fujiwara Michinaga (966–1027) and His Times.* Princeton: Princeton University Press.

—(1999), "Aristocratic Culture," in John Whitney Hall, Donald H. Shively and William H. McCulloch (eds), *The Cambridge History of Japan Vol. 2: Heian Japan.* Cambridge: Cambridge University Press, pp. 390–441.

McCulloch, William H. (1999a), "The Heian Court, 794–1040," in John Whitney Hall, Donald H. Shively, and William H. McCulloch (eds), *The Cambridge History of Japan Vol. 2: Heian Japan.* Cambridge: Cambridge University Press, pp. 20–80.

—(1999b), "The Capital and Its Society," in John Whitney Hall, Donald H. Shively, and William H. McCulloch (eds), *The Cambridge History of Japan Vol. 2: Heian Japan.* Cambridge: Cambridge University Press, pp. 97–180.

McCulloch, William H. and McCulloch, Helen Craig (1980), *A Tale of Flowering Fortunes: Annals of Japanese Aristocratic Life in the Heian Period, Vols I and II.* Stanford: Stanford University Press.

McDermott, Joseph (1999), "Introduction," in Joseph McDermott (ed.), *State and Court Ritual in China.* Cambridge and New Haven: Cambridge University Press, pp. 1–19.

McEwan, Gilbert J. P. (1983), "Distribution of meat in Eanna." *Iraq* Vol. 45(2) (Autumn): 187–98.

McGovern, Patrick E. (2003), *Ancient Wine: The Search for the Origins of Viniculture.* Princeton and Oxford: Princeton University Press.

—(2009), *Uncorking the Past: The Quest for Wine, Beer and other Alcoholic Beverages.* Berkeley, Los Angeles and London: University of California Press.

McGovern, Patrick E., Fleming, Stuart J., and Katz, Solomon H. (eds) (1995), *The Origins and Ancient History of Wine.* Amsterdam: Gordon and Breach.

Michalowski, Piotr (1990), "Early Mesopotamian Communication Systems: Art, Literature, Writing," in A. Gunter (ed.), *Investigating Artistic Environments in the Ancient Near East.* Washington DC: Smithsonian Institution Press, pp. 53–69.

—(1994), "The Drinking Gods," in Lucio Milano (ed.), *Drinking in Ancient Societies.* Padua: SARGON srl, pp. 27–44.

Mieroop, Marc van de (1997), *The Mesopotamian City.* Oxford: Oxford University Press.

Miller, Daniel (1995a), "Consumption and commodities." *Annual Review of Anthropology* 24: 141–61.

—(1995b), "Consumption as the Vanguard of History," in Daniel Miller (ed.) *Acknowledging Consumption.* London and New York: Routledge.

Miller, Margaret (1997), "Foreigners at the Greek Symposium?" in William J. Slater (ed.), *Dining in a Classical Context.* Ann Arbor: The University of Michigan Press, pp. 59–81.

Mintz, Sidney and Dubois, Christine (2002), "The anthropology of food and eating." *Annual Reviews of Anthropology*, 31: 99–117.

Mordaunt Cook, J. (1972), *The British Museum*. London: Allen Lane, The Penguin Press.

Moreland, John (2001), *Archaeology and Text*. London: Duckworth.

—(2006), "Archaeology and text: Subservience or Enlightenment?" *Annual Review of Anthropology* 35: 135–51.

Morris, Ian (1986), "The use and abuse of Homer," *Classical Antiquity* 5: 81–138.

Morris, Ivan (1967), *The Pillow Book of Sei Shonagon*. London: Penguin.

—(1979), *The World of the Shining Prince: Court Life in Ancient Japan*. London: Penguin.

Mote, F. W. (1977), "Yuan and Ming," in K. C. Chang (ed.), *Food in Chinese Culture*. New Haven and London: Yale University Press, pp. 193–258.

—(1999), *Imperial China 900–1800*. Cambridge and London: Harvard University Press.

Munn Rankin, J. M. (1956), "Diplomacy in western asia in the early second millennium BC." *Iraq* 18(1): 68–110.

Murray, Oswyn (1983), "The Greek Symposion in History," in E. Gabba (ed.), *Tria Corda: Scritti in onoredi Arnado Momigliano*. Como, Edizione New Press.

—(1995), "Forms of Sociality," in Jean-Pierre Vernant (ed.), *The Greeks*. Chicago and London: University of Chicago Press, pp. 218–53.

—(ed) (1994), "Sympotic History," in *Sympotica: A Symposium on the Symposion*. Oxford: The Clarendon Press, pp. 1–13.

Nader, Laura (1972), "Up The Anthropologist – Perspectives Gained from Studying Up," in Dell Hymes (ed.), *Reinventing Anthropology*. New York: Pantheon Books.

—(1997), "Controlling processes: tracing the dynamic components of power." *Current Anthropology* 18(5): 711–38.

Neer, Richard T. (2002), *Style and Politics in Athenian Vase-Painting. The Craft of Democracy ca. 530–460 B.C.E.* Cambridge: Cambridge University Press.

Nelson, Sarah Milledge (2003), "Feasting the Ancestors in Early China," in Tamara Bray (ed.), *The Archaeology and Politics of Food and Feasting in Early States and Empires*. New York, Boston and London: Kluwer, pp. 65–92.

Neumann, Hans (1994), "Beer As a Means of Compensation for Work in Mesopotamia During the Ur III Period," in Lucio Milano (ed.), *Drinking in Ancient Societies: History and Culture of Drinks in the Ancient Near East*. Padova: Sargon srl, pp. 321–31.

Nienhauser, William (1994), *The Grand Scribe's Records Vol. I: The Basic Annals of Pre-Han China (S'su ma Chien)*. Bloomington: Indiana University Press.

Nissen, Hans J., Damerow, Peter and Englund, Robert K. (1993), *Archaic Bookkeeping: Writing and Techniques of Economic Administration in the Ancient Near East*. Chicago and London: University of Chicago Press

Noonan, Thomas S. (1994), "What Can Archaeology Tell Us About the Economy of Khazaria?" in Bruno Genito (ed.), *The Archaeology of the Steppes: Methods and Strategies*. Naples, Istituto Universitario Orientale, pp. 331–45.

Notes and Queries on Anthropology (1929), Edited for the British Association for the Advancement of Science by A Committee of Section H. London, Royal Anthropological Institute.

O'Connor, Kaori (2013), *The English Breakfast: The Biography of a National Meal*. London: Bloomsbury.

Ohnuki-Tierney, Emiko (1995), "Structure, event and historical metaphor: rice and identities in Japanese history." *The Journal of the Royal Anthropological Institute* 1(2): 227–53.

Ooms, Herman (2009), *Imperial Politics and Symbolics in Ancient Japan: The Tenmu Dynasty*. Honolulu: University of Hawaii Press.

Oppenheim, A. Leo (1949), "The golden garments of the gods." *Journal of Near Eastern Studies* 8(3) (July): 172–93.

—(1965), "On Royal Gardens in Mesopotamia." *Journal of Near Eastern Studies*, 24(4) Pt 2 (October), pp. 328–33.

—(1977), *Ancient Mesopotamia: Portrait of a Dead Civilization,* Rev. edn completed by Erica Reiner. Chicago and London: University of Chicago Press.

Ortner, Sherry B. (1984), "Theory in anthropology since the Sixties." *Comparative Studies in Society and History* 26(1): 126–66.

Palaima, Thomas G. (2004), "Sacrificial feasting in the Linear B documents," *Hesperia,* 73: 217–46.

Parpola, Simo (2004), "The Leftovers of God and King," in Cristiano Grottanelli and Lucio Milano (eds), *Food and Identity in the Ancient World*. Padova: SARGON, Editrice e Libreria, pp. 281–312.

Percy, William Armstrong II (1996), *Pederasty and Pedagogy in Archaic Greece*. Champaign, IL: University of Illinois Press.

Peregrine, Peter N. (1998), "Comment in Joffee, Alexander (1998), alcohol and social complexity in ancient Western Asia." *Current Anthropology* 39(3): 314.

Philippi, Donald L. (1959), *Norito: A New Translation of the Ancient Japanese Ritual Prayers*. Tokyo: The Institute for Japanese Culture and Classics, Kokugakuin University.

—(1987), *Kojiki*. Tokyo: Tokyo University Press.

Pinnock, Frances (1994), "Considerations on the 'Banquet Theme' in the Figurative Art of Mesopotamia and Syria," in Lucio Milano (ed.), *Drinking in Ancient Societies: History and Culture of Drinks in the Ancient Near East*. Padova: Sargon srl, pp. 15–26.

Pittman, Holly (1998), "Cylinder Seals," in Richard L. Zettler and Lee Horne (eds), *Treasures from the Royal Tombs of Ur*. Philadelphia: University of Pennsylvania Museum of Archaeology and Anthropology, pp. 75–86.

Plutschow, Herbert (1995), "Archaic Chinese sacrificial practices in the light of generative Anthropology." *Anthropoetics* 1(2) (December). http://www.anthropoetics.ucla.edu/ ap0102/china.htm (accessed August 2014).

Pollock, Susan (2003), "Feasts, Funerals and Fast Food in Early Mesopotamian States," in Tamara Bray (ed.), *The Archaeology and Politics of Food and Feasting in Early States and Empires*. New York, Boston, Dordrecht, London and Moscow: Kluwer Academic/Plenum Publishers, pp. 17–38.

Poo, Mu-Chou (1999), "The use and abuse of wine in ancient China." *Journal of the Economic and Social History of the Orient* 42(2): 123–51.

Postgate, J. N. (1992), *Early Mesopotamia: Society and Economy at the Dawn of History*. London and New York: Routledge.

Powell, Marvin (1994), "Metron Ariston: Measure as a Means of Studying Beer in Ancient Mesopotamia," in Lucio Milano (ed.), *Drinking in Ancient Societies*. Padova: Sargon, pp. 91–119.

—(1996), "Money in Mesopotamia." *Journal of the Economic and Social History of the Orient,* 39(3): 224–42.

Praetzellis, Adrian (1998), "Archaeologists as storytellers." *Historical Archaeology,* 32(1): 2.

Puett, Michael J. (2004), *To Become a God: Cosmology, Sacrifice and Self-Divinization in Early China.* Cambridge, MA and London: Harvard University Asia Center for the Harvard-Yenching Institute.

Putz, Babette (2007), *The Symposium and Komos in Aristophanes.* Oxford: Oxbow Books.

Raaflaub, Kurt A. (2006), "Historical Approaches to Homer," in Deger-Jalkotzy, Sigrid and Irene S. Lemos (eds), *Ancient Greece: From the Mycenaean Palaces to the Age of Homer.* Edinburgh: Edinburgh University Press, pp. 449–62.

Rachewiltz, Igor de (2004), *The Secret History of the Mongols, Vols I and II.* Leiden and Boston: Brill.

Radner, Karen (2011), "Fame and Prizes: Competition and War in the Neo-Assyrian Empire," in Nick Fisher and Hans van Wees (eds), *Competition in the Ancient World.* Swansea: Classical Press of Wales, pp. 37–58.

Rath, Eric C. (2008), "Banquets against boredom: towards understanding (Samurai) cuisine in early modern Japan." *Early Modern Japan* 16: 43–55.

—(2010), *Food and Fantasy in Early Modern Japan.* Berkeley, Los Angeles and London: University of California Press.

Rawson, Jessica (1993), "Late Shang Bronze Design: Meaning and Purpose," in Roderick Whitfield (ed.), *The Problem of Meaning in Early Chinese Ritual Bronzes. Percival David Foundation of Chinese Art.* London: School of Oriental and African Studies, pp. 67–95.

—(1999), "Ancient Chinese Ritual as Seen in the Material Record," in Joseph McDermott (ed.), *State and Court Ritual in China.* Cambridge and New Haven: Cambridge University Press, pp. 20–49.

—(ed) (2007), *The British Museum Book of Chinese Art,* London: British Museum Press.

Redfield, James (1995), "Homo Domesticus," in Jean-Pierre Vernant (ed.), *The Greeks.* Chicago and London: University of Chicago Press, pp. 153–83.

Reiner, Erica (1995), "Astral magic in Babylonia." *Transactions of the American Philosophical Society New Series* 85(4): 1–150.

Riasanovsky, V. A. (1965), *Fundamental Principles of Mongol Law.* Bloomington: University of Indiana Publications.

Ricci, Aldo (trans.) (1939), *The Travels of Marco Polo.* London: Routledge and Kegan Paul.

Ridgway, David (1997), "Nestor's cup and the Etruscans." *Oxford Journal of Archaeology* 16(3): 325–44.

Roberts, J. A. G. (2002), *From China to Chinatown: Chinese Food in the West.* London: Reaktion Books.

Rolle, Renate (1980), *The World of the Scythians.* London: Batsford Ltd.

Root, Margaret Cool (1979), *The King and Kingship in Achaemenid Art.* Leiden: Brill.

Ruark, Jennifer K. (1999), "More scholars focus on historical, social and cultural meanings of food, but some critics say it's scholarship lite." *Chronicle of Higher Education* (USA), July 9.

Sachs, Abraham (1969), "Daily Sacrifices to the Gods of the City of Uruk," in J. B. Prichard, *Ancient Near Eastern Texts Relating to the Old Testament.* Princeton: Princeton University Press, pp. 343–5.

Sahlins, Marshall (1976), *Culture and Practical Reason.* Chicago and London: University of Chicago Press.

—(1991), "The segmentary lineage system: an organization of predatory expansion." *American Anthropologist* New Series, 63(2): 322–45.

—(1992), *Anahulu: The Anthropology of History in the Hawaiian Islands*. Vol. I: Historical Ethnography. Chicago and London: University of Chicago Press.

—(2004), *Apologies to Thucydides: Understanding History as Culture and Vice Versa*. Chicago: University of Chicago Press.

—(2008), "The Stranger-King or Elementary Forms of the Politics of Life." *Indonesia and the Malay World* 36:105, pp. 177–99.

Said, Edward (1978), *Orientalism*. London and Boston: Routledge and Kegan Paul.

Sancisi-Weerdenberg, Heleen (1989), "Gifts in the Persian Empire," in Pierre Briant and Clarisse Herrenschmidt (eds), *Le Tribut dans l'Empire Perse*. Louvain and Paris: Peeters, pp. 107–20.

—(1995), "Persian Food: Stereotypes and Political Identity," in John Wilkins, David Harvey and Mike Dobson (eds), *Food in Antiquity*. Exeter: University of Exeter Press, pp. 286–302.

—(1997), "Crumbs from the Royal Table: Foodnotes on Briant," in Pierre Briant (ed.), *Recherches Recent sur l'empire Achemenide*. Lyons: Maison de l'Orient et de la Méditerranée, pp. 297–306.

Sansom, George (1958), *A History of Japan to 1334*. London: The Cresset Press.

Sasson, Jack M. (2004), "The King's Table: Food and Fealty in Old Babylonian Mari," in Cristiano Grottanelli and Lucio Milano (eds), *Food and Identity in the Ancient World*. Padova: SARGON, Editrice e Libreria, pp. 179–215.

Schafer, Edward H. (1963), *The Golden Peaches of Samarkand*. Berkeley and Los Angeles: University of California Press.

Schiefenhovel, Wulf and Macbeth, Helen (eds) (2011), *Liquid Bread: Beer and Brewing in Cross-Cultural Perspective*. Oxford and New York: Berghahn Books.

Schmandt-Besserat, Denise (1992), *Before Writing*. Austin: University of Texas Press.

—(2001), "Feasting in the Ancient Near East," in Michael Dietler and Brian Hayden (eds), *Feasts: Archaeological and Ethnogaphic Perspectives on Food, Politics and Power*. Washington DC and London: Smithsonian Institution Press, pp. 391–403.

Schmitt-Pantel, Pauline (1990), "Collective Activities and the Political in the Greek City," in Oswyn Murray and Simon Price (eds), *The Greek City from Homer to Alexander*. Oxford: Clarendon Press, pp. 199–215.

—(1994), "Sacrificial Meal and Symposion: Two Models of Civic Institutions in the Archaic City?" in Oswyn Murray (ed.), *Sympotica*. Oxford: Clarendon Press, pp. 14–33.

Scholliers, Peter (2012), "The Many Rooms in the House: Research on Past Foodways in Modern Europe," in Kyri W. Clafin and Peter Scholliers (eds), *Writing Food History: A Global Perspective*. London and New York: Bloomsbury, 59–71.

Scholliers, Peter and Clafin, Kyri W. (2012), "Surveying Global Food Historiography," in Kyri W. Clafin and Peter Scholliers (eds), *Writing Food History: A Global Perspective*. London and New York: Bloomsbury, pp. 1–10.

Sherratt, Andrew (1999), "Cash Crops Before Cash: Organic Consumables and Trade," in Chris Gosden and Jon Hather, (eds), *The Prehistory of Food: Appetites for Change*. London and New York: Routledge, pp. 13–34.

—(2006), *Bread, Butter and Beer: Dietary Change and urbanisation in early Mesopotamia and Surrounding Areas 6000–3000 BC*. Unpublished manuscript, cited in Jill Goulder (2010), "Administrators' bread: an experiment-based re-assessment of the functional and cultural role of the Uruk Bevel-Rim Bowl." *Antiquity* 84:351–62.

Sherratt, Susan (2004), "Feasting in Homeric epic," *Hesperia* 73(2) (April/June): 301–37.

Simoons, Frederick J. (2001), *Food in China: A Cultural and Historical Enquiry*. Boca Raton and Boston: CRC Press.

Simpson, St John (2005), "The Royal Table," in John Curtis and Nigel Tallis (eds), *Forgotten Empire: The World of Ancient Persia*. London: British Museum Press, pp. 104–31.

Slotsky, Alice L. (2007), "Cuneiform Cuisine: Culinary History Reborn at Brown University, SBL Forum", Online: http: //sbl-site.org/Article.aspx?ArticleID=703 (accessed September 2, 2011).

Sourvinou-Inwood, Christiane (1990), "What is *Polis* Religion?" in Oswyn Murray and Simon Price (eds), *The Greek City from Homer to Alexander*. Oxford: Clarendon Press, pp. 295–322.

Spieser, E. A. (1954), "The case of the obliging servant." *Journal of Cuneiform Studies* 8(3): 98–105.

Steele, John (1917), *I-Li or Book of Etiquette* (2 vols). London: Probsthain.

Steiner, Ann (2002), "Private and public: links between symposion and syssition in fifth-century Athens," *Classical Antiquity* 21(2): 347–80.

Sterckx, Roel (ed.) (2005a), "Introduction," in Roel Sterckx (ed.), *Of Tripod and Palate: Food, Politics and Religion in Traditional China*. New York and Basingstoke: Palgrave Macmillan, pp. 1–8.

—(2005b) "Food and Philosophy in Pre-Buddhist China" in Sterckx, Roel (ed) 2005 *Of Tripod and Palate*, New York: Palgrave Macmillan: 34–61.

—(2011) *Food, Sacrifice and Sagehood in Early China*. Cambridge: Cambridge University Press.

Stol, Marten (1994), "Beer in Neo-Babylonian Times," in Lucio Milano (ed.), *Drinking in Ancient Societies: History and Culture of Drinks in the Ancient Near East*. Padova: SARGON srl, pp. 155–83.

Strong, Roy (2002), *Feast: A History of Grand Eating*. London: Jonathan Cape.

Suter, Claudia E. (2007), "Between Human and Divine: High Priestesses in Images from the Akkad to the Isin-Larsa Period," in Jack Cheng and Marian H. Feldman (eds), *Ancient Near Eastern Art in Context: Studies in Honor of Irene J. Winter by Her Students*. Leiden and Boston: Brill.

Sutton, David E. (2010), "Food and the senses." *Annual Review of Anthropology* 39: 209–23.

Tchen, John Kuo Wei (1999), *New York Before Chinatown: Orientalism and the Shaping of American Culture 1776–1882*. Baltimore: Johns Hopkins University Press.

The Times, Saturday October 3, 1885, p. 9; issue 31568; col D.

Thomason, Allison Karmel (2004), "From Sennacherib's bronzes to Tarhaqua's feet: conceptions of the material world at Nineveh." *Iraq*, 66: 151–62.

Thompson, R. Campbell (1903), *The Devils and Evil Spirits of Babylonia*. London: Luzac and Co.

Thucydides (2009), Martin Hammond (trans.), *The History of the Peloponnesian Wars*. Oxford: Oxford University Press.

Thureau-Dangin, F. (1921), *Rituels Accadiens*. Paris: Editions Ernst Leroux.

Tubielewicz, Jolanta (1980), *Superstitions, Magic and Mantic Practices in the Heian Period*. Warsaw: Wydawnictwa Uniwersytetu Warszawskiego.

Turner, Victor (1967), *The Forest of Symbols*. Ithaca, NY: Cornell University Press.

Twiss, Katheryn (2012), "The archaeology of food and social diversity." *Journal of Archaeological Research* 20: 357–95.

Tyson Smith, Stuart (2003), "Pharaohs, Feasts and Foreigners: Cooking, Foodways and Agency on Ancient Egypt's Southern Frontier," in Tamara L. Bray (ed.), *The Archaeology and Politics of Food and Feasting in Early States and Empires*. New York and London: Kluwer/Plenum, pp. 39–64.

Ustinova, Yulia (2005), "Snake-Limbed and Tendril-limbed Goddesses in the Art and Mythology of the Mediterranean and Black Sea," in David Brown (ed.), *Scythians and Greeks. Culture Interactions in Scythia, Athens and The Early Roman Empire*. Exeter: University of Exeter Press, pp. 64–79.

Van Buren, E. Douglas (1948), "Fish-offerings in ancient Mesopotamia." *Iraq* 10: 2, (Autumn): 101–21.

Vanstiphout, H. L. J. (1992), "The Banquet Scene in the Mesopotamian Debate Poems," in R. Gyselen (ed.), Banquets d'Orient. *Res Orientales,* vol. IV, pp. 9–21.

Vernant, Jean-Pierre (1989), "At Man's Table," in Marcel Detienne and Jean-Pierre Vernant (eds), *The Cuisine of Sacrifice Among the Ancient Greeks*. Chicago and London: University of Chicago Press, pp. 21–86.

Von Falkenhausen, Lothar (1993), *Suspended Music: Chime-Bells in the Culture of Bronze Age China*. Berkeley and Oxford: University of California Press.

Von Verschuer, Charlotte (2003), *Le Riz dans la Culture de Heian: Mythe et Réalité*. Paris: Institut des Hautes Etudes Japonaises.

Waines, David (1987), "Cereals, bread and society: an essay on the staff of life in medieval Iraq." *Journal of the Economic and Social History of the Orient* 30(3): 255–85.

Waley, Arthur (1918), *A Hundred and Seventy Chinese Poems*. New York: Alfred Knopf.

—(1937), *The Book of Songs*. London: George Allen & Unwin.

—(1965), *The Tale of Genji: A Novel in Six Parts by Lady Murasaki*. London: George Allen & Unwin.

Watson, James L. (1987), "Feasting from the common pot: feasting with equals in Chinese Society." *Anthropos*, 82(4/6): 389–401.

Wengrow, David (2008), "Prehistories of commodity branding." *Current Anthropology* 49(1): 7–34.

—(2010) *What Makes Civilization?* Oxford and New York, Oxford University Press.

Wiessner, Polly and Schiefenhovel, Wulf (1996), *Food and the Status Quest*. Providence, RI and Oxford: Berghahn Books.

Wilcox, George (1999), "Agrarian Change and the Beginnings of Cultivation in the Near East," in Chris Gosden and Jon Hather (eds), *The Prehistory of Food: Appetites for Change*. London and New York: Routledge.

Wilkins, John (2000), *The Boastful Chef: The Discourse of Food in Ancient Greek Comedy*. Oxford: Oxford University Press.

—(2012), "Food and Drink in the Ancient World," in Kyri W. Clafin and Peter Scholliers (eds), *Writing Food History: A Global Perspective*. London and New York: Bloomsbury, pp. 11–23.

—(2014), "Archestratus: naughty poet, good cook." *Petits Propos Culinaires* 100: 162–86.

Wilkins, John and Hill, Shaun (2011), *Archestratus: Fragments from the Life of Luxury*. Devon: Prospect Books.

Wilkins, John, Harvey, David and Dobson, Mike (eds) (1995), *Food in Antiquity*. Exeter: University of Exeter Press.

Wilkinson, Toby C., Susan Sherratt and John Bennet, (eds) (2011), *Interweaving Worlds*

– *Systematic Interactions in Eurasia, 7th to 1st Millennia* BC. Essays from a conference in memory of Professor Andrew Sherratt. Oxford: Oxbow Books, pp. 37–60.

Willerslev, Rane (2011), "Frazer strikes back from the armchair: a new search for the Animist soul. (Malinowski memorial Lecture 2010)." *Journal of the Royal Anthropological Society* 17(3): 504–26.

Winter, Irene J. (1985), "After the Battle is Over: the Stele of the Vultures and the Beginning of Historical Narrative in the Art of the Ancient Near East," in Herbert L. Kessler and Marianna Shreve Simpson, *Pictorial Narrative in Antiquity and the Middle Ages*. Center for Advanced Study in the Visual Arts, Symposium Series IV. Washington DC: National Gallery of Art. pp. 11–32.

—(1986), "The King and the Cup," in Marilyn Kelly-Buccellati (ed.), *Insight Through Images, Studies in Honor of Edith Porada*. Malibu: Biblioteca Mesopotamica 21, pp. 253–68.

—(1993), "Seat of kingship/a wonder to behold: the palace as construct in the ancient near east." *Ars Orientalis* 23: 27–55.

Wiseman, D. J. (1952), "A New Stela of Ashurnasirpal II." *Iraq* 14: 24–39.

—(1983) "Mesopotamian Gardens." *Anatolian Studies* 33: 137–44.

Woolley, Sir Leonard (1934), *The Royal Cemetary, Ur Excavations*, vol. 2. London: Trustees of the British Museum and of the Museum of the University of Pennsylvania.

—(1938), *Ur of the Chaldees: Seven Years of Excavation*. Harmondsworth and New York: Penguin Books.

Wrangham, Richard (2009), *Catching Fire: How Cooking Made Us Human*. New York: Basic Books.

Wright, James C. (2004a), "A survey of evidence for feasting in Mycenaean society," *Hesperia*, 73: 2: 133–78.

—(2004b), "The Mycenaean feast: an introduction." *Hesperia* 73(2), Special issue: The Mycenaean Feast: 121–32.

—(2006), "The Formation of the Mycenaean Palace," in Sigrid Deger-Jalkotzy and Irene S. Lemos (eds), *Ancient Greece from The Mycenaean Palaces to the Age of Homer*. Edinburgh Leventis Studies 3. Edinburgh: University of Edinburgh Press, pp. 7–52.

Wright, Katherine I. (Karen) (2014), "Domestication and inequality? Households, corporate groups and food processing tools at Çatalhöyük." *Journal of Archaeological Research* 33: 1–33.

Wu, David Yen Ho and Cheung, Sidney C. H. (2004), *The Globalization of Chinese Food*. London and New York: Routledge.

Wu, David Yen Ho and Tan, Chee Beng (2001), *Changing Chinese Foodways in Asia*. Hong Kong: Chinese University Press.

Yiengpruksawan, Mimi Hall (1994), "What's in a Name? Fujiwara Fixation in Japanese Cultural History." *Monumenta Nipponica* 49:4, 423–53.

Yoffee, Norman (1995), "Political economy in early Mesopotamian States." *Annual Review of Anthropology* 24: 281–311.

Zeitlyn, David (2012), "Anthropology in and of the archives: possible futures and contingent pasts. Archives as anthropological surrogates. *Annual Review of Anthropology* 41: 461–80.

Index